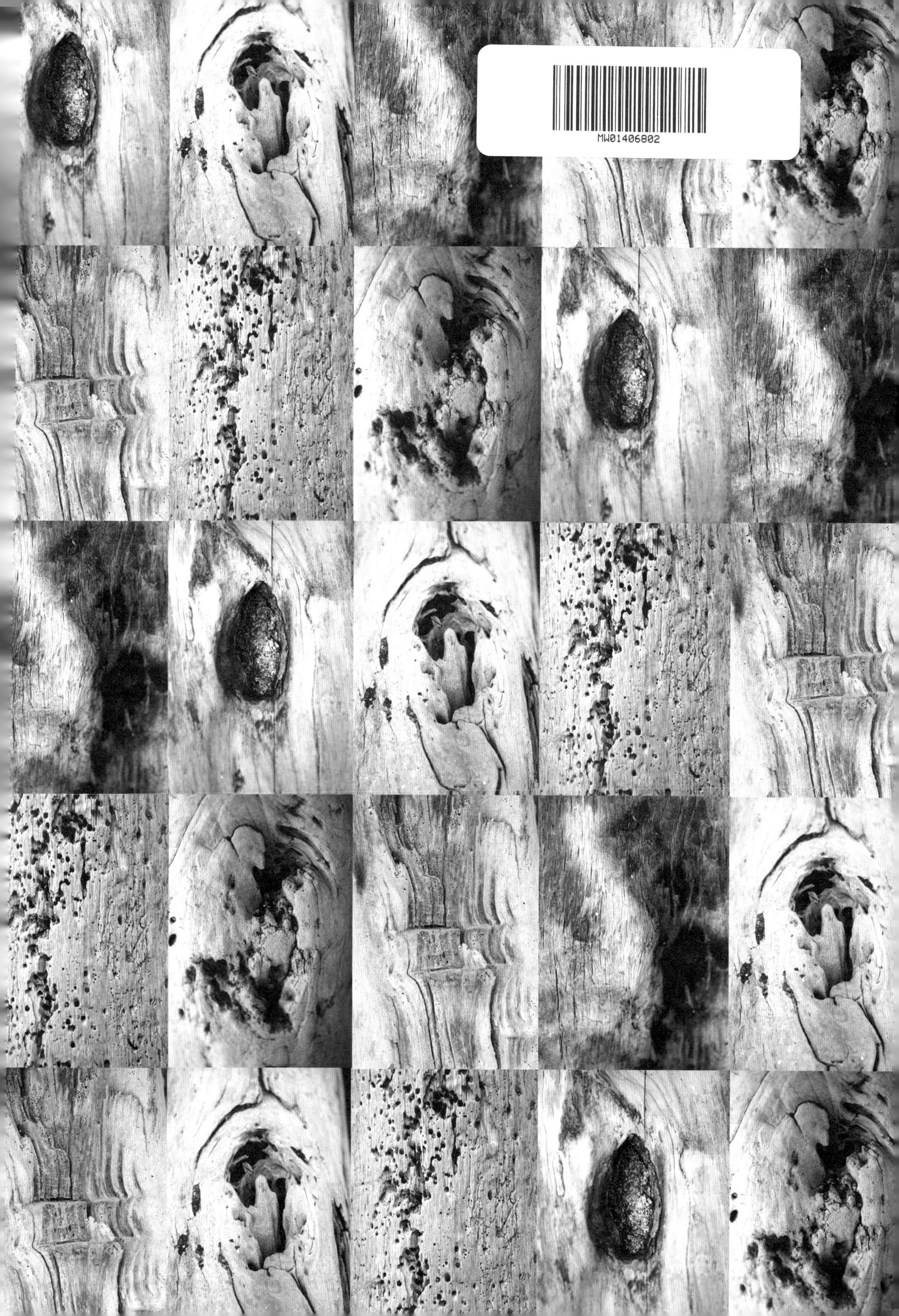

BALI

SUSTAINABLE VISIONS

BALI

SUSTAINABLE VISIONS

SECOND EDITION

PHOTOGRAPHY BY
ISABELLA GINANNESCHI

TEXT BY
DUNCAN MURRAY KIRK

ABBEVILLE PRESS PUBLISHERS
NEW YORK   LONDON

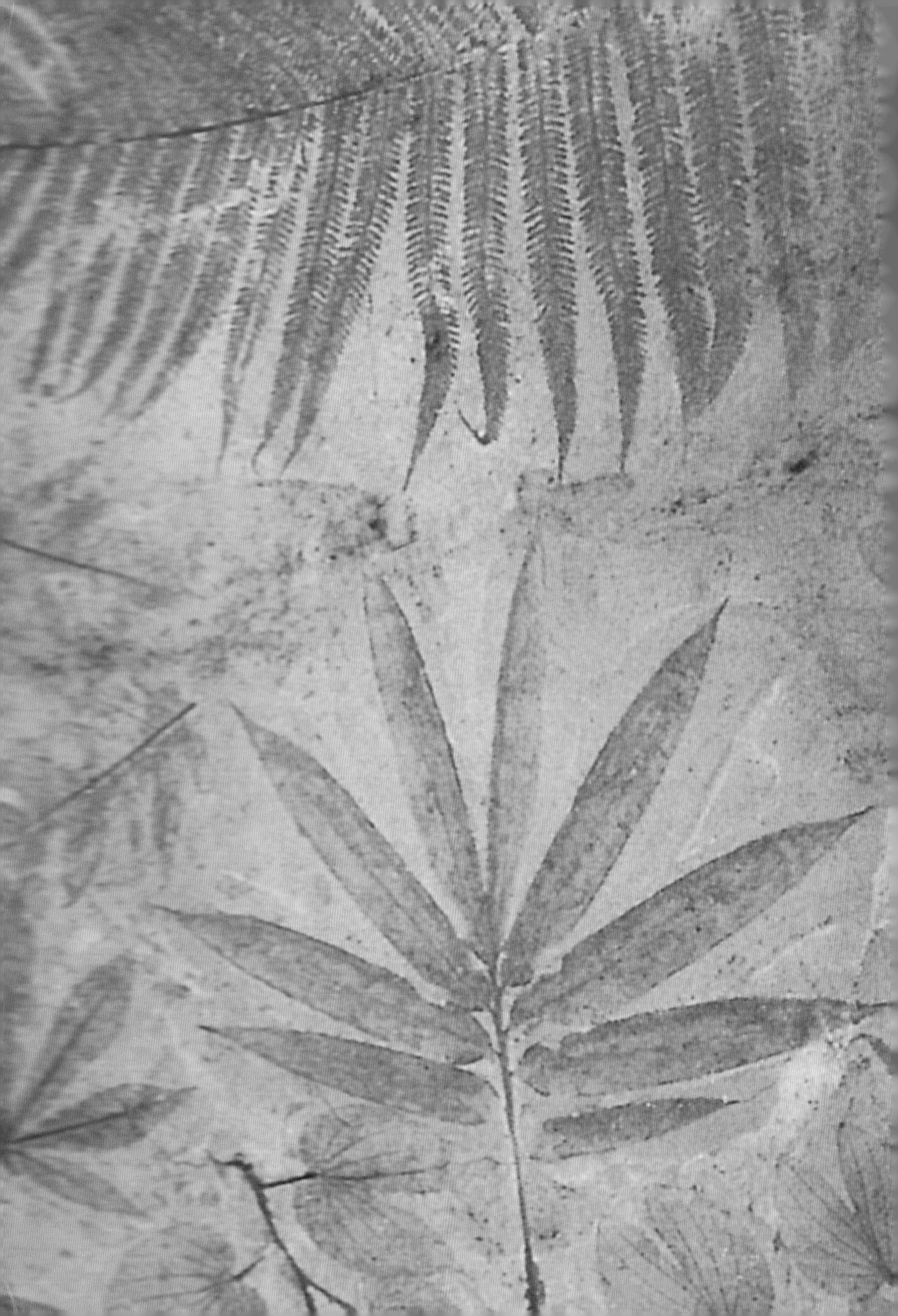

CONTENTS

INTRODUCTION 7

MARRYING NATURE 13

MUD, EARTH, AND BRICKS 29

BAMBOO 53

MATERIALS RECLAIMED 83

KNOCKDOWN HOUSES 107

GREEN 131

METAL AND GLASS 151

LIVING WITHOUT WALLS 177

ROOFS 213

ACKNOWLEDGMENTS 227

FEATURED PLACES 229

INDEX 236

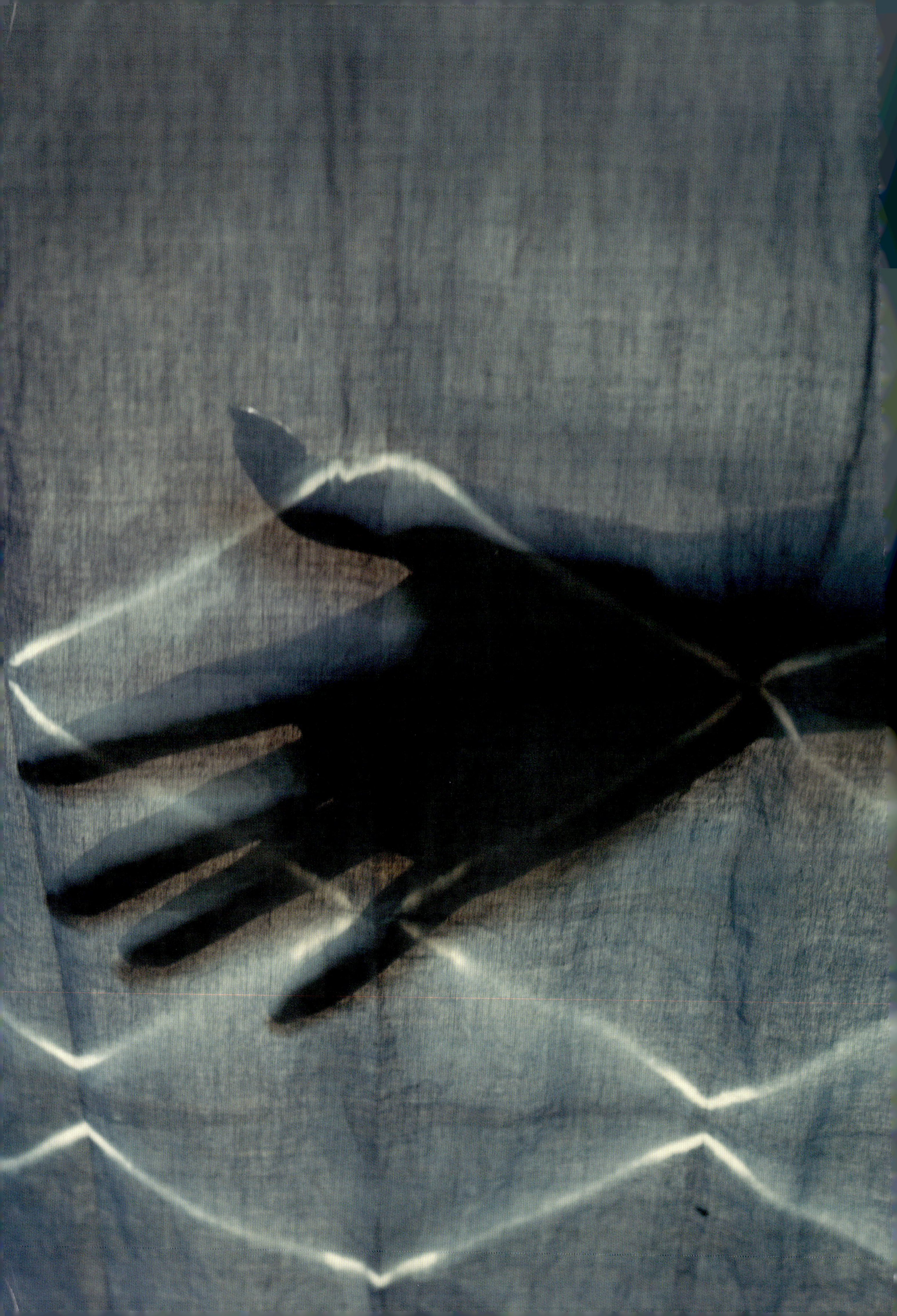

INTRODUCTION

According to the U.S. Environmental Protection Agency, "Sustainability is based on a simple principle: Everything that we need for our survival and well-being depends, either directly or indirectly, on our natural environment. Sustainability creates and maintains the conditions under which humans and nature can exist in productive harmony, that permit fulfilling the social, economic and other requirements of present and future generations. Sustainability is important to making sure that we have and will continue to have the water, materials, and resources to protect human health and our environment."

This book does not attempt to provide universal solutions for sustainability, but shows how members of the tropical elite have incorporated sustainable principles in their own architecture and interiors, without sacrificing glamour or quality of life. Their example can encourage us to be thoughtful and to care about our own actions and impact, wherever we are and wherever we go.

In Bali, one has a strong sense of being in the present, which creates a great potential for creative thinking. For this reason and others, Bali has attracted to its shores many creators, visionaries, and artists. Things were very basic when this tribe arrived, and they were introduced to a simple way of living, without the electricity and services they were accustomed to in their own countries. They had to be inventive and create the life they were looking for, and there was ample room to do it.

Many of them shared an environmental consciousness that was reinforced by the local culture. Traditionally, the Balinese had no official land ownership but held the understanding that they were caretakers of the land; through their care and devotion, they would receive constant and bountiful gifts from nature.

The early Balinese created a unique irrigation system called the *subak*. In use for the past nine hundred years, the subak captures the life-giving water high up on the volcanoes and channels it throughout the island's rugged terrain, making use of naturally occurring physical boundaries. Dependent on island-wide social cooperation between farming villages, the subak is perhaps the world's finest example of sustainability as a cooperative endeavor; it shows that we humans really can take a unified approach to life and survival.

However, in the last twenty-five years, an influx of tourists and rapid economic development have damaged the subak, as well as the island's ecology as a whole. The leaves used for wrapping food have been replaced by plastic bags, which are burned daily. Bicycles and tuk-tuks have given way to more cars, motorbikes, and buses than the infrastructure can handle; the old soundtrack of bicycle bells has been drowned out by the roar of engines. Cement buildings proliferate and eat away at the beautiful rice fields that are supposed to serve as green belts. Trash washes up on the shore and piles up on the streets.

Alongside these man-made problems persist the age-old challenges presented by nature herself. Struck by the magical beauty of Bali, one can easily forget the hazards of living on this small volcanic island just a few degrees south of the equator—earthquakes, fierce tropical storms, humidity, and bucketing downpours. Anyone building here must take into account the rugged topography, the climate, and the indoor-outdoor lifestyle that comes with it.

The artists, architects, and visionary entrepreneurs featured in this book have responded to the inspiration and challenges of Bali with designs that make use of old, new, and reclaimed materials such as bamboo, thatch, wood, stone, iron, glass, and canvas—even mud. Often they have borrowed from the island's own architectural heritage, which has always been based in sustainable materials; they have reimagined the traditional bamboo houses found in mud-walled villages, the *lumbungs* used to store rice, and especially *bales*, *wantilans*, and other types of pavilion. The knockdown wood houses of Java—*gladaks*, *joglos*, and *limasans*—have also been adapted for use as standalone bedrooms and studios. Some structures combine these traditional forms with high-tech environmental solutions such as water catchment, retrieval, and redistribution systems; hydroponics and aquaponics; the strategic use of shade to enhance interior and exterior convection; and new types of solar-, wind-, and water-powered electrical generators. All, however, bear the personal touch of their creators, often expressed in fanciful twists and wild inspirations.

Isabella's photography creates an intimate portrait of the style generated by a new way of thinking. The people behind these designs have finely tuned their visions to nature without neglecting elegance or luxury. Each member of this visionary tribe brings his or her own experiences and passions to the endeavor. As I interviewed them, it became obvious that their personal journeys and philosophies were just as important as the details of their design process. I decided to relate the text to the photographs organically rather than rigidly, to focus on the stories behind the buildings. These stories are told in the interviewees' own words, usually verbatim but sometimes paraphrased. Together their voices offer a strong and abiding message about the importance—and possibilities—of sustainable design.

Most of the sustainable buildings herein belong to a tropical elite, and indeed, that is part of their appeal. However, the younger generation whom we interviewed for this book are keen to simplify these designs and make them affordable to a broader public. This reflects a renewed concern for the environment among the current generation of Balinese. They are demanding more integrity and transparency in business practices, and many companies are taking their ecological impact very seriously at last.

We hope this book will encourage you to take a fresh approach to living sustainably, whether in the tropics or not. We all need to find workable local solutions to reverse the present madness of our global conditions. In the long run, sustainability is really the only issue of importance, and it can only be addressed with education and positive action.

Sustainability is based around long-term solutions and renewable resources—but change is a constant, as are changes in perception!

Nearly a decade after the original publication of *Bali: Sustainable Visions*, we felt it was time for a new edition. This time we have stayed in Bali proper, although we know that Rote, Lombok, and Sumba have some inspired new constructions, not least at Nihiwatu Resort, Claude Graves's former gem.

We have revisited certain projects that illustrate ongoing sustainability as well as creative evolution, and we have followed up with some of the original pioneers featured in the first edition, including Arief Rabik, who has a bamboo-growing project operating in twelve countries and is a shining star for sustainability; Elora Hardy, who continues her career as a bamboo design guru; and Sebastian Mesdag, who is now producing indigo. We revisited the Potato Head Beach Club and followed designer Maximilian Jencquel in his new endeavors. And we went back to the Bambu Indah resort, where John and Cynthia Hardy have opened up a heavenly river playground and renovated the original knockdown houses into two-story structures.

We have also introduced new innovators, such as the engineering consultancy Eco-Mantra, which helps developers and architects build eco-friendly resorts and destinations. They are particularly concerned with the problems of energy consumption, groundwater depletion, and trash on Bali. CEO Sean Nino Lotze heads up a team with cutting-edge sustainability knowledge. Eco-Mantra was founded by Nino, Maitri Fischer, and Wayan Lam in 2015. Nino and Maitri had grown up on Bali and were disturbed by the changes they found when they returned from studying and working abroad. As they explain it,

> It was just as Joni Mitchell said: "They paved paradise and put up a parking lot." The changes affected more than just idyllic "paradisal" landscapes. Development brought with it real problems and was visibly affecting the environment. By 2014, visitors had tripled to 10,160,945 per year. It was clear that local infrastructure and government policies were unprepared. Bali had surpassed its carrying capacity, and the environment and local communities were under immense pressure. Enter Eco-Mantra. Driven by our love of Bali and our passion for the environment, we seek to preserve the beauty of our island home.

Two other sustainability innovators pushing in a positive direction are Cezary and Kinga, who have created and oversee an excellent, over 90 percent sustainable resort on Nusa Penida and a home in Ubud called Uma Jiwa. This sensational dwelling was a design collaboration between Elora Hardy's Ibuku and Abbie Labrum's Earth Lines Architects.

Another eco-conscious designer on Bali, Norm vant Hoff, is in the process of creating bird-proof glass. This new product was not yet available at the time we went to press, but we are confident that Norm will realize his ambition of decreasing the very high number of deaths that birds suffer from impacts with glass.

We hope this new edition of *Bali: Sustainable Visions* will awaken more readers to the complex interplay of development, governance, and sustainability, which requires careful consideration. Nature must always take the central position and lead the way. We trust that common sense and free speech will grow into best practices, and that our view of the world will become more circumspect. We have to, en masse, adopt a nonexploitative and regenerative mindset: sympathetic, compassionate, and aware, filled with gratitude for the blessings and bounty of our planet's nature.

Bamboo tunnel at the Potato Head beach club and resort, Seminyak.

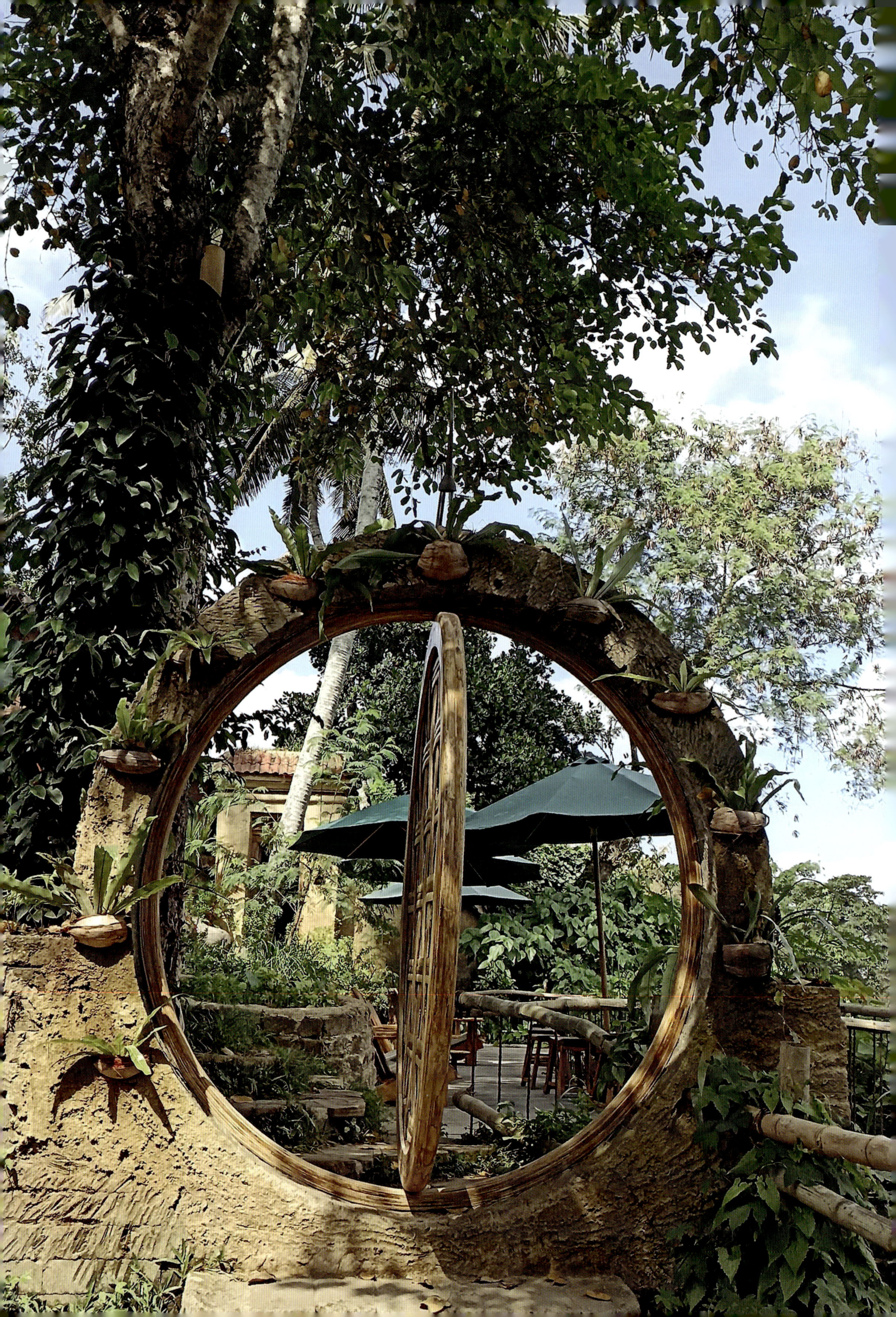

MARRYING NATURE

The Balinese aspire to a life of balanced harmony, both in this world and in the unseen or parallel world. Their unique variant of Hinduism combines ancient animistic beliefs with the concepts of karma and service to the ancestors. The ancestors are reborn in their descendants, and fields and buildings are linked to gods and birthrights. The spiritual life of the Balinese is outstandingly complex and includes the whole community.

On arrival the visitor is immediately struck by the warmth and kindness of the Balinese people, as well as by the colorful offerings placed daily at all intersections of roads and paths to protect against bad spirits that may lie in wait for the unaware or unsuspecting. Offerings are made to a myriad of deities, including the gods of machinery, so your rental car's glove compartment may well conceal a *tekor* (banana leaf) filled with dried flowers and herbs, and possibly even meat, feathers, and bones.

The focal point of Balinese prayer is the largest of the volcanoes, Mount Agung, and temples radiate outward from this central hub all the way to the sea, like the spokes of a bicycle wheel.

A new building's positioning is of great consequence, and the high priests must consult the gods and historic texts to ascertain an acceptable location and orientation. In recent years this rule has been flouted by developers and corporate hotel chains, and many planning officials have been corrupted by

14 MARRYING NATURE

Evoking an intergalactic vessel that has landed at the edge of a cliff, the spa at Intaaya, a sustainable resort on Nusa Penida.

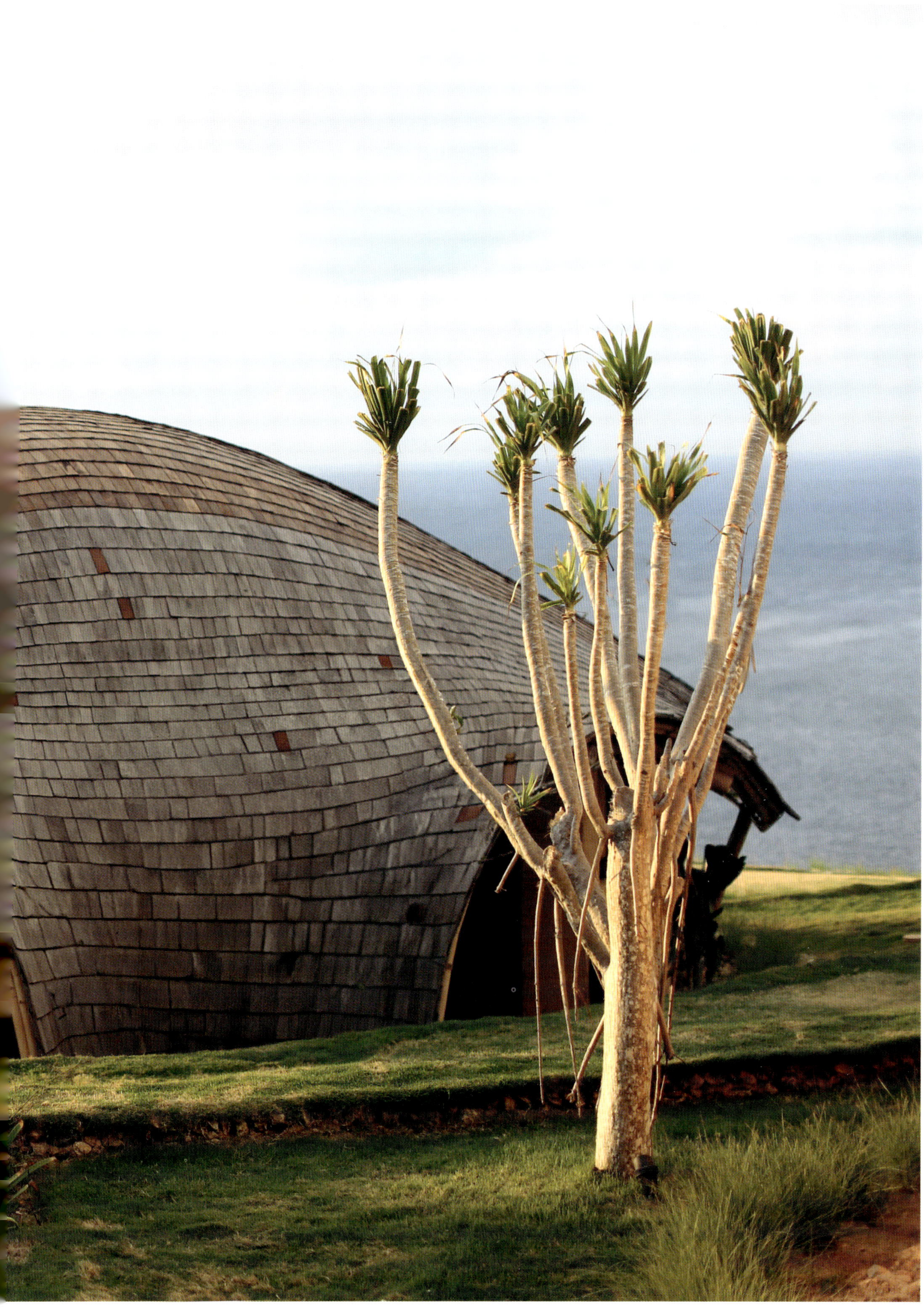

bribery. This has led to a tremendous degradation of Bali's ecology and overstressed its infrastructure.

We are fortunate to have among us in Bali a small group of visionary designers who aim to offset the rabid practices of the concrete merchants and bring eco-friendliness and sustainability into the architectural dialogue. But before we introduce some of these pioneers, our first step is to survey the indigenous architecture, the locally available sustainable materials, and their traditional uses.

Balinese architecture evolved from the people's concepts of social organization, their community-based social relationships, and their philosophy and spirituality. It incorporates animist, Buddhist, Hindu, Majapahit, and Dutch influences. Traditional Balinese buildings used natural materials such as thatch roofing, bamboo poles, woven bamboo, coconut wood, teak wood, mud, and stone.

Roofs were usually made from thatched black sugar-palm fibers, alang-alang grass, lontar palm leaves, dried coconut leaves, or shingles of ironwood or bamboo. Foundations and walls were constructed of red brick and cut river stones.

The Balinese developed sophisticated sculptural techniques, carving interior and exterior ornaments from sandstone and andesite. Temples and palaces are exquisitely decorated with both wood and stone carvings, mostly in floral patterns. Fierce statues guard the gates of palaces, temples, and villages, and other sculptural embellishments abound, such as the waterspouts in the form of goddess nymphs, skulls, fish, or dragons that are found in bathing places.

Balinese gardens are designed to accommodate the natural topography of the site and to look like unspoiled tropical nature. Water gardens are laid out in more formal designs, with ponds and fountains. A "floating pavilion" is a pavilion surrounded by ponds, which are usually filled with water lilies, papyrus, and lotus. Pools and fountains are used for recreational bathing as well as for ritual purification.

Emerald Starr is known for having redesigned the waterways at Tirta Gangga, the great water palace of East Bali. We meet at Villa Agung, part of Villa Campuhan, the magnificent estate that Linda Garland designed for Starr's friend Rob Cohen. The setting for our meeting is idyllic, with Mount Agung towering above and the ocean rolling in at the bottom of the garden. Villa Agung has a sublime majesty, and the spatial arrangements offer the roving eye a new vision at every turn.

> I moved to Hawaii in 1984 and bought a farm and expanded into permaculture and edible gardens. I was privileged to meet Mark Nelson, who has a PhD in wastewater treatment, at one of Linda Garland's first bamboo conferences, back I think in the late eighties. Mark Nelson and the Biosphere Foundation had developed a certified design system of constructed wetlands with a specific ratio of plant mass, biomass, and water flow, called Wastewater Gardens.
>
> I became the first person to bring it to Indonesia, and my first project was nine systems in Sacred Mountain Sanctuary. Over the years it has proved to the government its hygienic effectiveness and gained approval, and Wastewater Gardens are now widely used: villas, malls, hospitals, everywhere.
>
> Tirta Gangga Water Palace was basically cement, water, and grass. The bathroom was a little room where you squatted on stone over a channel of running water and it was washed down into the rice fields for the farmers to deal with. Hygiene was an is-

sue, and we realized that if we renovated the palace more people would come; so we gave Tirta Gangga Wastewater Gardens.

In 2006 I went to Nashville and, with about two hundred others, was trained personally by Al Gore to make presentations for his climate reality project, which grew into his film *An Inconvenient Truth*.

In 2007 I brought this message to Indonesia and patched a government attaché into Al Gore's training. Presenters are now all over Indonesia and the awareness is always spreading.

We have adapted some mangrove trees successfully into Wastewater Gardens, but the reefs are still being damaged by acidic runoff, and only Wastewater Gardens and constructed wetlands can help deal with this problem. We really need many more now, especially for the water table in Kuta and Legian. It is an environmental tragedy in the making.

We have gone terribly wrong, and it's time to right those wrongs, be sensible, and use obviously sustainable materials for our own needs, and the planet's. The chemical and oil industries should invest in cleaning up their own environmental damage. Obviously crops like bamboo and hemp should lead the way in future building materials.

Did you see *Hemp for Victory*, the 1942 film? We can thank William Randolph Hearst for demonizing hemp. Why? Because he owned forests!

The clouds are threatening and the air temperature has dropped as we head to our evening meeting with Claude Graves to discuss Nihiwatu, his resort on Sumba, an island southeast of Bali, and the Sumba Foundation founded by him and his wife. Their plan for a resort that would seriously support its surrounding community has had stellar success, and Nihiwatu has won numerous awards, including most recently the 2013 Condé Nast World Savers Award and the 2014 Tatler Travel Award for the world's best resort in the Style & Soul category.

My wife, Petra, and I planned and evolved a resort microsystem that was overlaid by the Sumba Foundation. The resort is a vehicle to enrich us, the community, and now the whole island.

In the 1980s, in Kenya, I built a mud building and quarried stone out of necessity, not out of any knowledge of sustainability. I didn't get fully into the sustainability aspect of development until we were a few years into the Nihiwatu project. Our plan was focused on what is now called responsible development; sustainability would come later. We had to really think about what we were doing out there in the middle of nowhere. It would not be right for us to build an Aman-standard resort and bring in Javanese construction labor to build all of it and then Balinese hotel staff to operate the property. That typical development mentality would have excluded the local people we grew to respect and love so much.

We hadn't thought about these issues until we settled in Sumba and started consolidating the land for our project. We realized that there were two ways to realize our vision: import everything for the benefit of suppliers in Bali and Java or create it locally for the benefit of the Sumbanese villagers. This island was so poor, so desperate, and so in need of help; it was clear that of course

The glorious Wastewater Gardens created by Emerald Starr at Villa Campuhan estate in Jasri, East Bali. Linda Garland designed this estate for Rob and Barbara Cohen, in collaboration with Sumatran master carpenters. Constructed without screws or nails,

the guest villas and the main house are open to the mountains
and the sea.

we should do it all here, no matter how much harder it would be for us. We would need to train up staff from zero. No locals could read or write Indonesian, let alone English, so we really had to start from scratch.

In the beginning Petra and I decided we would give a third of the money we made to projects that would help the community around us. It was a noble goal, but at some point I came to the realization that our target of one-third was not going to make much of an impact on the overwhelming needs we were seeing in the villages. By then I knew that if we were going to help the community in an impactful way we would have to have an entity that could stand alone from the resort. We tried to set up the foundation in Switzerland, three years before opening, but we just couldn't get it right; we didn't have the right advice and the right people with us.

When we first opened Nihiwatu, before the foundation was established, we needed to get our guests to support our vision of helping the Sumbanese community, and clearly the business alone was not going to be able to do it. Our first guests generously gave between a hundred and five hundred dollars; I knew they could afford a thousand dollars or more, and I also knew they were thinking, Will my money really go into the community, or will it go to building the resort? The idea was definitely working, and clearly our guests wanted to get involved, but donating directly to us was a problem that needed solving.

Some years after we opened, and only with the help of our first guests, we set up and registered the foundation in America. Having an American-based 501(c)(3) foundation gave our American guests the ability to donate to the many community development projects I was setting up and get a tax write-off. That changed everything. Almost overnight the donations grew from two to three hundred dollars to five to ten thousand dollars. Today the average donation is in the range of ten thousand dollars.

Sumba was so poor and needed help; there was no end to the problems the villagers were up against. I listed around a hundred things the communities desperately needed and then prioritized the most important in each area. My hopes at the time were to help maybe five schools and ten to twenty of the villages immediately around us. As it turns out, we are now in 430 villages and helping twenty-five thousand people with water. We have five clinics, a whole battery of nurses and doctors, malaria training schools, and malnutrition and organic farming projects. We've been able to reduce malaria by 85 percent and increase enrollment in schools by 300 percent. Students who received scholarships from us years ago are now actively educating and contributing to their own communities or working for Nihiwatu or the Sumba Foundation. It is a perfect circle. It has exceeded my highest hopes and is something I'm proud to have created.

The foundation has hundreds of water wells. Before the wells, the women and children spent the majority of their day carrying water. When they don't have to do that anymore the impact is immediate; the kids start to go to school and the women start to make blankets that provide family income. We have five malaria clinics strategically placed so that no sick person has to walk more than three kilometers to reach one. To fight malnutrition, improving diets and farming techniques have shown remarkable results.

We create generational change and teach the kids in grades 1 to 6 why this food they are eating is beneficial to them and what the food chain is and about protein, everything—the nutritional values and diet. We do this to help create a healthier community, one that has a better ability to care for itself. Once that's achieved, the next thing is to create employment so that these communities can become sustainable. This is where tourism comes in.

Our resort creates the opportunity for involvement by the guests. If you can get your guests involved in projects that are helping people in need, it generates repeat business, as those who became involved in the community projects always return to see the results of their donation. If you have repeat business you need to spend less on marketing. It also adds great value to the guests' vacation experience when they can have the satisfaction of integrating with the community, whether it's helping kids with school, malnutrition, malaria, or water.

All of this grew out of that idea that if you get other people involved it creates a perfect model: a for-profit business side by side with a nonprofit business. They both help and benefit each other.

So, I've covered the responsibility aspects of our development. I'll move on to the sustainability aspects. For me a good sustainable development is one that will be able to maintain itself through time without adversely impacting, in any way, its immediate and regional environments, and it should be profitable for it to work.

Creating power is the least sustainable aspect of remote hotel developments. We looked very seriously at solar power, but it was quoted at almost one and a half million dollars and we'd still need generators! Wind wouldn't work where we were, so we had to go with fuel-guzzling generators.

The very first step in the development planning was to reduce consumption everywhere we could. Installing LED lights and water-saving devices, using local plants that did not need much water—these were some of the key components in reducing our consumption to the bare minimum.

But Nihiwatu is a very high-end resort property, and we don't cut corners under the guise of ecotourism. There are pools and plunge pools, kitchens and bars all over the place, air-conditioning everywhere—it has everything high-end clients expect, and to provide that for them we have a huge fifteen-hundred-dollar-per-day bill for diesel fuel and oil to run the generators. I decided to make a Sumba Foundation biodiesel project that would make and sell the biofuel to our resort. So instead of buying diesel from the oil company, all of that money went to the community of farmers who sold us the coconuts we needed to make the biodiesel. But still, at the end of the year it's a lot of money for the business to bear.

Water is another major problem for these kinds of developments. At Nihiwatu it's a very limited resource; it's precious. When it runs out it can cost upwards of eight hundred dollars a day to buy just to keep the resort operating. It is imperative to reduce con-

Palm oil trees (*Elaeis guineensis*) planted for shade and biofuel next to the natural stone swimming pool at Panchoran, designer Linda Garland's former estate in Nyuh Kuning, Ubud.

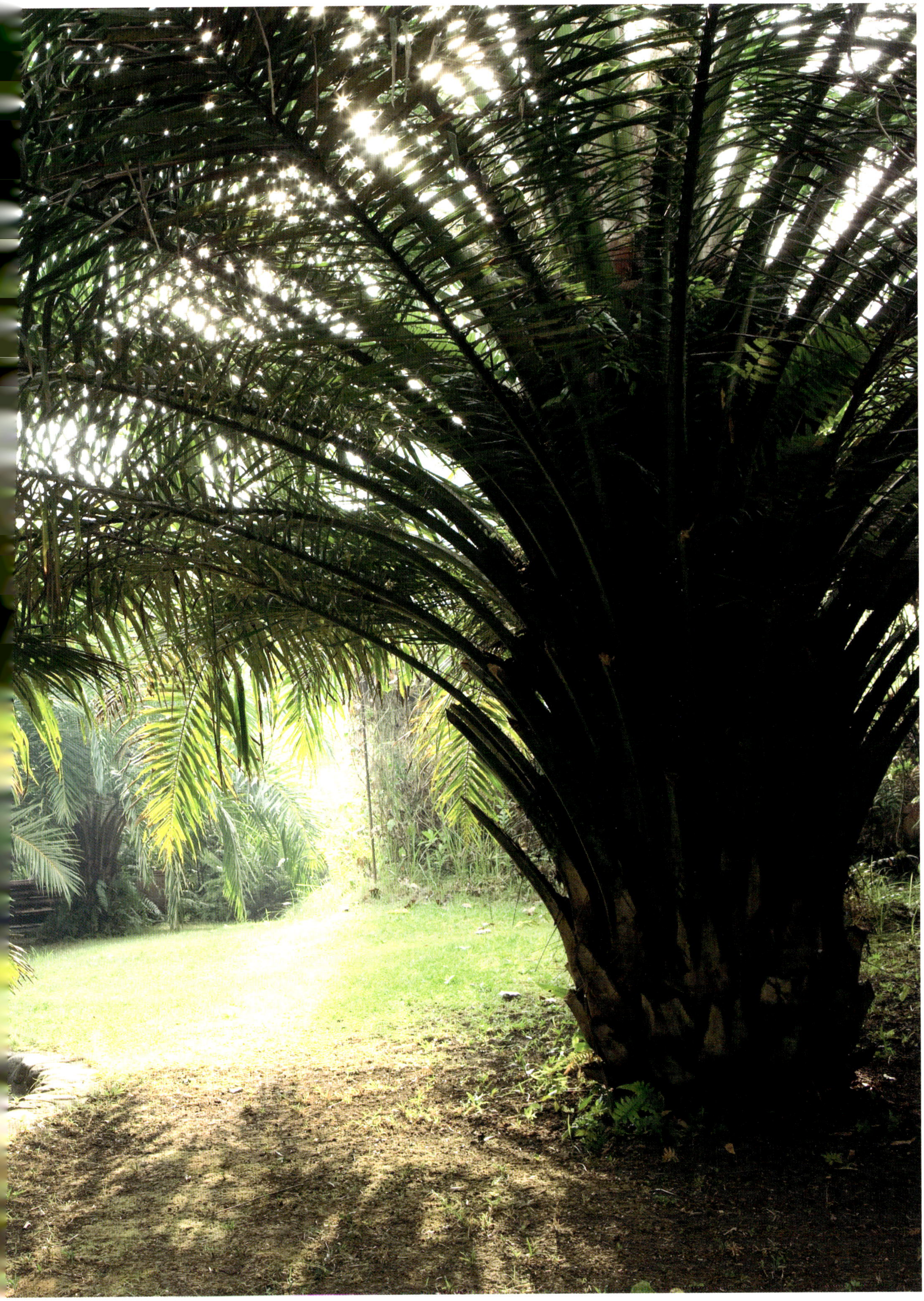

sumption and to reuse it as much as possible. We have deep-bore wells, and reservoirs to trap seasonal rainwater; we also built berms to build up groundwater levels. We reuse water by treating it to a level where it can be used in gardens, but we only get to use that water twice. I'd like to have the ability to constantly recycle all the water that's consumed; that would really change things. We are trying a few simple things like evaporating salt and gray water in trays for drinking water. It works, but it would be difficult to scale up enough to support a resort's needs.

There are a lot of new and constantly evolving technologies that are becoming more efficient and cost effective; however, most are still based on solar and wind. In my opinion they are at best supplemental sources of power. After all, they'll only work when you have sunlight or wind, and when you don't have enough of that then it's back to running generators and the problems that come with them.

For the past five years I've been working with some brilliant scientists on a solution that will end the power and water problems many remote developments have to deal with. I expect to have the first unit in Sumba around August 2015. This will be powering our latest sustainable development in Sumba, called Haweri.

This unit generates power without using fuel. Future versions will have attachments that can flash-steam and distill 90 percent of the water used in the resort, even wastewater coming out of the hotel's toilets. The recycled water would be drinking-quality water; that's where I'm going with it.

The power generator has been running in the California test facility for two years now. The boys have been constantly fine-tuning it. It's now certified in the U.S. and just about ready for production later this year. I'm not going to say it will change the world, but it will change things. At this point we are unable to reveal the nature of the invention, but we are sure from our test results that it will be a huge breakthrough in this technology.

It's funny, the local people are so superstitious; I heard a story from a junior minister of tourism that I'm on Sumba looking for gold. After twenty-seven years, I must be the worst gold prospector on the planet!

Another superstitious story: a friend of mine, during the rainy season, would dash into the house to get out of the rain; the locals think that Clayton has a laser and is shooting the clouds with it to stop the rain!

Early on a story went around that John Hardy was stealing the sacred water with his river vortex project! [See page 138.] I think that when Linda Garland built her first bamboo house the locals almost killed themselves with laughter; they simply didn't understand the concept of style!

I think the corporations who use plastic packaging should be responsible for cleaning up the oceans, but it will never happen. There are biodegradable plastics, and it will take government regulation to force their adoption, but let's face it: the corporations own the governments.

I know someone is developing a kind of plastic packaging from tapioca, and of course there should be plastics and fuel made from hemp and not our dwindling fossil fuels. Hempcrete is a fabulous building product, and apart from continuing to sink carbon, it is incredibly strong and continues to grow stronger. I hope these changes come quickly. It's common sense.

How would I describe my design signature? Without a doubt it is integrating responsible development with sustainability, changing lives along the way. That is my influence, to help with guidelines and solutions.

Seven years later, we met up with Elora Hardy for lunch at Rüsters in Ubud. At our meal, which included a series of delightful moments, such as a chance meeting with Sebastian Mesdag (see pp. 32–40), Elora reminded us of what makes sustainable architecture on Bali so special—namely, that it appeals first of all to the spirit.

I use bamboo because it is beautiful and has personality; Dad saw it too. It was apparent early on that not many people were motivated solely by bamboo being a sustainable product or not. They wanted it because we caught their hearts. I never sold the building just because it was sustainable! I only got commissioned because they believed I could make a space that made them feel closer to who they wanted to become; part of that was by bringing them closer to nature. But trying to route it through the value system of the logical mind, making decisions about sustainability, is not the way it worked. Our clients felt we understood their dreams, and we caught their hearts.

There are two forms of bamboo construction: post and beam, and grid shell structure, where you're getting away from compression and into tension. The whole thing must have tension to be strong. The webbing between each of the ribs is what makes it strong, a very particular arrangement and very specific tested connections; all of it, the entire surface, is doing work. The advantages are that you get to create forms that look and feel different, and shapes that you can't do otherwise.

In future, the bamboo poles will be split and laminated and turned into beams that the whole industry can use.

My perceptions haven't really changed, but my appreciation of collaboration has increased. We've done more work overseas, with projects in Costa Rica, Panama, Thailand, and the Philippines, and more with mixed materials, not just bamboo.

The magical wastewater garden at Uma Jiwa, a house in Ubud designed by Ibuku Studio and Earth Lines Architects.

Down by the river. The river bend at Bambu Indah, John and Cynthia Hardy's eco-luxury boutique hotel on Sayan Terrace, Ubud, accommodates half a dozen natural pools.

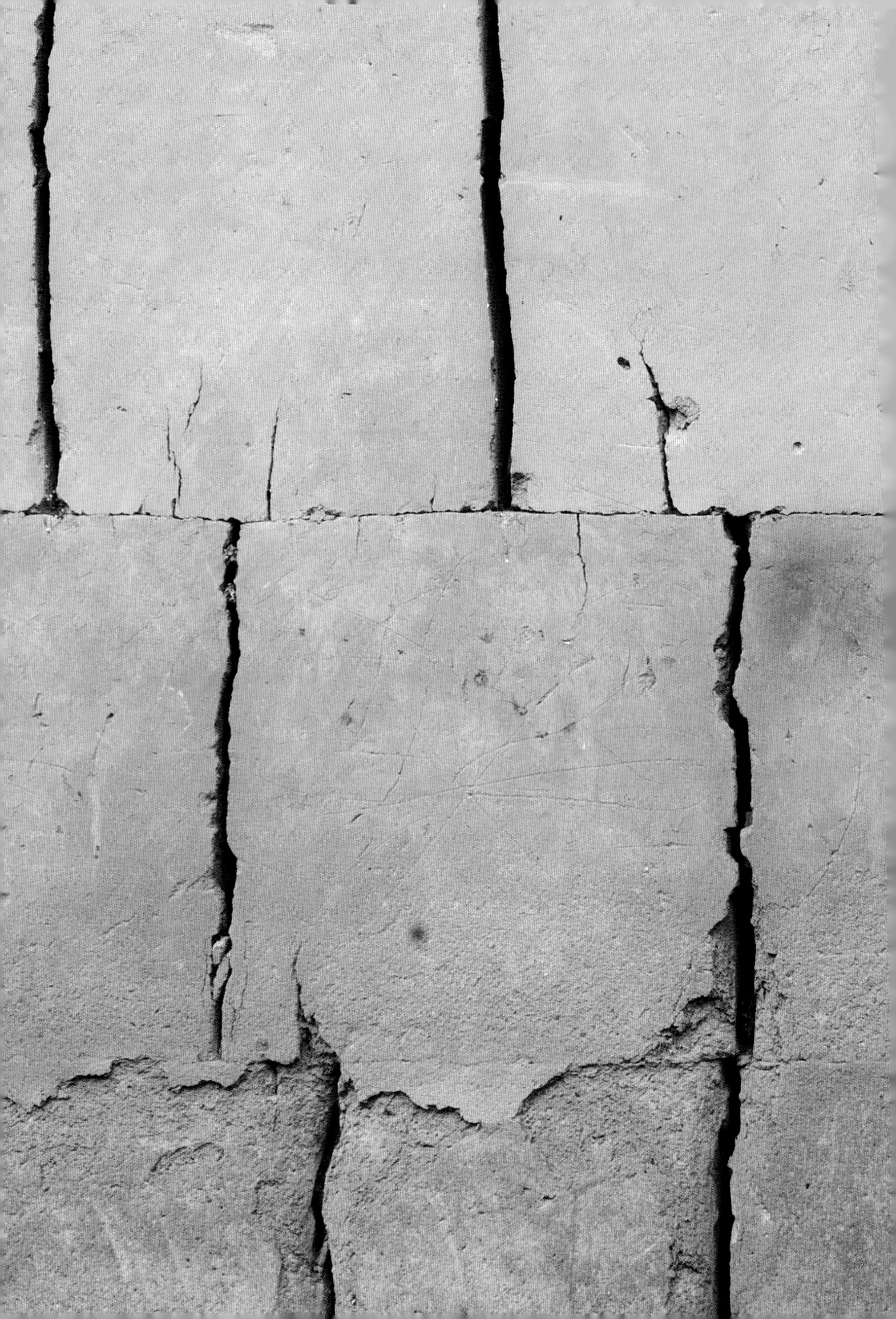

MUD, EARTH, AND BRICKS

Mud is slippery, gooey, messy, and great fun to play in. It is a child's joy and a parent's nightmare.

Making an earth wall or dwelling is closer to baking a cake than building; finding the right recipe to use is a matter of trial and error, and depends on what soil is available.

Prehistoric hunter-gatherers, though nomadic, still needed shelter from the elements and security from predatory animals. The first temporary dwellings were made from immediately available materials—such as earth—and positioned around a central hearth with a fire, which would have been avoided by most predators.

Mud is durable enough to make permanent structures, so when humans developed agriculture and desired fixed habitations, they built mud walls to encircle a common area. This marked the birth of the village.

Mud is still a chief building material in many areas of the globe. Close to one-third of the world's population lives in mud-brick houses. A remarkable quality of these structures is their durability, with some mud buildings lasting for a thousand years. Earth-based homes are naturally insulated, cool in summer and warm in winter. They are extremely resistant to earthquakes and are naturally healthy, with no pollutants in the mixture to cause allergies.

The mud gate of a traditional residential compound in Kebek Puhu Village, with woven bamboo cages for fighting cocks visible within.

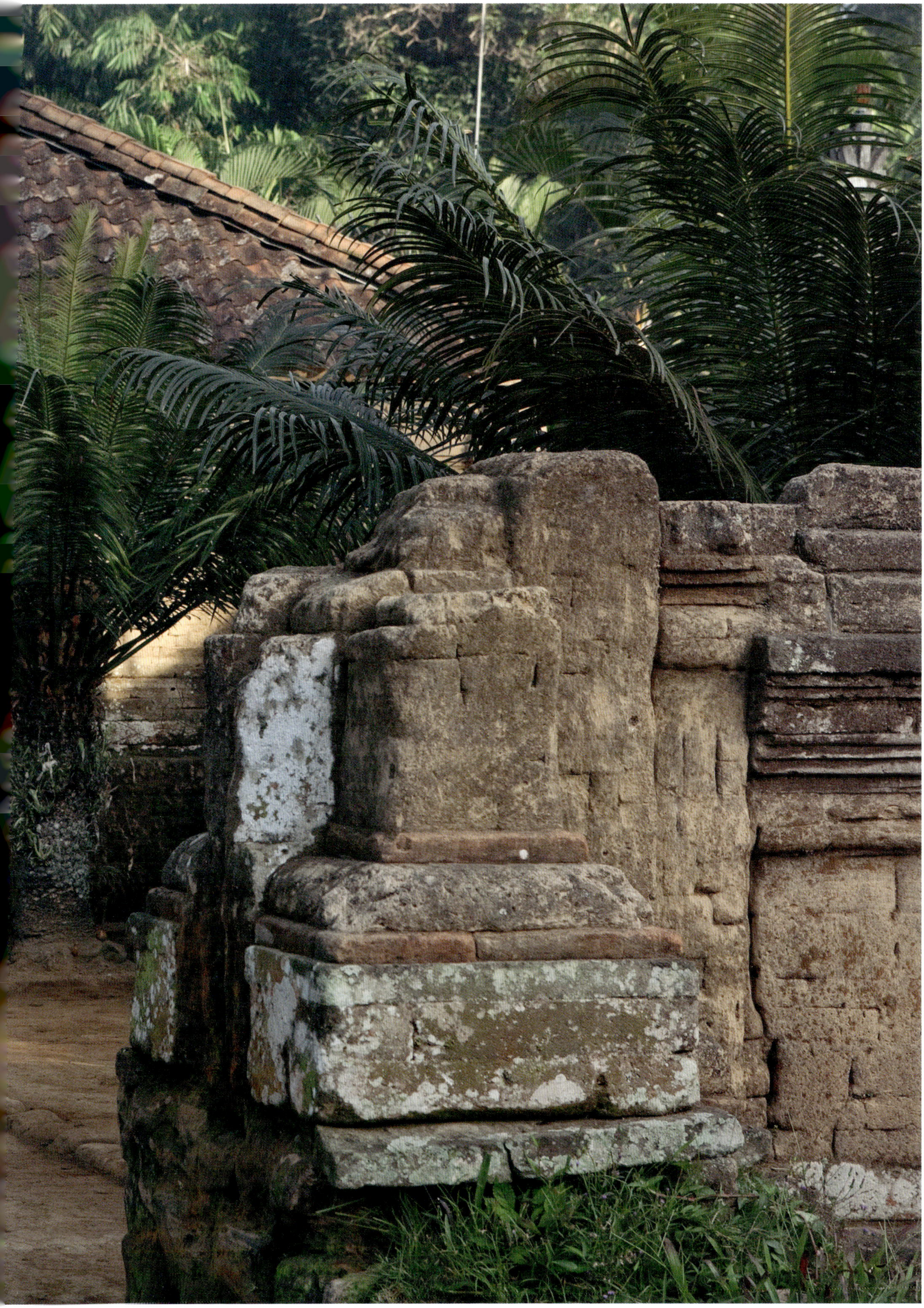

Varieties of earthen building include rammed earth, cob, mud brick, and adobe. Rammed earth requires a mixture of sand and clay and is compressed in a mold. Cob is clay-rich mud with straw or rice husks mixed in for strength. Mud brick and adobe are made by molding cob into bricks.

The Balinese traditionally used mud to build the boundary walls around *desas* (villages) and in the construction of their family compounds of several houses with a communal kitchen. In recent decades, though, cement has progressively replaced traditional vernacular construction, and the practice of earthen building has almost vanished, along with the associated technical skills and knowledge—although the mud-brick recipe used by Balinese women, historically the hardworking hands behind these walls, has survived: "Mix blood in it, and eggs."

Mud buildings are now as rare as hen's teeth in Bali. There are remnants of walls and the odd kitchen, but all are neglected, and piles of cement bricks stand ominously in the courtyards. These last mud structures will be knocked down and replaced by the kind of drab cement boxes that only the beautiful natural surroundings can make acceptable to the roving eye.

Puhu, north of Ubud, is one of the very few mud villages left on the island. We head up to visit Sebastian Mesdag, who undertook a field study of the earthen buildings there and has built mud walls around his own house. We meet on the dusty open space in front of the village *bale banjar* (assembly pavilion). Our luggage is transferred and we head to his remote property over four-wheel-drive-only terrain.

Mesdag's house overlooks a jungle forest capped with volcanoes. His wife, Ayu, and their toddler daughter, River, greet us warmly and show us to our wooden jungle cabin accommodation among ferns and trees in a gully below the main house. River carries her live Australian feather-footed silky chicken as if it were a teddy bear. We sit on the veranda of the cabin to talk, with the occasional interruption of River's cry when her chicken timidly tries to fly away.

> The most impressive walls are the ones built using the cob technique: the walls are thicker, and the rhythm of the joints and vertical cracks gives the impression of massive stone walls. In most cases, compound walls have been erected without stone foundations or protective capping—the "boots and hat" of a good earth wall—but the inhabitants will tell you that they have withstood the extreme rains for a long time and that they are even getting harder as time passes. This soil hardens when exposed to air.
>
> Earth has great potential as a low-carbon-footprint material, because it's locally available and doesn't need to be fired; it can be transformed into a construction material through a very simple process, using mainly labor.
>
> Sustainability is not about pushing a self-serving ecological agenda but reestablishing a balance in nature that, with luck, will allow us to coexist in harmony for years to come. This will only be achieved if nature comes first.

Some years later, we return to Puhu to see Sebastian's latest venture, an indigo plantation and dyeing operation. He tells us how this new project is a natural outgrowth of his relationship to the land, and to the community.

> When I first bought the farm, I slept in a bamboo hut. Having no electricity or running water allowed me to explore the surroundings. We had to go on a hike to a waterfall to bathe or a river to cook, and so on. This allowed me first to fall in love with the land

Nineteenth-century oars from Mentawai hang on a mud wall at Bambu Indah, John and Cynthia Hardy's eco-luxury boutique hotel on Sayan Terrace, Ubud. In the foreground is a *rumbi*, a rice storage pot made by the Batak people of Sumatra.

A mud wall at the entrance of the Pawon House, Bambu Indah.

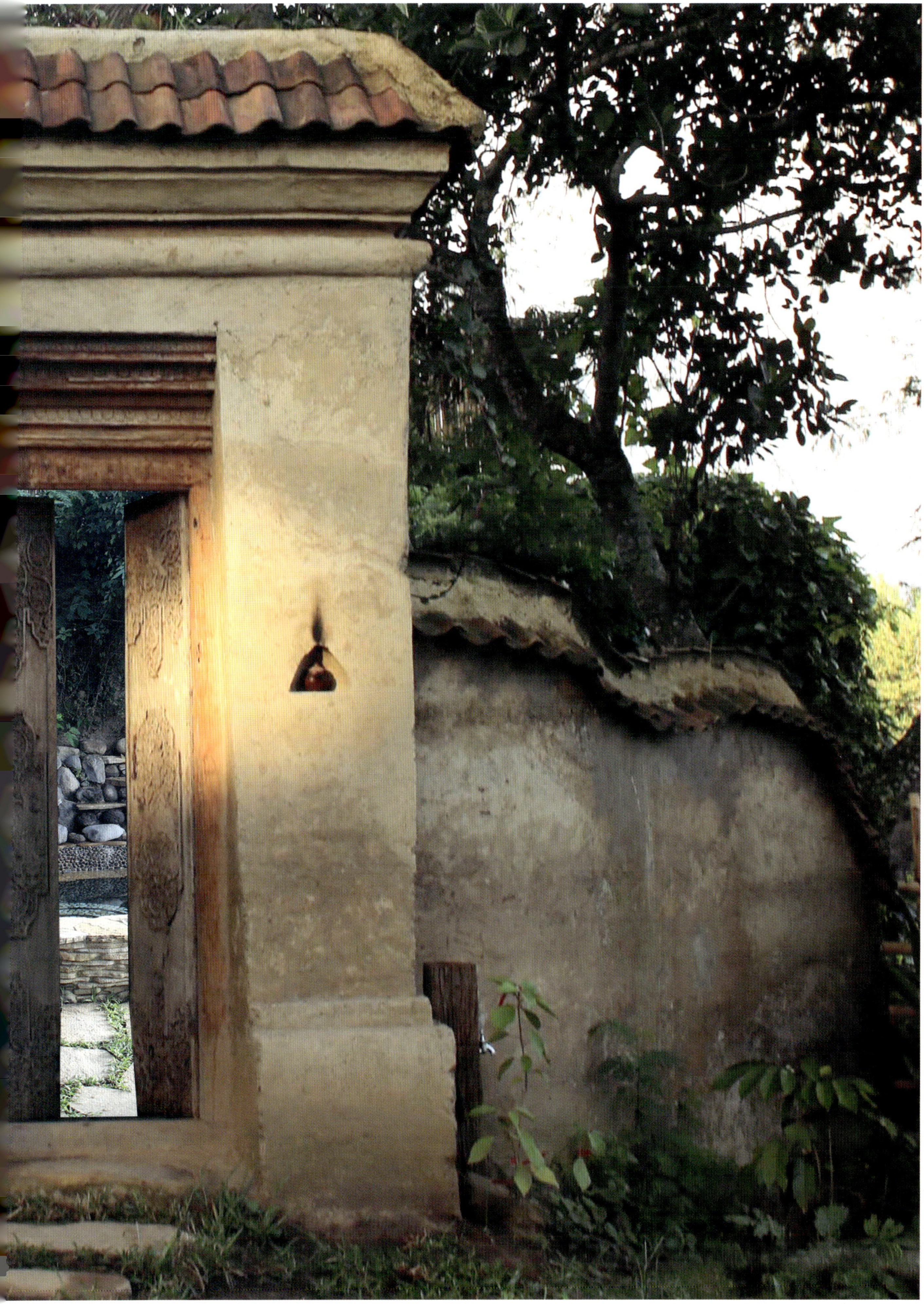

A wall made of mud mixed with chopped rice husks, Bambu Indah.

and later come to respect it fully. I had time to get to know native trees, and with the help of the village we started planting trees. Not trees that are directly and obviously beneficial to humans but instead to all native living creatures.

I had visited protected holy forests, where small temples are hardly visible and the forest becomes the main focus, and the sounds of nature that dwell in it are overwhelming. This made me realize I wanted to live in such an environment. To build the house took six years working with the villagers and simple tools. We did it practically all by hand, and took breaks to savor the process. Stood back, enjoyed the view, and gradually and organically framed it. Windows became paintings that during the day change and during the years mature. Instead of building a tree house, the small seedlings are slowly becoming giant trees that embrace the house and hide it from the world. We rarely cut a branch, and if we do it becomes a family affair. Each piece of wood has a story, and each stone was placed with the help of many. The process, as I mentioned, was long.

The philosophy behind the indigo is similar. It takes time and involves the help of the community. We use every part of the plant, and once the dye is extracted the leaves are given back to the land. From the beginning we knew we never wanted to work for others or make this part of our life a business. This part of our life is a practice and a way for us to share a philosophy that hopefully also inspires others to pursue it.

Being surrounded by indigo and working with it, and in an environment we have played a big part in creating, is a privilege. You realize how giving nature is. How the simple act of planting a seedling can be so rewarding for years to come not only for your life but for those who follow. A dream here in Bali can become a reality in one's lifetime, as things grow so fast.

We found out later that the land we bought had been rice fields, and once the water source had gone it was planted with other crops. There were trees only on the edge of the property, marking the boundary with the neighbors' land, and the soil was infertile, this being the reason they decided to sell. All topsoil had been washed away by the heavy rain in the area, and the land looked tired. The first thing we did was to replant local trees. We collected saplings from different parts of Bali, trees that would bear fruit not for us but for birds and other native animals. To do this we asked members of every family in the village to help plant a small forest. We asked them to bring trees that would grow big. Now eighteen years have passed, and some trees are more than a meter [3 ft.] in diameter and at least forty meters [130 ft.] high. In Bali trees tend to shed their leaves twice a year, which is great for bringing back a healthy topsoil.

The indigo we plant does not like the sun at all and needs a very damp condition to grow. As we did not want to irrigate or maintain it, we managed to create the perfect balance for it to grow naturally. A flock of chickens walk freely, moving the topsoil and eating insects that if not controlled could potentially damage the crop. Usually not much grows under shade, but our indigo does and acts as a net when the heavy rains come, holding the topsoil from being washed away. To the untrained eye it doesn't even look as if we have a plantation growing, as the forest and the crop

A shower at Intaaya, a sustainable resort on Nusa Penida, with rammed-earth walls by Elie Gaborit of Earth Construction Bali.

Another rammed-earth wall at Intaaya.

grow side by side. This I would say is the most sustainable plantation I have seen.

It is a hot day on the Bukit Peninsula, but the trees cast deep shadows and cool breezes waft around us. At the Temple Lodge, a boutique hotel for surfers in Bingin, near the famed Uluwatu surf break, we are in a sort of time warp of recovered timbers, driftwood, stone, and mud, all stylishly put together with a charming restaurant on the cliff's edge overlooking the mesmerizing waves. The food is exceptional, fresh and organic. We are shown to a *limasan* (knockdown wood house) built of mud and reclaimed teakwood, whose bathroom boasts a bamboo-and-alang-alang roof pierced by a gigantic stone lingam that summons thoughts of Stonehenge. A large lap pool is positioned along the length of the building. We have penciled in an after-surf meeting with Mario Ilotte, the proprietor.

I was an industrialist, so my concerns were machinery, time, engineering, science, and production. When I moved from Italy to South Africa, I joined the Waldorf School, which stimulated me toward appreciation of all the forms of nature. I was forty-nine years old. In these buildings there are some aspects of the free-form thought that is taught by the Waldorf School. There is no geometry, just a flow. I guess that if I walk away from this, in ten years nature would completely reclaim it. In a way I am very proud to make a place that can disappear back to nature if we don't maintain it!

When I was building this place, I was in an artistic state of mind, and my free-flowing approach brought up all sorts of problems. So I would go surfing and clear my mind completely, and afterward the gods would present me with an answer, sharpening my sensibility to recognize the treasures that surround us.

I have used reclaimed wood, driftwood, bamboo, mud, reeds, alang-alang, and stone; all have come from the local area and are sustainable resources.

I didn't have an architect. I just kept adding to the place as materials kept finding their way to me. On numerous occasions I would see huge logs washed up on the beach and I would get a group of men together and we would haul them up the cliff to be used later in many different ways.

The log that we used as the headboard for the oversize bed in the limasan, we hauled up and had about twenty people balancing it until it slipped out of control into the swimming pool. It took us a whole day to get it out of the pool. Thank the gods that the helpers and the guests in the pool were young and fast enough to jump out of the way as the log plunged in.

A blank canvas is very menacing and won't stimulate you, but if you have odd and different things around you, they will indicate a place where they should be and then form becomes recognizable. If you draw boxes, it is for calculating time and money, not to shape the structure that you are creating. In other words, one is a process for money and the other is a process of creation. The materials will show you the way artistically and sustainably. I suggest that students and architects gather a junk shop around them filled to overflowing with materials that they wish to use.

When the Temple Lodge was our private home, I had a dream. I was sitting at the end of a long table with my wife, Cristiana, and

41

A limestone sink at Intaaya in front of a rammed-earth wall.

A mud-walled pathway to the jungle, between a traditional bamboo kitchen and a temple.

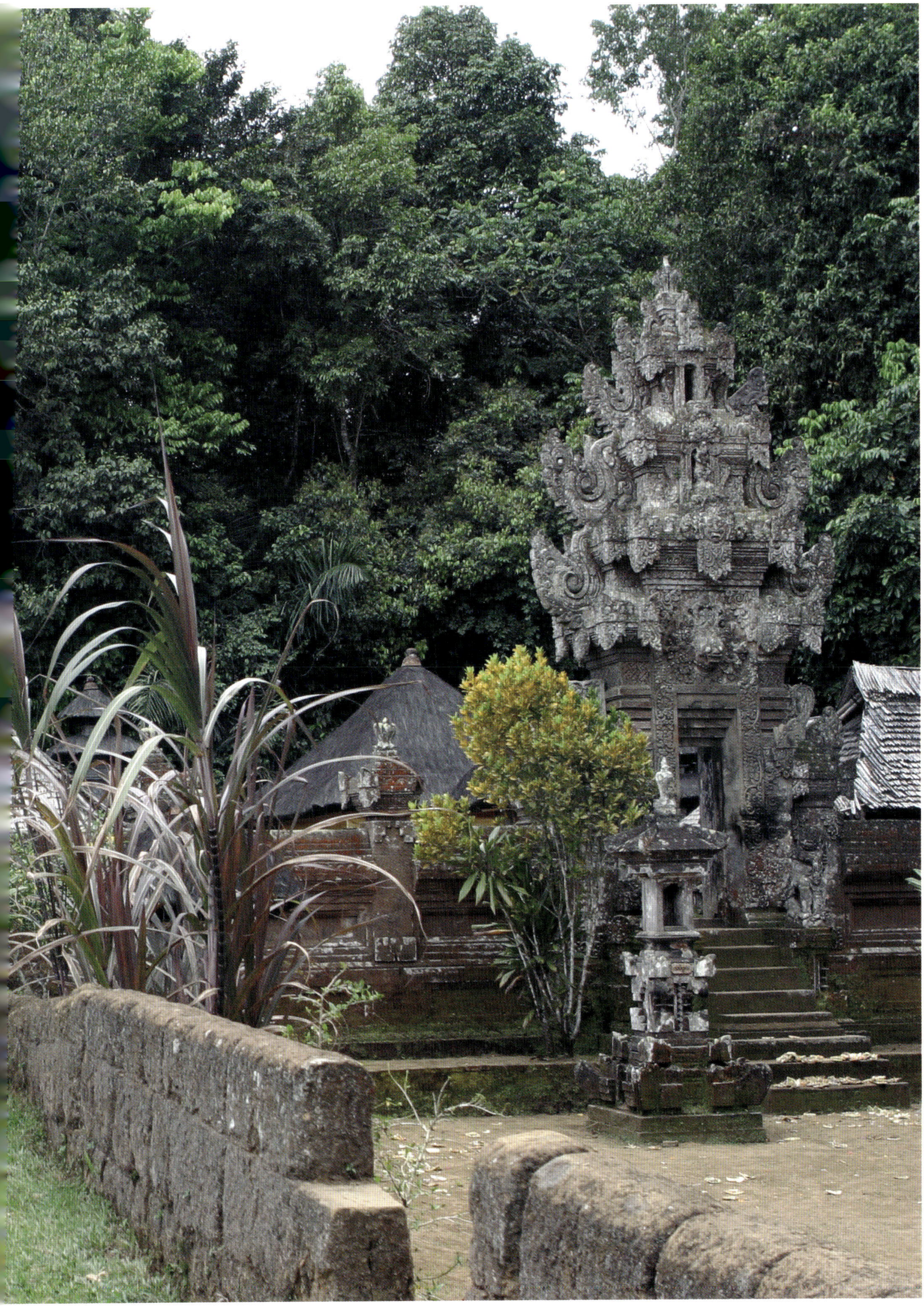

A poolside dwelling with mud walls and an alang-alang roof, at the Temple Lodge, Bingin, designed by Mario and Cristiana Ilotte.

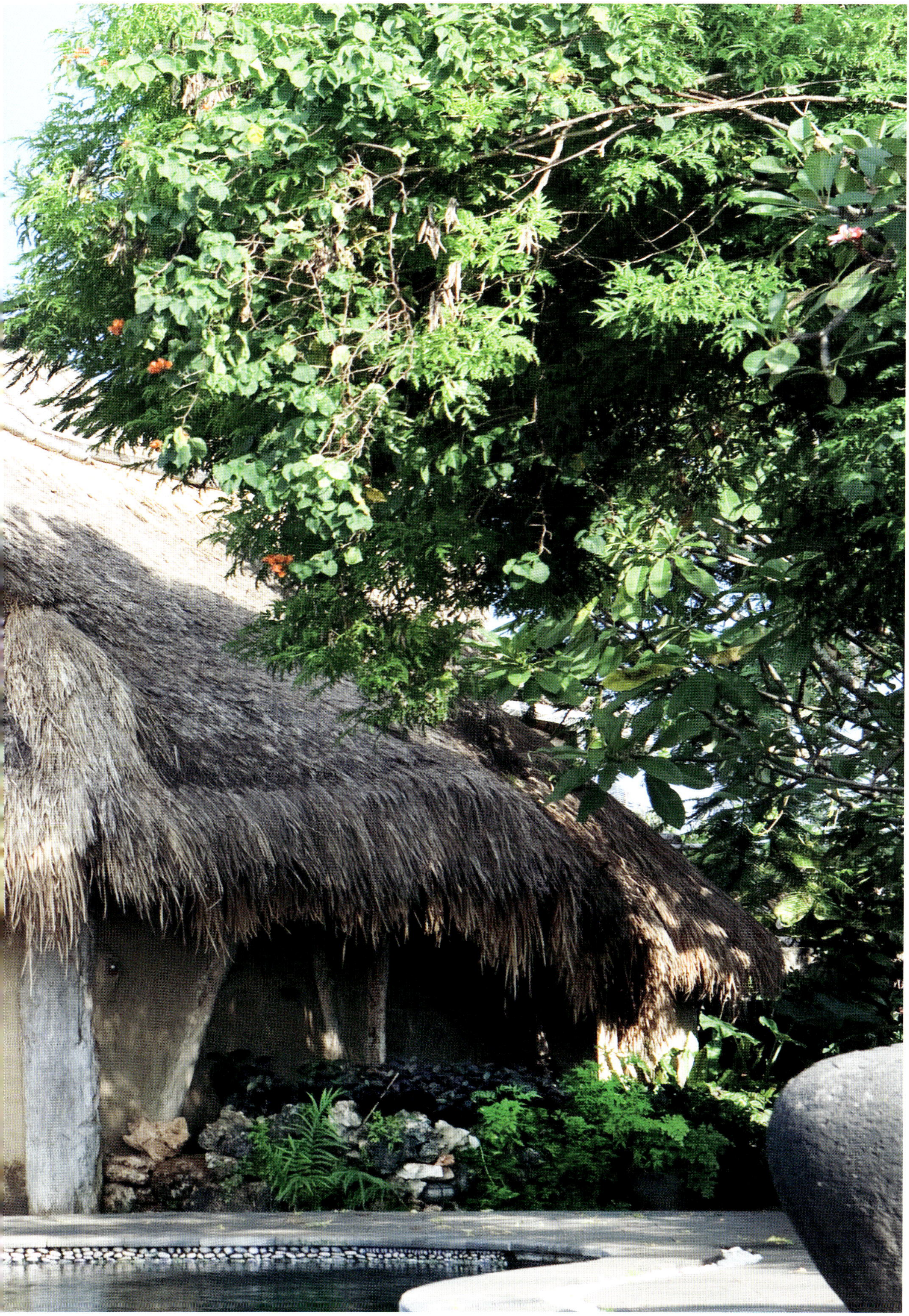

Reclaimed teak boards and a louvered window rest atop a mud-brick wall at the Temple Lodge.

Mud walls are freely combined with windows, tiles, shutters, and timber panels in the buildings of the Temple Lodge.

The red-brick entrance to Rumah Rubah, a house in Tumbak Bayuh designed by
Maximilian Jencquel, with a carved wooden archway and doors.

we were looking at each other over the candles. It seemed like life was boring even though we had everything. You know, I have seen people with fifty-meter yachts begging their friends to come on board. Community is very important. I wanted something more than possessions that impress; I wanted a better quality of connectedness and life.

After I built my house, Cristiana and I added a small restaurant and some more rooms. In the restaurant we have two big tables in the Italian style of the *tavolata*, a mixed table for single people and lone wolves. All of a sudden we have hundreds of friends and I'm making new ones; we belong to a community.

I like the idea that nature is a perfect provider of shelter for humans, not the skyscrapers of New York. If you live there you don't even want to see a little beetle or fly in your house. Those people come here and are scared of bugs, even geckos or crickets, but especially bacteria. They want a sterile, hermetically sealed, temperature-controlled enclosure, because they are so out of touch with nature. People want security and have become addicted to it. I know people who feel secure with 100,000, and I know people with 100 million who are insecure, with sick, depressed minds. Isn't it all about connection to nature?

The Temple Lodge is like a *kampung* [hamlet] of rustic and primitive styles from all over the archipelago, and it feels very grounded and real in its natural and elegant simplicity of unpolluted old times . . . with Wi-Fi.

My son said to me that he didn't want money, he wanted me to buy a big block of land and protect it for posterity. This touched my heart and I agreed. It will be held in trust and will remain as it is forever.

I will not stop building, turning my dreams into reality. I have a project on Rote, which is quite remote, and this will make it easier to control.

Did you read about the French mariner who went to Tahiti? He mixed his poo with seaweed and grew potatoes and carrots and survived happily. Well, we've put a sign on our anaerobic toilet: "Your poo is precious to us!"

A house temple nestled under a *timbul* (breadfruit) tree at Rumah Rubah.

A dreamy mix of terra-cotta bricks and minimalist lines at the
Potato Head beach club and resort, Seminyak.

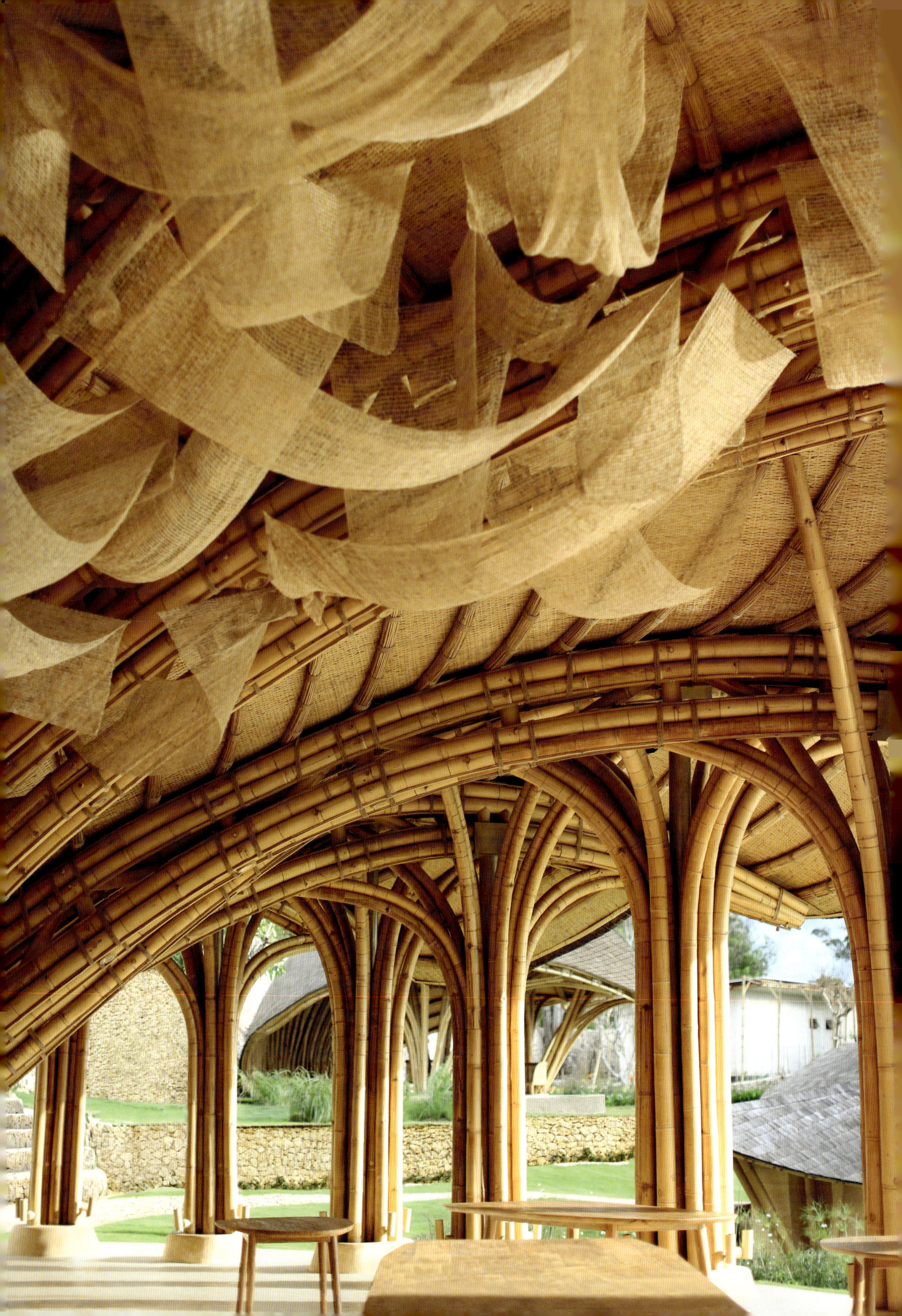

BAMBOO

Some are introduced to bamboo in moments of agony, as the headmaster thrashes out "six of the best" with his bamboo cane. Some may hear the sound of a bamboo flute or an *angklung*, a musical instrument not unlike a xylophone. Some live in jungles where bamboo provides food, shelter, and tools for living.

Today Bamboo also promises a sustainable, cost-effective, and ecologically responsible alternative to the widespread clear-cutting of our world's precious forests and timberlands.

Dotted prolifically all over the tropics, bamboo is one of the fastest-growing plants in the world: some species can grow as much as a foot in a single day. Of all natural building materials, bamboo is perhaps the most flexible, sustainable, and diverse. Related to pampas grass, sugarcane, and even corn, bamboos include over a thousand species of woody perennial grasses. They are a recent addition to Earth's flora, having evolved 30 to 40 million years ago, well after the demise of the dinosaurs.

It has been estimated that bamboo is used by at least half of the world's population every day. More than a thousand different products are made from bamboo. Bamboo shoots are a popular ingredient in Asian cuisine. Entire bamboo farms have been established to provide fresh bamboo shoots, which are tastier than canned. Bamboo wine is made from the fermented juice of the plant.

Framing beauty on top of a cliff at Intaaya, a sustainable resort on Nusa Penida designed by Pablo Luna Studio.

Some bamboo stems have the same tensile strength as steel and are used to reinforce concrete. Bamboo is used to make scaffolding, cooking utensils, furniture, toys, and even mountain-bike frames. Bamboo pulp is turned into paper and fabric, and small polished stem segments are sometimes used in jewelry and necklaces. Bamboo can be made into weapons, too, including bows and arrows and sharpened stakes. In Sumatra, native hunters fashion blowpipes from bamboo to shoot poison darts. The *shinai*, the wooden sword used in the Japanese martial art of kendo, is made from bamboo strips.

Everywhere there are flowers and ferns, and the jungle spills over into the narrow road before us. The scenery seems to get more and more green as we trundle north through the rice fields, away from the coast and tourist bustle. Hundreds of kites are blazing across the blue sky. We feel a balmy breeze and hear the rattle of wooden cowbells, punctuated by the sound of a spoon tapping against a bowl, which announces a *kaki lima* (food stall on two wheels) wheeled by a small man dressed in dazzling colors.

As we gradually ascend the slopes of the volcano, the surrounding vegetation becomes even more impossibly lush and green. At almost every bend in the road a shrine appears, and in the rice fields sit bivouacs, sometimes anchored by a solitary tree, for shelter from sun and rain, a place for a drowsy snooze out of the midday sun. We drop down into a gully carved by the river, where artisans cut and fashion the exposed stone into long bricks.

Passing through a village where terra-cotta is made, we drive up a street lined red with drying tiles and roof ornaments. The street is sprinkled with shops built with reclaimed timber doors and columns, some plain, some carved with intricate details. Sculptures of ancient dieties covered in fine moss add their green energy to the bric-a-brac for sale.

Past the village, huge banyans come into view, each one's base wrapped in checkered cloth, a pattern called *poleng* that has been used ceremonially by the Balinese for centuries. Though all nature is sacred, these trees are especially so.

Every mile or two we see a temple with giant stone gates carved with defenders of spiritual realms, until we turn off through a village dotted with the remains of ancient mud walls and enter a driveway lined with a living fence of thin but tall bamboo.

A stone path leads down to a large three-story bamboo house with a prominent thatched roof made of alang-alang. There is a feeling of deep serenity; the jungle and the house are breathing together in harmony. It is the natural feeling of indoor-outdoor living typical in tropical climes, but this place, called Panchoran, has a special elegance and good taste created by the visionary interior and landscape designer Linda Garland.

The term *gypsetter* might have been coined just for Linda Garland, as she is known for her nomadic tendencies. She jets from one paradise to another, leaving her mark on all who encounter her wisdom and vision. She's been called Bamboo Linda, and her creative genius is known around the world; she has created tropical retreats for the likes of Chris Blackwell, Richard Branson, and David Bowie. Linda is known particularly for her work with bamboo and for her nonprofit Environmental Bamboo Foundation, which aims to expand the uses of bamboo and bring ecological awareness to a global audience.

Her beautiful Balinese team welcomes us into her domain with silver-rimmed bamboo cups of delicious coconut water with lime, palm sugar, and mint. We greet Linda and, sipping the cooling nectar, we talk of friends, smooth travels, calm seas, and the immediate issue: the plight of the world's ecology.

> It's very serious, the destruction we are seeing here. The handicraft industry has huge orders for bamboo wind chimes, and it's

decimating the bamboo plantations. They're cutting it down and chopping it into bits! They don't know how to manage bamboo, and by that I mean harvest it properly to maintain its sustainability.

My family lived on a farm after the Second World War. Nothing was wasted and everything was precious. If I didn't finish my lunch I'd have to eat it for dinner. You used everything with care and respect. Since the advent of supermarkets, almost half of the produce in the world is now thrown away!

When you grow up with forests, you know which tree you are going to fell. You plan its future, how it's going to be used. All along the line there's a kind of respect. We never cut a tree that wasn't past its prime. My family made all our energy from our lakes, from water wheels, so we were completely self-sustaining, without knowing that was unusual.

My aunt Margaret "Peggy" Hall started the largest underwater national park in the world in the Bahamas. She would go out in her tugboat, *Moby*, catch young poachers, and say to them, "I am sending you to university!" She sent 150 of them off to Florida to study environmental conservation, and they would return later as wardens and guides. They didn't just conserve but regenerated species. It has taken forty or fifty years to do a couple of hundred miles, but most of the things that are extinct in the rest of the Caribbean are thriving there.

I'm financing a book about her work with young Bahamians that contains local information for the local people, and it's filled with information gathered by the people she sent off to university.

The heat from global warming is ending up in the oceans, and it's starting to bubble up. When it hits the surface area, the blue-green algae won't be able to grow. We rely on the algae for cloud formation; they emit tiny particles that water droplets condense around. Ocean acidification is horrific, too.

I always walked a lot, and in Indonesia I would see bamboo that was only shoots and I would return a few weeks later and see the poles towering over me up in the sky. I was also intrigued by the creative uses the locals found for it. I got very depressed after flying over Kalimantan and seeing beautiful forests and returning a week or so later to find that they had been clear-cut. Not a tree standing!

One day I went to the Natural History Museum in London, and when I walked in I saw on one side of the entrance a meteorite and on the other an enormous bamboo pole. I took it as a sign. I did some research there, which is difficult for me as I am dyslexic, but I did find that there was one organization in Canada that was doing bamboo research, the International Development Research Centre (IDRC). Canadian industry was interested in pulp for paper, and they had found out that paper was produced from bamboo pulp in India.

I went to the IDRC office in Singapore and they told me they were doing lots of projects relating to bamboo; I asked them where the projects were so I could go and actually see what they were doing. When I was traveling for my design business, I would go and check out these research projects.

Bamboo is the sustainable product of the future. If you look at the need for resources based on population growth, bamboo is actually able to keep up with it. It has the tensile strength of concrete and steel, so it's a really strong fiber, and it's guilt free—we don't have to devastate the planet's forests.

When they dropped the atom bomb on Hiroshima, three things survived at ground zero: gingko, bamboo, and, famously, cockroaches. Bamboo has an incredible ability to deal with toxicity because of its high silica content. You can grow it on degraded or abandoned land. It's also a really efficient method of water collection; it's a pipe system that collects and stores water. It adds 35% more oxygen and 50% more water to a water table. There are field studies on compromised water tables in India; after bamboo is planted it lifts the water table, and dry wells are now producing water where before there was none. I had always thought that bamboo was the timber of the future, but actually it's the water provider of the future.

The first time I saw it was in the mountains of Ecuador. An interesting American guy called F. A. McClure, who passed away in 1970, had a $2 million budget from the U.S. Department of Agriculture to do bamboo research there.

I went to see the Indonesian bamboo he had planted in the mountains. I got there and there was a river running through the property. I commented on how lucky McClure was to have found a property with a river running through it. The caretaker said that when McClure got the land there was no river, but after the bamboo was planted it pulled the water table up and created this river.

When you talk to old people on the island of Flores, where my son Arief Rabik sources his bamboo [see page 55], they say you are not allowed to cut the bamboo because it is their water. In Colombia they say they are planting water. This is big.

At Panchoran I planted 275 species of bamboo on the hill on the other side of the river. There was one little trickle of water from this hill going into the river during the rainy season; now we have six waterfalls! I always knew that water was going to become a issue, so I bought land with its own spring.

The Environmental Bamboo Foundation is mainly focused on the scientific side of bamboo. After ten years of research I received an honorary PhD for my work on how to prevent the powder post beetle from destroying bamboo, and actually my borax technology made it possible for people like John Hardy to build structures that last. Before that, the bamboo would last only a few years, so no one was using it for building.

We work like a kind of brokerage; I know the specialist in each field and I put the specialists together for free to further the agenda. Very often these people don't really know what they need, but I can see the direction and recommend the right people.

When my son Arief was young, I sent him all over the world to very inspiring people. I sent him to Belgium to see a guy who was doing bamboo tissue culture and then to South America to the architect Simón Vélez to learn new ways of joining bamboo for building. He was doing this as a kind of holiday project, and it added to his knowledge, and he got it! He has now taken the mantle from me and is carrying on the work. He is an environmental chemist who has written a book with Ben Brown, *Towards Resilient*

The late designer Linda Garland's famous bamboo sofa. It all started with a sofa. . . .

59

Bamboo Forestry, that we make available through our foundation and website. The most important thing is sustaining the bamboo with correct agricultural practices. Arief's book addresses this; it's a sort of bamboo farming for dummies.

In 1995, I hosted the Fourth International Bamboo Congress. I had been to several conferences and they were very dry and not at all stimulating. Everybody was isolating into their particular research; the people were not seeing the global context. When I put on the conference, I brought a lot of big-picture thinkers and had open-forum sessions where we would pull in scientists, engineers, architects, and government officials to discuss bamboo's role in the future of the planet.

Before the conference I had about twenty volunteers at Panchoran, working and living there free; we took a lot of photos and wrote a lot of articles and created a sexy ready-made editorial. One article gave the whole breakdown on the money side of it. With most business people, if you talk about bamboo in terms of profit, they take notice, but if you talk about it in terms of the environment, they fall asleep right in front of you.

We sent that article out to the media and we got incredible coverage: two pages in *Forbes* magazine, six pages in the *Telegraph* color supplement, two specials on CNN, *Asiaweek*, *Wired*—we got it everywhere. Thirty-five hundred people flocked to the conference from fifty-two countries. Its energy was upbeat and positive. We weren't talking about problems but about solutions and how to make them happen. Conference attendees were inspired to start hundreds of new projects all over the world.

One great thing happened at the conference because we had such good high-end publicity. A guy from Aveda was sent to us by Fritjof Capra, the author of *The Tao of Physics*, and Gunter Pauli, who wrote *The Blue Economy*. He stood up and said, "Every Aveda store in the world"—some five hundred stores—"will put bamboo flooring in."

At the time, Chinese bamboo flooring had just been developed and it was a several-million-dollar industry; it now turns $20 billion a year, but Indonesia has done nothing.

We had funding approved from the the U.S. to protect and catalog Indonesian bamboo, and we had thousands of people involved. But then Newt Gingrich got in a snit fit with Indonesia, and with a single stroke he wiped out all funding just after our international conference; we had a real global buzz going on and it just stopped it in its tracks. I had to let go of thirty specialists overnight; unbelievably sad things happened and the momentum we had created was stopped just as we were gathering and steamrolling ahead.

I couldn't get the Indonesian government to listen after forty presentations; they have strict controls on what can be planted. Bamboo is a grass. The government's forestry division controls 70 percent of Indonesia's land; you can't plant bamboo because it's not a tree. Now, with the new president, Jokowi, we have a partial allowance; he is progressive and hopefully will recognize bamboo's benefits and change the laws.

My biggest eco-blunder? I had designed some bamboo furniture that became very popular, and almost all the giant bamboo in Bali was wiped out because so many people copied it. I decided

I wouldn't design anything else until I could do reforestation. You must be careful of unforeseen consequences; instead of helping I had inadvertently nearly caused a catastrophe.

Edison tried two thousand different carbonized filaments for his lightbulb. It's said that one day he was fanning himself when he noticed a fiber coming loose from the bamboo handle of his fan. He took it and carbonized it, and it lasted much longer than any other filament. So he sent his assistants out to collect all the different species of bamboo. The prime minister of Japan was interested in Edison's work, and he met them. He sent them to Kyoto, where the samurai had selected a particular bamboo from the forest for their arrows. Edison's company used this madake bamboo for all their lightbulb filaments for fourteen years, until they realized how durable it was, so they synthesized an inferior filament with built-in obsolescence to make more profit. If you go to the Smithsonian you can still see one of the original bulbs still working!

The original needle for gramophone records was made of bamboo. After playing the record you would resharpen it. So you've got light and sound because of the silica content. It's a very sophisticated high-tech material. I talked with NASA scientists and asked them why they hadn't used bamboo in the spaceships. They said, "The bosses wanted us to come up with something new. Can you imagine if we had proposed bamboo?"

It has been a roller-coaster ride. I was a successful designer, but my work on behalf of bamboo has been extremely expensive, with frustration, delays, and humiliation. I had to face doors being slammed in my face. And it has taken its toll. I always said to the kids, "I am committed to the process but not the outcome," and that you must keep moving ahead if you feel it is important.

My advice for architects and design students is to use natural materials. They create a very different frequency in a house and make people feel much calmer. When you live with synthetic materials, there is no resonance and you feel dislocated; you don't vibrate with the house. When you go into a wooden or bamboo house, there is a resonant frequency and you feel more connected. Bamboo's silica content helps shield you from electromagnetic frequencies [EMF].

I remember I was having trouble sleeping and I realized all the electrical wires were running under my bed. I asked a friend to come and do some EMF tests. We relocated the wires, and then I could sleep. During the tests she noticed that wherever I had embedded the wires into or disguised them behind bamboo, there was no EMF, and so we discovered its shielding properties.

So because electromagnetic frequencies really disturb and damage your cellular balance and overstimulate your cells, my advice to students is that you should try to use bamboo as a component in your house.

My design signature? I have always been inspired by traditional and tribal art and architecture. I try to reinterpret it, in a respectful way, for contemporary living spaces.

The tipping point is right now. Interestingly, the insurance companies have had so many enormous claims related to environmental disasters that they and some corporations have realized that it's better for their bottom line to look after the environment.

> If you drew up a list of all the people responsible for the environmental devastation I am sure you would find that they grew up in a third-floor concrete flat with a dead geranium in a window box, without any connection to nature. This is a huge problem, as city folk have little idea about nature and the natural world.

Arief Rabik is Linda Garland's son, and in Klungkung, on Bali's southern coast, he has commited his energy to the sustainable manufacturing of bamboo beams, boards, and flooring of incredible strength, beauty, and durability.

At the only big traffic circle on the road to East Bali, we take a wrong turn and find ourselves at a beach market where a kind man offers to show us the way to Arief's factory and proceeds to ask a dozen people if he can borrow a *bebek* (scooter). Finally successful, he escorts us gracefully to the gate.

Arief and his wife Joanna are taking delivery of a huge industrial press. They break away to greet us, and Arief shows us around the huge factory, identifying all the processes in his production line. He is the leading manufacturer of architectural bamboo in Indonesia. We adjourn to the boardroom to chat.

> My father is Pak Amir Rabik, a crazy out-of-the-box thinker who opened a small made-to-order furniture workshop in Kuta in 1973. My dear mother is Ibu Linda Garland, an open-minded and aware person.
>
> I think environmental awareness came in the late seventies to Sumatra and Java and of course Bali. My brother Karim, a painter, used to discuss the issue very eloquently. We were using words like *sustainability* even before Deepak Chopra came along to tell us what they meant. So my introduction to eco-friendliness was through my family, not through education. My mother was so passionately into environmental issues that I was sucked into the vortex.
>
> In 2005, with the help of my American teacher, I was working for USAID's Environmental Services Program as a field chemist in Java. I worked with about thirty incredible scientists, working on saving Java's watersheds. It was a nine-month adventure and education on U.S. aid.
>
> After that, I started a small business called Sustain a Clump. Basically we were looking at how to manage a bamboo clump so that it remained in optimum health and how to marry the needs of the user and the needs of the bamboo.
>
> Actually, it's remarkable that if you do the harvesting using an age ratio it remains sustainable. So Ben Brown and I have written a book about it, called *Towards Resilient Bamboo Forestry*. It took seven years to work it out after talking with all the world's leading bamboo authorities. It's a system of localized bamboo forestry.
>
> My biggest eco-blunder was in bamboo forestry. I came up with a harvesting program for bamboo using lichen as an aging marker. We thought one layer of lichen grew on the bamboo each year, and that we could tell how old the bamboo was by counting these layers. So if you had four layers it was a four-year-old bamboo. Done! We were going to save the bamboo world! Later we discovered that in more humid areas lichen grows two or three times a year, so our system was flawed.
>
> My father and I built what we think was the tallest bamboo structure in the world, a seven-story, twenty-eight meter [92 ft.] high Tibetan pagoda, at the Boom Festival in Portugal. We built

A play of veiled curves with a clifftop view of the sea at Intaaya. Fishing nets animate the lines of the bamboo structure.

Designer Linda Garland collected the entire genetic heritage of Indonesia's bamboo on this plantation at Panchoran, her former estate in Nyuh Kuning, Ubud.

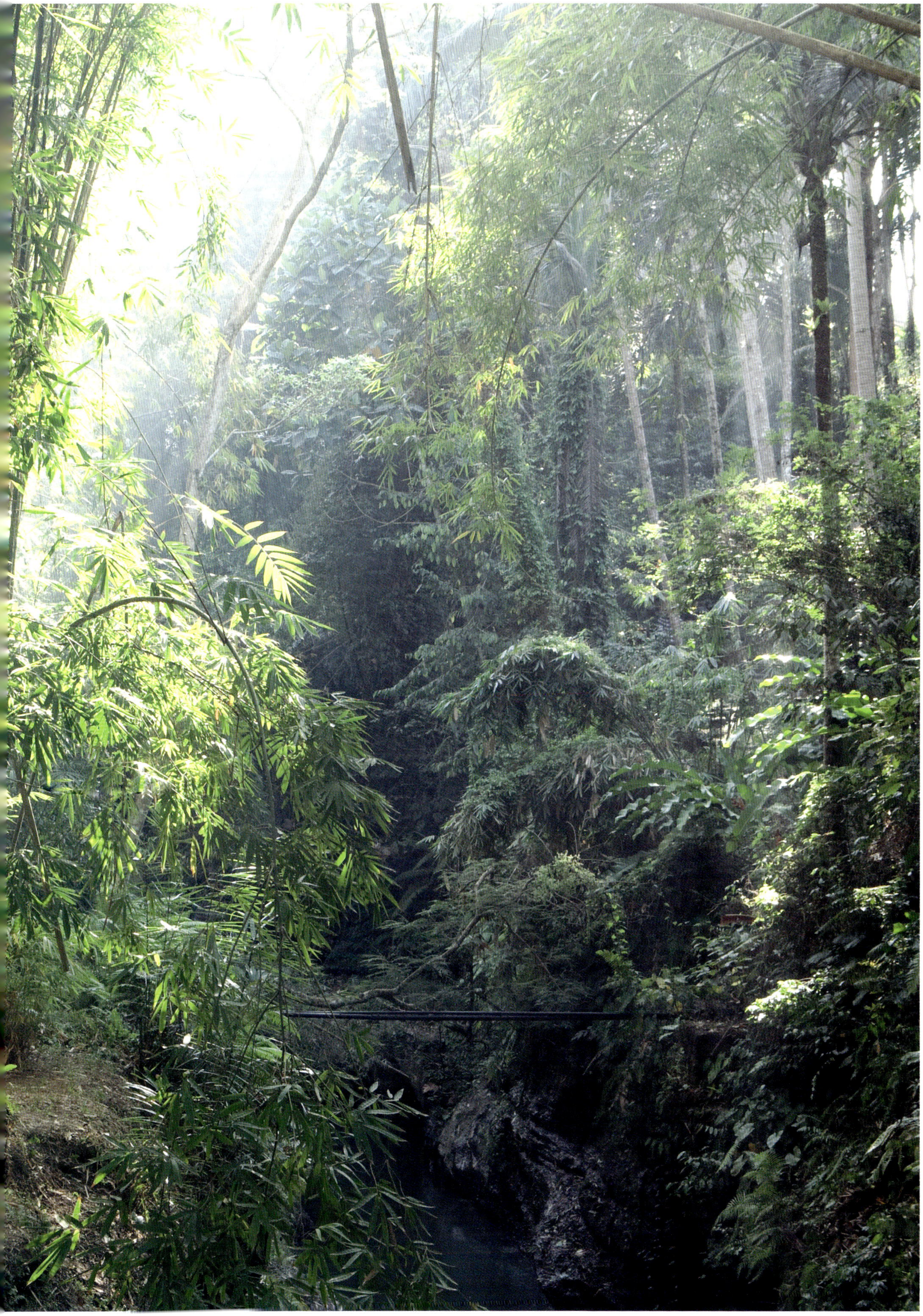

A harmonious juxtaposition of "see-through" buildings at Intaaya.

this incredible eight-pillar octagonal spire that was cross-linked with steel cable and put a pagoda roof on it. We were given three months to finish this thing. We couldn't get a crane operator to come out into the desert, so I had to learn how to use one myself, in a single week. About a month into the project, the temperature rose to 47°C [117°F] on the ground, and the winds were incredible. It was very scary, because if bamboo splits it kind of flicks sideways. With bamboo you really must know how to use it. Anything over six meters [20 ft.] requires very specific bamboo, because the fibers all run one way, and if you haven't chosen correctly they can split and it can get very dangerous. But somehow we pulled it off, and we also built a huge *wantilan* [pavilion] as a convention center, a three-story *meru* [tiered shrine], a labyrinth, a tree house, a big swing, and an archery thing. Still today they say that the most beautiful Boom Festival was designed by Amir Rabik.

I am very impressed by a new business called Ecospecifier, which connects builders with green products and materials. They ask all the right questions of the suppliers and provide a tremendous network and hub for positive products with real information.

There is also a beautiful book called *Wikinomics*, by Don Tapscott and Anthony D. Williams, that discusses creative collaboration in industry. It is possible when we all lose our egos. Sustainability just won't happen until we all collaborate!

My design focus is more on the engineering side, analyzing how a material behaves in different situations. We have a modern view and a traditional view, and they are in an ongoing conversation. The traditional uses of rapidly renewable materials were all very specific and limited. In order to expand those uses, you must really understand your material and what to do with the traditional parameters and methods of quality control.

When I started the business, I used bamboo, alang-alang, and coconut wood, but I discovered that coconut wood must be at least eighty years old, so I don't use it anymore.

We harvested two meter [6½ ft.] long strands of mature alang-alang for Therese Poulsen's house in Nyuh Kuning. We stripped out the young central pieces, which is where the rot usually starts. Most alang used today is about eighty centimeters [2½ ft.] long.

Therese Poulsen's house is a wantilan, and we used a quad-block system. Each column is made up of four bamboo poles, so you don't need to make a fishmouth to join a beam to a column; you can use bolts and have columns going in both directions, and it's much stronger. My mother brought this information to me. The technique was invented in Germany in the 1800s and used for pine. We reclaimed old Javanese *bengkel* [workshop] sliding doors to use in Therese's house, too.

Recently Arief and I caught up at a garden party that Susanna Perini gave for her fellow designer, Paul Ropp:

I've been either on the road or in the forest. It's kind of a weird thing launching a social forestry program internationally in twelve countries, and this is a new institution: the Bamboo Village Trust. It's a trust fund that basically raises $275,000 for a village-level champion, who creates an operational plan, a business plan, a benefit-sharing plan, and a tenurial access plan over a year. The

The bathroom of the main three-story *wantilan* (pavilion) house at Panchoran. A copper sink harmonizes with *bedek* (woven bamboo) in a variety of naturally occurring and smoked colors.

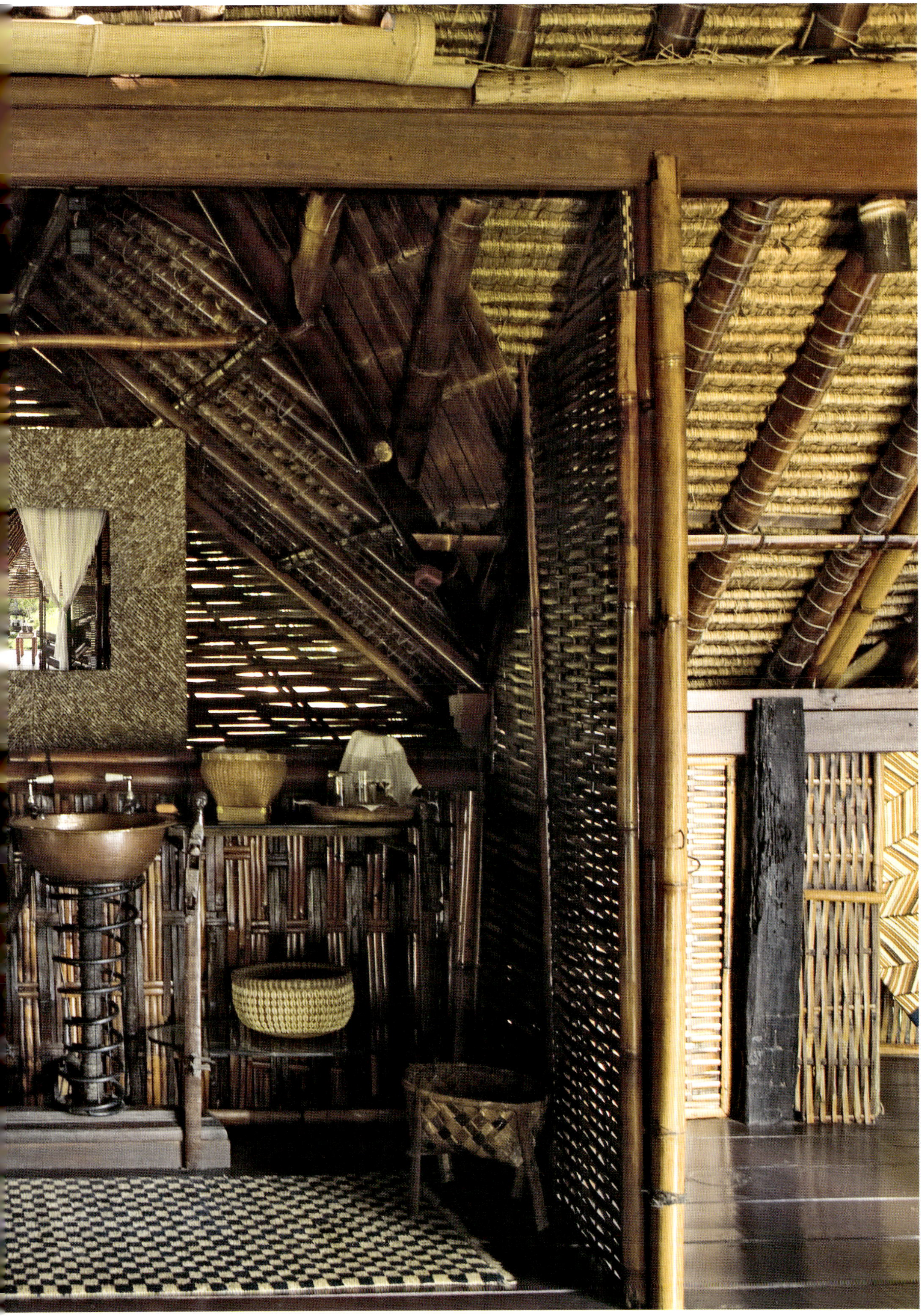

champion is helped by all these smart people who look at land condition, village preparedness, government support, access and ease of doing business, risks and threats, gender-positive potential, and the potential for the integration of bamboo to other agro-commodity supply chains. Then once they are clear with the vision of how it can be done, 2,000 hectares [4,900 acres] of land can be restored and actually make money.

They go to two hundred households and they say, do you wanna join in on this plan? And they do another year of iterating the plan per household. Basically each household is given 10 hectares [25 acres] of land. And they're planting about 35 to 90 bamboos per clump if it's an asper, or giant bamboo, and it's a mixed planting that will include other species, based on the hydrology.

We're creating what we call a restoration economy using bamboo for its superpower ecologically. Actually sustainability is something that's been an oversight for most people when they speak about bamboo. There are many layers of assumptions that the bamboo that people use is sustainable, or is promoting sustainable forestry, etc. Unfortunately, the data shows that before World War I, there was somewhere between 20 to 27 million hectares [49 to 67 million acres] of bamboo under cultivation in Indonesia. And now we're closer to 1 million hectares [2.5 million acres]. The trend is actually showing exploitative harvesting of bamboo and basically just no valuing of it; that's because all those old traditions of using bamboo were deemed "poor man." It's still got that stigma here, I'm afraid. I've learned something new in the last few years, which is that it's not just because of technology making other building materials available that it's been deemed a poor man's wood. More importantly, and more critically, the techniques of using bamboo are seen as "poor man" techniques; all the preservation and weaving techniques are seen as kind of subpar. Handicrafts are seen as inferior to machine-made, so actually that's killed a whole culture of natural resource management.

The methods that we're using with the bamboo are an example of a nature-based solution, or NBS. All UN bodies have created a list of Sustainable Development Goals, which will rely on these nature-based solutions. An NBS is not a compatible alternative in every situation, but it turns out that 50 to 70 percent of the time it's very applicable, especially in rural and suburban environments. So actually it's cheaper, more effective, and you tick many more boxes in a holistic solution. So long as we have the rigor to do more things.

Integrated strategies, all these multidisciplinary approaches that have been popping up over the last twenty years, are finally coming together. Nature-based solutions are very complex, and the thinking needs to be at that level of complexity. The first go at kind of trying to capture all of that was the Sustainable Development Goals; it was a first iteration. It's flawed, but it's an amazing first go.

One thing since the last time we talked, I was invited to be part of the *Laudato si'* (*Praise Be to You*). It's an encyclical of Pope Francis, a kind of environmental think tank; the subtitle is "On Care for Our Common Home." And this 184-page encyclical mentions everything from microplastics to circular economies. It was published in 2015, a few months after the Paris Agreement was signed.

It was an acknowledgment by the Catholic Church, one of the most conservative bodies in the world, that we were causing the destruction of nature. And the church could actually have an environmentally minded leader, the pope, who could challenge the whole institution. What he had said is that we have turned our lands and our home into a pile of rubbish and waste, and how can we evolve our minds? *Laudato si'* is about making all things new, so that we do not create this pile of rubbish and waste in our home. And he ties in all of these amazing ways of thinking.

My journey really in the last seven years has been very much about how we link the public sector and the private sector. I won an award from the Climate Breakthrough Foundation, which has the IKEA Foundation behind it, the Packard Foundation, the Good Energies Foundation, the Oak Foundation. They gave me an award of $2 million plus a whole bunch of support, what's called wraparound support of about $50,000 per year. And then a match fund as well. It was a kind of $3 million package in the end, to basically have me explore the strategy I created in my book with Ben Brown, *Towards Resilient Bamboo Forestry*, in 2007. We can truly scale at a global level, or at least during my tenure at an international level, this bamboo-based agroforestry system, because of thought leaders like Paul Hawken, Johan Rockström, and others. Do you know who Johan Rockström is? Nine planetary boundaries! He is probably one of the most important thought leaders in sustainability. Rockström pointed toward these rapidly renewable biomass species that could basically maintain the water and soil resources that are foundational to our ecosystem. These are resources and assets of the planet with trillions and trillions of dollars in value, which are just every single year being leached and degraded in so many different ways.

The valuation of those assets is critical, but so is the actual activation of some systems. We also need to make apparent to the human mind the value of those assets and those systems, because these are cycles that are quite hard to understand and ephemeral in nature. They're there and then they're not, depending on El Niño, factors like that. They're very complex, but they're assets. They're dynamic assets. They're ecosystem assets.

I was given this award to basically create a system, and so we came up with the Bamboo Village Initiative. Now we're using the Bamboo Village Trust to launch the initiative to an inflection point where basically we've proved the model enough that anyone can just take a look at the data. It has to be a data-driven approach with all the context very clearly laid out on those enabling conditions of village preparedness, government support, access needs for doing business, risks and threats, and gender. We say that without a minimum of 50 percent female participation, where women are actively getting compensated to work on a clear target for the restoration of these assets, it won't work.

The men can't do it alone. They have conversations and create programs and put themselves forward aspirationally. They say, I can do ABC, and it's impossible for them to do that. But they're forced by government systems and bureaucracies and partisan politics, with parties that are looking to get voted in, to make these outlandish claims of capacity that is just not there. When someone like me is given a few million dollars to look at all the

The entrance to Therese Poulsen's former residence in Nyuh Kuning, a wantilan house built by Arief Rabik. A rice cluster hangs from the key ring for auspicious protection.

The former Poulsen residence employs the quad-block system of construction, with columns consisting of four bamboo poles. The bamboo in the ceiling has a dark smoked finish.

Another interior view of the former Poulsen residence.

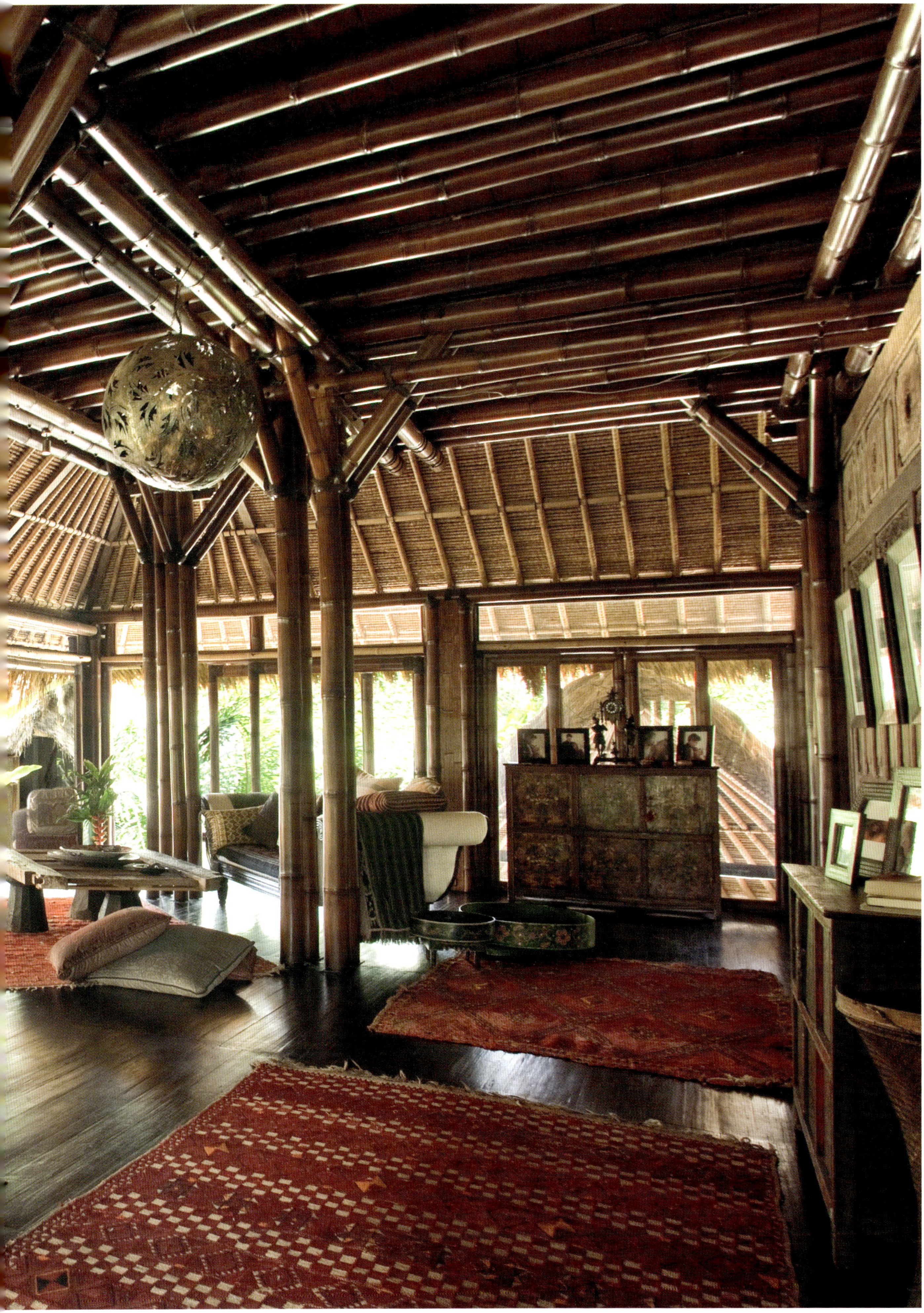

data, it's clear the capacity is not there. They're forced to make these sensational, outlandish claims of being able to create a tomato program through the whole of the island of Flores and create an economy of $10 million per annum. Basically some fantasy numbers on a spreadsheet!

We humans right now are fixated on a growth mindset. But it's not really a growth mindset—it's a boom-bust mindset, and it leads us into a destructive and degrading cycle of plundering resources. It's so illogical and irrational, but you know everyone's on this train. How can we stop this unsustainable economic growth mindset and replace it? We're trying to identify all the parameters that we need to take into consideration when designing our growth.

There are these assets and there are these cycles, and there are all of these people who have been regarded as inconvenient or not allowed to be real actors, like women; women have to stay at home and do ABC. That is rubbish in a sustainable system. If you look at all the sustainable systems, historically, they had full active participation of women. The women were driven and focused on targets, be it seasonal targets or dynamics within the community, etc. They were very clear, and they took positions. The moment you take away that empowerment, that integrated decision-making, you're stuck in silos and the system fails.

In the context of this global challenge and this ideological challenge, I'm much more coherent and mindful. It is much more about the simplicity of being mindful. All of us have to step out of our doors every day and be mindful that half the things we're doing or all the things we're doing are actually unsustainable, even if our intention is to be sustainable. I was told just the other day I'm wearing gold and the whole concept of wearing gold is incredibly unsustainable and supports all of these systems that are unsustainable. And so I need to think twice about wearing gold. And then I was told that I wear jade and that was representative of the Han and their whole dynasty of exploitation. You're wearing shoes, and you know, the nails that hold it together came from a mine, whatever. Having said that, I do, for example, believe in sustainable plastics, or the way that I think of it is sustainable polymers. I do believe in fast-growing bio-based materials.

So what's happening with hemp? Well, what's happening is that there are over ten thousand species and actually probably approaching twenty thousand species of ferns, grasses, perennials like hemp, seed species, even ficuses, that all need to be integrated into systems with low or zero external input from humans. And then we can sustainably coppice, not harvest, them. This is a kind of terminology we've been working on, we're not completely there yet, but you know, coppicing is what you do to a willow, where you just harvest the branches of the willow and you don't take the trunk. And that's what we do with bamboo. Yes. The trunk of the tree is underground, what you see above the ground are branches. We just harvest the great-grandmother branch. We don't harvest the grandmother branch, or the mother, or the baby. And that allows for enough of a canopy of photosynthetic leaves to continually pull from these climatic cycles. Humans didn't realize that you need to have a critical mass of these green things in order to sustain the roots, the mycelium, the macro-invertebrates of the soil, the micro-invertebrates, the soil itself, etc., all depend on these bloody green things! And if we're not even able to manage that, how can we go beyond bamboo, go beyond hemp, and actually think in terms of whole ecosystems? Because there's a hemp in every landscape across the world. There's a bamboo in every landscape. It may not actually be a bamboo, and it may not be hemp. It's that indigenous species. And we have to understand that there are all these little microbes and mycelium and whatever that have been evolving for up to 300 million years in these landscapes. They've evolved to work together, and when we disturb them we're basically causing ecological diversity to fall off a cliff. We do it under the auspices of growth and scientific and technological advancement, and yet we are crippling the very foundation of our existence.

Yeah, I know, it's crazy, man, isn't it? In five generations or ten generations they're going to look back at us and laugh. But we are where we are. We're all trying our best, and actually I do think that artificial intelligence will bring coherence to these systems. It's too much for a brain to try to even take it on. And therefore you can't have definitive answers; you just have a range of answers. And then you have a range of capacities and potentials.

The individual being educated isn't as important as the collective being educated. So a village needs to be educated, not just an individual in the village. The village has to grow in its capacities, and those capacities have to be developed socially and integrated economically. This is a whole different way of thinking than I was taught in university!

The perfect example of that is big pharma. I don't think a doctor is really being a doctor, because she hasn't got the full knowledge. She's only got the pharma chemical knowledge, and it's not treating root causes. It's always, let's deal with the symptoms!

Every landscape has its benefits. Every landscape has its anti-inflammatory. Every landscape has its antioxidant. Every landscape has all that the inhabitants of that landscape need, if they can create this socio-ecological alignment, which is complex.

But in ten to twenty years, and in drier areas unfortunately thirty or maybe fifty years, you can develop a full thirty layers of ecosystem alignment that create the resilience to allow a very clear carrying capacity of X amount of people to live on that land. We're talking probably in 5,000 to 7,000 hectare [12,000–17,000 acre] scales here, and they can live off of that system sustainably, on a low external input. That will include some areas of conservation forestry for mating and reproduction, areas for harvest, and areas for all the different parts of these systems can be developed and grown and supported and designed. To achieve that level of coherence, we will probably need some AI modeling, not only to create the table, the matrix, the framework, but also to have sensors to track and then keep feeding into the model and develop how Dubai needs to look in fifty years, how Rote needs to look in thirty, hopefully twenty years. And this socio-ecological alignment can use bamboo—a fast-growing, shallow-root species.

But guess what? Bamboo on its own doesn't work. It needs a medium-root species to be right there, right underneath it, to steal the water that infiltrates past the bamboo. And guess what? That medium-root species needs to have a deep-root species that

Tribal style in the Sumba House at Bambu Indah, John and Cynthia Hardy's eco-luxury boutique hotel on Sayan Terrace, Ubud. Three *kris* (ceremonial daggers) hang at right.

The central column supporting the traditional alang-alang roof of the Sumba House at Bambu Indah.

The "intelligent wall" at the Potato Head beach club and resort, Seminyak, is made from cement and leftover brick and represents the Tika, a traditional Balinese calendar. Potato Head Design Studio with Andra Matin and OMA.

has taproots and what have you to pull out carbonic acid that's literally pressurized to thirty bar or dissolved CO_2 aquifers that are thirty to fifty meters [100–160 ft.] deep. These roots can get into those layers and pull out potassium and different minerals. They bring it up into the canopy and then express it out through leaves and fruits and what have you in bioavailable forms. It would be impossible for humans to even comprehend how to do that.

So bamboo would kill the world if it's just bamboo on its own. Bamboo works in a village, a village ecologically, a village socially, and a village economically. And it takes a village. And that's the thesis that I'm driving. We have to think in terms of these complex systems, and unfortunately they're a nightmare to get our heads around.

I used to think that, you know, we're going to get to the year 2000—this is how naive I was—we're going to get to the year 2000 and technology is going to take over and it's going to be wonderful. And that was the sort of psychological brainwash that somehow I inherited. The techno fix. It was a strong narrative. Oh my God. And when we got to the year 2000, it was like, uh, nothing's happened. We've got Y2K. We've got the failure of computers coming up on New Year's Eve. And then that was it. There was no sort of massive breakthrough. I think humans just have inertia. I think they have homeostasis. They have resistance to change. Everyone wants to grow in the system that they're in.

If you go to these communities—I'm very much speaking Paul Hawken here, so I'm basically wearing his hat—it's the individuals in those communities who took twenty, thirty, fifty years to change their mind. They see they can have a growth trajectory within those sustainable models. That is the equivalent of greed. It's very self-serving, but they see themselves as part of the collective, and it provides a completely different framing for their ambition. I think what we express as greed is a result of testosterone or something. It probably does come from ego. Oh, I need more than you, you know what I mean? And then you buy into the sustainable model yourself, you say, that would be good for me—that's a sort of naive greed, isn't it? Yeah. And so I think the solution is in there. How do we hack these minds? Not in a day, not a year, not a decade—this is multiple decades, but we need to start planting the seeds of this kind of collective thinking. It's not any one of these reductionistic approaches that works against all these reductionistic forces of palm oil and gold and whatever it is; you can't fight it with one thing. It's not a reductionistic solution to a reductionistic problem. It's a holistic one. We've been talking about being holistic, and yet we're reductionistic in our narrative of being holistic. It's a bit of a worry, isn't it?

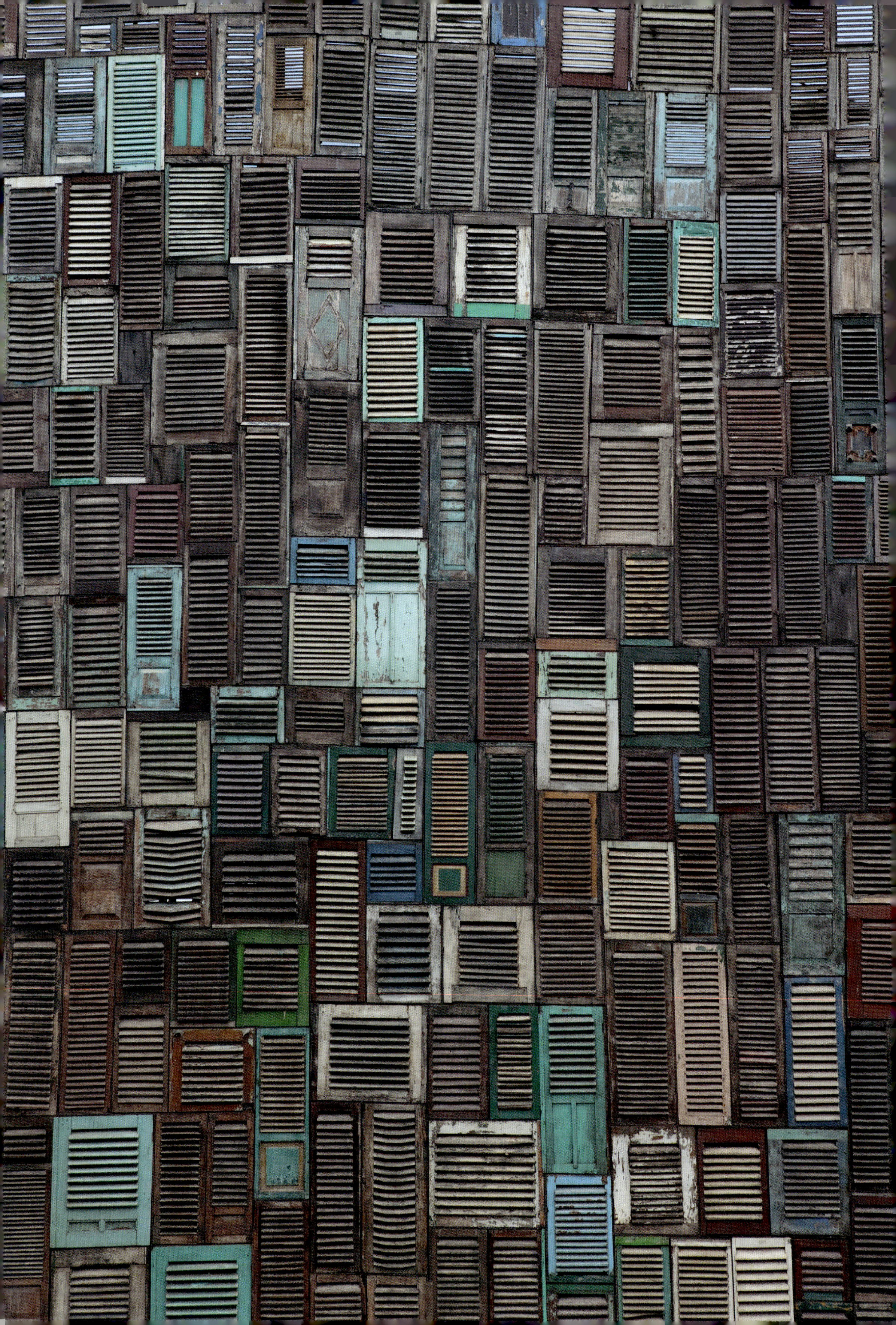

MATERIALS RECLAIMED

Teakwood and ironwood are reclaimed or recycled for construction all over the archipelago. Many other materials, including stone, are also reclaimed from old buildings. Argument rages over the use of stone brought from other islands. The removal of river stones is damaging and accelerates erosion, but some stone is collected from surface land, in order to make it usable for agriculture. This is true of the stone collected from Sumba for use in the Suarga Sustainable Boutique Resort, on the Bukit Peninsula.

The sheer size of the bamboo roof at Suarga is impressive, almost overwhelming—17,760 square feet (1,650 m^2) of bamboo shingles. The resort is on a cliff top overlooking the Indian Ocean, directly above one of Bali's premier surf breaks.

Frederik E. A. Wittesaele and his wife, Karolien D. A. Verschelden, have invited us to be the first guests to stay overnight in the first completed bungalow.

Frederik is a successful textile professional. He hails from Flanders and spent most of his career in Jakarta before setting his sights on a radically new project. He asks us to join him for a dinner catered by his head chef, where he tells us how he came to create this iconic place.

A woven mesh ceiling made of recycled plastic strips from PET bottles at the Potato Head beach club and resort, Seminyak. Potato Head Design Studio in collaboration with Lim Masulin of BYO Living.

85

At Bambu Indah, John and Cynthia Hardy's eco-luxury boutique hotel on Sayan Terrace, Ubud, this elevator basket offers visitors access to the six natural pools by the river. A sixty-foot (18 m) dive in a tunnel to heaven.

I'm from the Belgian coast—it's all covered in concrete now—and I've lived most of my life near a shoreline. I lived a long time in Jakarta and always had my work in the factories there, but I would visit beautiful places. I always liked nature.

We wanted a traditional-looking resort with minimalist lines. We looked at strand-woven bamboo back in 2008 or 2009, and this was when I stumbled on using wood sustainably.

The wood you see has mostly been reclaimed from Borneo and East Java and painstakingly documented in order to obtain the FSC [Forest Stewardship Council] Chain of Custody Full Project Certification. Some of these timbers are five hundred to maybe a thousand years old, according the wood sections we measured. We've had countless adventures sourcing piers, bridges, and complete ironwood roads built on stilts alongside the Mahakam River in East Borneo, and repurposing the wood for structural beams, planks, and posts in the resort's forty-eight pavilions. Even an unoccupied Bank Indonesia branch in Samarinda was completely dismantled and reclaimed, mainly as teak planks for the villa walls throughout the resort. The huge beams of an old merbau bridge in Gresik, East Java, obtained a new life in Suarga's bathroom sinks and pavilion floorings. We dismantled a Chinese merchant's house from the 1800s in Jalan Karet, in the old part of central Surabaya, where we found a huge volume of very big teak beams and rasamala wood floorings. Rasamala is an as-good-as-extinct hardwood species from Central Java that was used during the Dutch colonial era for boat building and factory structures.

Altogether we've used a huge amount of reclaimed wood—in fact, by now some five thousand cubic meters [6,540 cu. yd.], which translates to twenty-five hundred cubic meters of net usable timber.

We needed many unusally big sections of recycled Borneo ironwood (also known as *ulin* or *billian*). This very important tree is one of the most durable and heaviest timbers in the world. It is now threatened by illegal logging, lack of regeneration, and difficulties in cultivation. Ironwood grows slowly, just half a centimeter [$3/16$ in.] per year. The current demand for it is fueled by its popularity among the Chinese as a coffin wood (as it is resistant to insects and rot).

When Karolien and I decided to buy and recycle this wood, it was our first important move toward building the resort. The big main building in bamboo we conceived of later. We wanted an iconic centerpiece, but in wood it was simply not possible and it didn't feel like the right thing to do. We didn't want alang-alang thatch roofs, so we decided to try bamboo shingles in a special layering design. I found a tiny photo on the Internet of Panyaden School in Chiang Mai, Thailand, and we followed the idea and tried to create a finish inspired by the texture of an armadillo. We cut and reversed the bamboo and tried it on twenty square meters and it worked out perfectly. We now have one of the largest all-bamboo roofs in the world, and it looks amazing.

All the bamboo was treated in a borax treatment facility in Bali. The preservative used is a mixture of boric acid and chili, which results in the formation of disodium octaborate, which is easily soluble in water. Boron salts are effective against borers, termites, and fungi (except soft rot fungi), and are widely recognized en-

A sweeping entrance corridor at the Potato Head Beach Club,
lined with antique Javanese shutters.

MATERIALS RECLAIMED

Sustainably sourced and reclaimed wood and stone create Zen bliss in the courtyard of Rumah Rubah, a house in Tumbak Bayuh designed by Maximilian Jencquel. The courtyard is constructed above a basement equipped to make this home almost entirely sustainable.

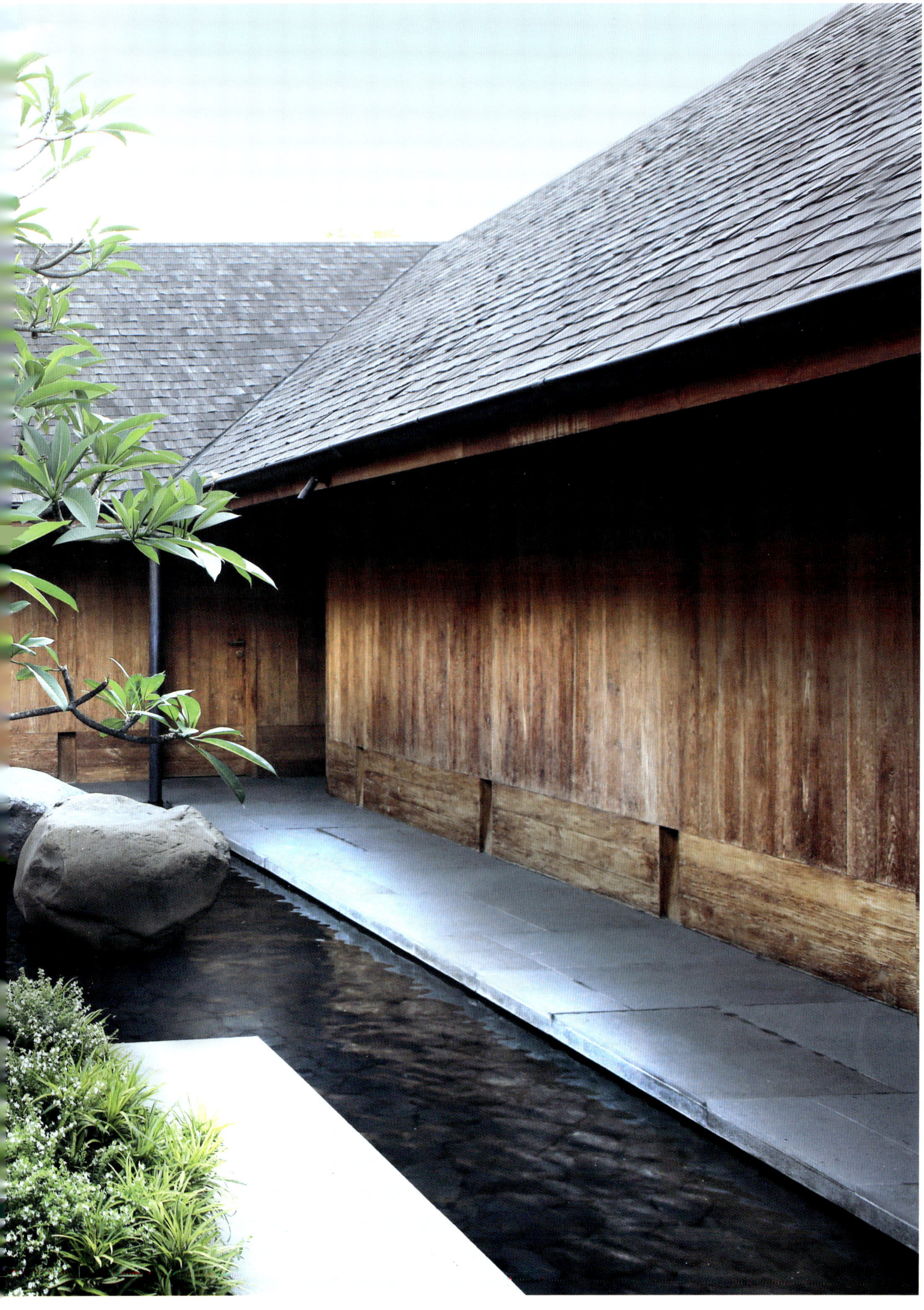

A *wantilan*-style roof over the dining area at Rumah Rubah adds ventilation.

A teak wall glows in the sunlight at Rumah Rubah.

vironmentally acceptable and safe for mammals. The bamboo is soaked in a solution in a heated open basin for several days. In the latest treatments we also smoke the shingles as an extra precaution.

Suarga's landscaping uses carefully selected dry-climate vegetation typical of the Bukit area where the resort is situated. This is to save water and to sustain local wildlife. Below our gardens we have constructed wetlands to harvest the water and keep reservoirs for the dryer periods.

Karolien and I use the three-pillars sustainability principle—people, planet, and profit. As responsible investors we require a return on our investments; our footprint must be sustainable; the community must benefit. We must create our own energy on-site.

Our array of solar panels generates an average of 440 kilowatt hours of power throughout the day and stores part of this energy overnight. It is necessary to have a generator on standby to ensure the batteries maintain a minimum 45 percent charge, for the cloudy days or when the resort has major peak loads during events or full occupancy. We keep the energy usage from the generator to a bare minimum.

We have used an anaerobic bacteria system from Jakarta for the sewage treatment rather than traditional septic tanks with air ventilation systems. This is to avoid using excess electrical energy.

Gray water from the kitchen, showers, and baths goes into the garden's constructed wetlands and Wastewater Gardens.

We embraced local and regional skills by employing native Sumbanese workers to place the Sumba stone, while hiring a team of Javanese craftsmen for the woodwork and Balinese locals for bamboo work. We employed all our teams on equal terms and are very grateful especially to our team from Sumba for their long-term commitment over the last four years.

The LED lights are sourced from the U.S. and Europe and assembled into lamp holders in China. We have used them for four years without any breakage, and therefore they are proving to be a sustainable product. We are using fans made from bamboo blades that have won awards for their design and energy efficiency, using only 15 to 25 watts. Every single energy-consuming device has been checked for its power consumption before procurement as a strict rule to respect our sustainability goals.

We have special air conditioners for the beds that use on average 250 to 300 watts. They use 680 watts to start off, but once the unit is cool they use less than half of that. Our rooms use 6 or 7 kilowatts per day for all functions.

During my travels I found huge rubber pipes, around twenty centimeters [8 in.] wide, that had been used as pipelines. I realized I could run all my electrical wires through one pipe. So we acquired these retired pipes and ran all our cables through them. All the rooms are interconnected by this smart system.

Workers from Madura [an island next to East Java] helped us a lot with the sourcing of the recycled wood. They are exemplary recyclers, as they dismantle complete buildings and ships!

We did a study of wind generators, but here on the Bukit we don't have enough consistent wind except in August and December, and even then at night it drops off. For us, more solar would

A detail of the courtyard pool at Rumah Rubah, capturing the wabi-sabi aesthetic.

94 MATERIALS RECLAIMED

Another detail of the dining area at Rumah Rubah. The bangkirai wood that covers the pool deck extends into the dining and living areas.

The kitchen at Rumah Rubah is well appointed with teak, Grigio Argento marble, and black Indonesian andesite.

A salon and media library looking out on the dining area at Rumah Rubah. Reclaimed ironwood was used in the construction of the roof.

be better. The best current technology is not yet available for commercial use. We are generating 350 kilowatts today, but sometimes 500 kilowatts on very sunny days.

Our biggest eco-blunder? Our Sumba team made some sixty-five thousand limestone *batako* bricks from the limestone on Suarga's property. This was a mistake, because limestone likes to absorb water. When we used our regular cement to build with them it would just fall off, so we had to switch to a different cement. Yes, this was a blunder that started out with sustainable thinking.

For me everything is about education. Good education could solve a lot of the world's most pressing problems. I was lucky I could study engineering. They should teach sustainability in schools.

Suarga's design signature is its imposing scale and that it is designed to last. Meanwhile, the interior lends a welcoming atmosphere that will soon be completed with locally inspired decorative elements.

Just across the bridge, on the other side of Padang Padang Cove, lives Stephen Palmer, a veteran surfer and businessman, and a founder of Little Tree Bali, a supplier of green building materials. His house incorporates not only reclaimed teakwood but also a number of energy-saving features. Stephen was away on a snowboarding trip, so he answered my questions by e-mail.

Sustainability was a progressive awareness for me, starting back in the early seventies with the *Whole Earth Catalog*, one of the best books ever. Around 2006 I became more and more aware of the need to be eco-friendly. In my house I have used FSC-certified laminated finger-joint timber, nontoxic timber finishes, and recycled teak timber.

I consider it ecologically friendly to use refrigeration-foam panels in roofs and under any sun-exposed terraces, to reduce heat load and air-conditioner use.

The house has an insulated western wall with minimal windows to block the most intense sunlight. The windows in that wall have large trees and bamboo planted in front of them to keep direct sunlight from entering the building.

I put in five hundred thousand liters [130,000 gal.] of underground rainwater tanks that collect roof water for home use. This was done out of concern that the farmers below were being deprived of water for their fields. The rainwater tanks last the entire year, from rainy season to rainy season, and a filtration and water activation system make it better than bottled water.

I did not think enough about solar energy and designing my house to use minimal electricity. However, I have installed LED lighting throughout, plus energy-efficient computer-controlled pumps and energy-efficient air conditioners and fans.

If you're designing your own more sustainable, energy-efficient, and human-friendly building, put your plan out there in the public arena for input and feedback. Everyone wants to do it all themselves, and 99.9 percent of the time it turns out that better designs and materials could have been chosen. This might be hard, as we all have egos and want the accolades, but the earth suffers, so we have to get over that, and soon.

My design signature is evolving. I doubt I will build again the

French doors and a wantilan roof provide ventilation at Rumah Rubah.

Teak doors channeling the gentle breezes at Rumah Rubah.

A *lesung*, the traditional mortar used to process rice and grains, was converted to a sink at the Suarga resort, Padang Padang, Uluwatu.

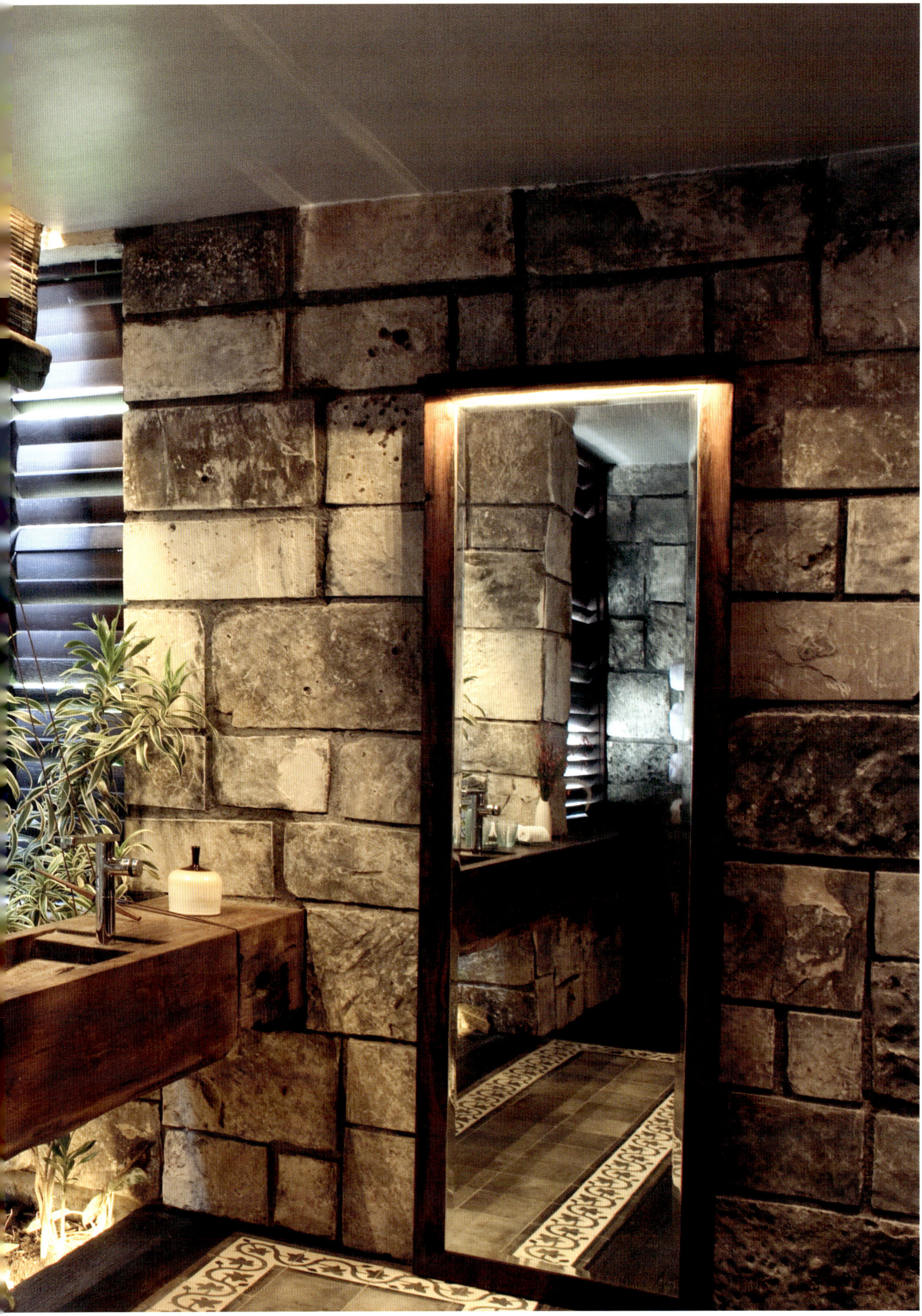

Villa Agung, the main house at the Villa Campuhan estate, designed by Linda Garland for the movie director Rob Cohen, offers a perfect view of Mount Agung. The ceilings are supported by reclaimed ironwood utility poles.

> way I have before. I am becoming more attracted to the idea of "less is more," in terms of size and number of components.

Recently we returned to one of the places featured in the first edition of this book, the Potato Head beach club and resort. Huge beach clubs have proliferated in Bali, but Potato Head was one of the first, and it is leading by example. Sustainability is at the core of Potato Head's DNA, and it has an R&D team dedicated to finding circular solutions. Their mission is to promote a zero-waste lifestyle without compromising their products, services, or experiences. The iconic facade of the Potato Head Beach Club, crafted from 6,600 upcycled antique shutters sourced from around Java, is emblematic of their approach.

Potato Head Studios, a new beachfront hotel in the complex, is a marriage of contemporary techniques with traditional Balinese architecture. It is built mostly of recycled materials, including discarded bricks used in the cement, recycled plastic bottles woven into the ceilings, and waste from the construction process used to build the floor at the Circle Store and Amphitheatre.

Each room features stylish furniture and amenities made from recycled plastic and planet-friendly materials, conceptualized by celebrated British designers Max Lamb and Faye Toogood and fabricated by Balinese artisans using indigenous techniques. Each guest checking in to the Studios receives a zero-waste kit from Potato Head's own Waste Lab, to reduce the use of single-use plastic while starting the conversation about design and waste reduction as a vehicle for change.

Potato Head's current project is to build a bigger collective to help ease Bali's waste burden. Alongside hospitality industry peers, Potato Head is building a waste centre in Batubelig Banjar that will enable partner businesses to reduce the waste they send to landfills. The aim is to roll out the scheme to other Bali districts in the near future, eventually bringing the island as close as possible to zero waste to landfill.

Potato Head's recent attainment of B Corp status means that its efforts to create "Good Times while Doing Good" have been officially recognized. Gaining certification was a long and painstaking process, with every aspect of the brand's operations carefully examined to make sure Potato Head can be included among companies that meet "the highest standards of verified social and environmental performance, public transparency, and legal accountability to balance profit and purpose."

Even as the hospitality industry continues to pursue greater sustainability, private homeowners on Bali are doing so as well. Gildas Loaëc was kind enough to give us permission to photograph Rumah Rubah, his house in Tumbak Bayuh. *Rumah rubah* means "fox house" in Indonesian—perhaps not a surprising choice for Loaëc, cofounder of the multifaceted lifestyle brand Maison Kitsuné, which is named for the shapeshifting trickster fox of Japanese folklore.

Designer Maximilian Jencquel and Eco-Mantra's team of engineers collaborated to design Rumah Rubah as a sustainable yet luxurious residence. The timeless architecture is inspired by Maximilian's international upbringing and infused with elements of the local Balinese culture and Asian culture generally, using natural materials such as lava stone and plenty of teak.

Maximilian told us:

> The wood is from sustainable plantations in Indonesia, according to the contractor who did all of the procurement. We used Eco Mantra and their team of environmental engineers for Rumah Rubah and came up with solutions to optimize energy and water efficiency. We are catching the rain and harvesting the sun!

Teak chairs on a reclaimed-wood veranda overlooking the Wastewater Gardens at Villa Campuhan. In the background is a guesthouse with walls of *bedek* (woven bamboo).

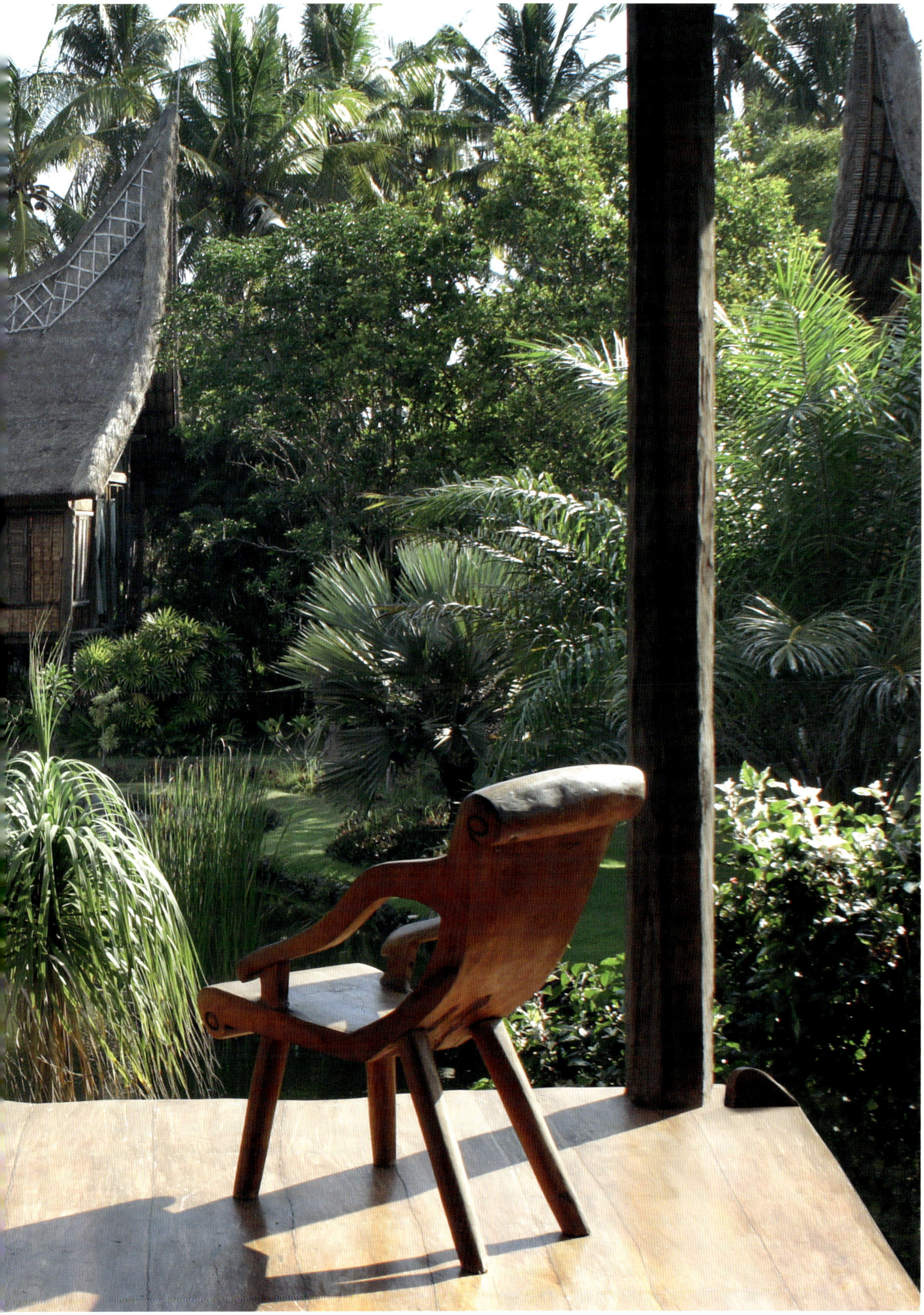

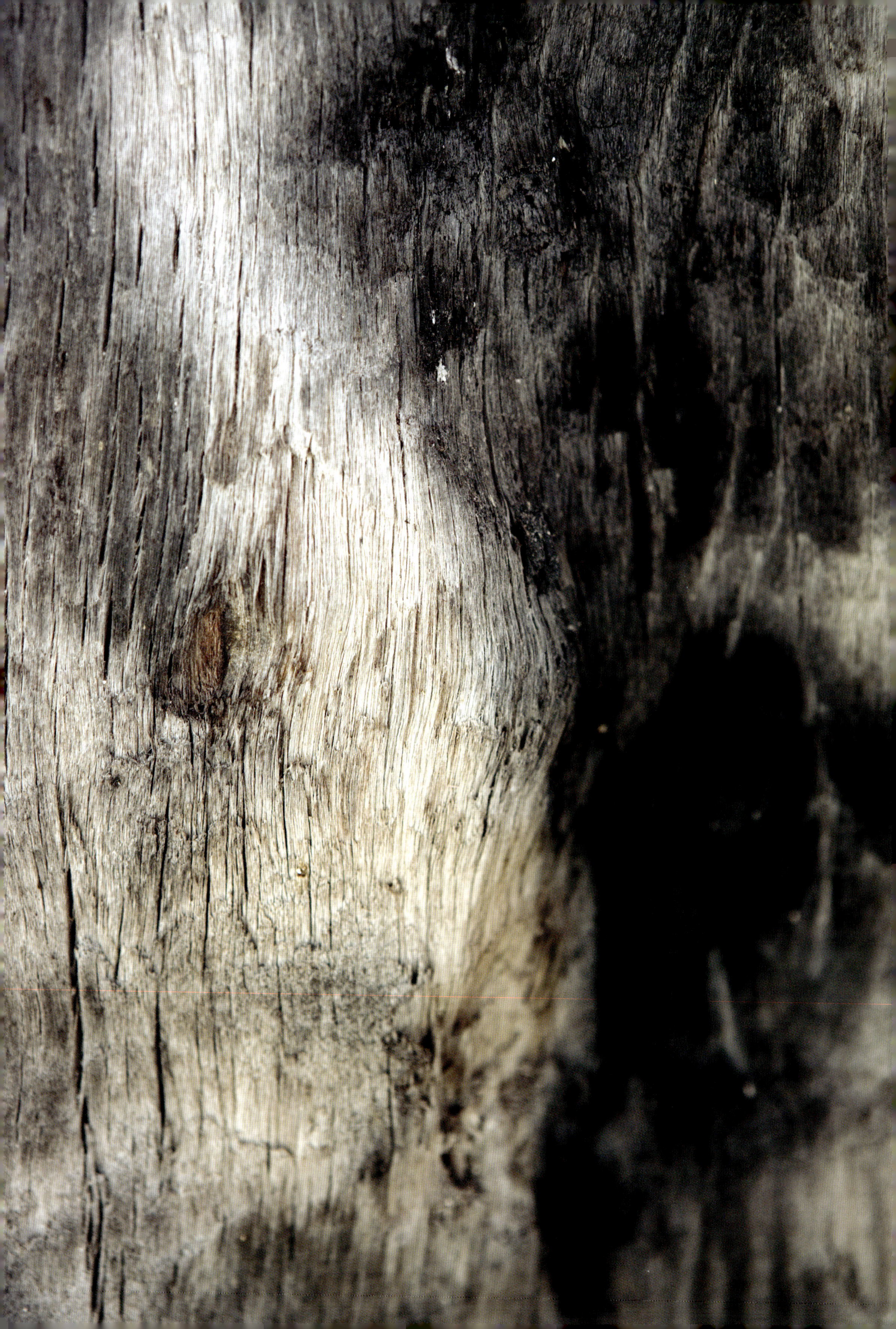

KNOCKDOWN HOUSES

Several types of knockdown wood house from Java have been adopted in Bali. The smallest is called a *gladak*, and two larger varieties are the *joglo* and the *limasan*. Most are made from teak, and the roofing is usually either terracotta tiles or ironwood shingles (*sirap*). The trademark of the joglo is a tall central roof supported by four large central columns. Neither the limasan nor the gladak has central columns, so nearly all the interior space is usable. All these buildings are designed to be moved easily and have coded joins so that they can be erected quickly, with a minimum of mistakes. Some of the timbers are richly carved, particularly above the uprights of a joglo, but most are made from simple hewn timber.

The foundations are minimal, and as "traditional" homes they are subject to almost no building regulations, unlike concrete slab construction, so they have become more prevalent in the current real estate climate.

Bud Hart has built his home, Hartland, on the ridge of Sayan Terrace, outside Ubud. The buildings on the estate include a joglo and a modified gladak.

> I don't know the definitions or categories of what is considered "sustainable" or "non-sustainable" material. For example, because Sumba stone is excavated within the country in order to clear farmland, does that mean it's sustainable? Even though

Seen from the natural spring-fed pools, the circle of houses overlooking the Ayu River gorge at Bambu Indah, John and Cynthia Hardy's eco-luxury boutique hotel on Sayan Terrace, Ubud.

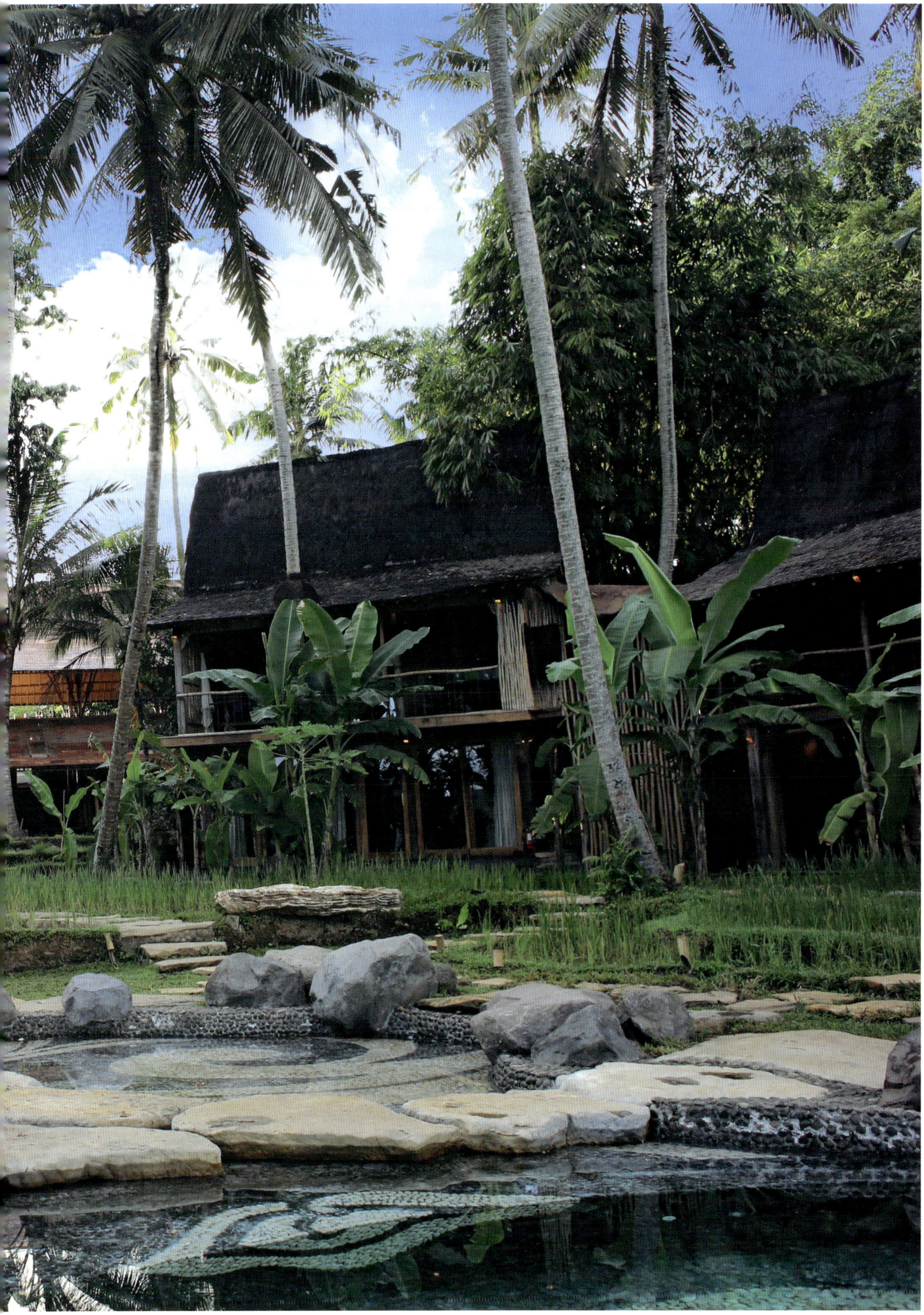

a fair amount of petrol is probably used to transport it to Bali? But I used every last piece of stone—for the retaining walls, steps, house walls, pool, etc. Even the broken stones, rubble, I pounded into powder and used for pigment in the polished cement walls and floors, and in the grouting. The buried teak logs from Java I used not only for the buildings, but for making all the furniture on-site, as well as shelves, switch plates, you name it.

I used earth from the land for mud walls and terracing for the organic vegetable gardens. I grew my own bamboo to be used later for fences and natural barriers. There are living fences from other plants and trees grown locally. I made tables from discarded tree stumps on the building site.

For me, sustainability started unconsciously, as a way of life in my cowboy childhood. I grew up in a sheep-trading and cattle-ranching family in southern Colorado in the 1950s—sheep drives to the high country, branding calves, round-ups, the whole works. We lived in an "off-the-grid" cabin during the long summers (before there was even a grid to be off of), with a windmill and natural springs for water, no electricity, no phone, an outhouse, a true icebox, a wood-burning stove, recycled bunk beds (from train cars), Coleman lanterns, and candles. Our playhouse was a sheep camp. Our furniture was made from wagon wheels, and our decorations were found objects.

My dad used government subsidies to help pay for soil conservation and water systems to collect rainwater in ponds for the animals. We used the wool from some of the sheep to make blankets. A steer and a ewe were slaughtered each year and kept in the freezer to feed the family. The message was that you use what you have and take care of it so it'll last, whether it's topsoil or boots.

The message became conscious when I took a couple of ecology courses in college. Then I spent thirty years living in New York City, where there was no eco-anything. But when products came to market that were "eco-friendly," I bought those, and I still loved wearing my lizard cowboy boots, repaired with gaffer tape.

I was much more concerned about the sustainability of human life during the holocaust of AIDS in the 1980s and into the early '90s. I was very engaged in that effort. First, take care of your own body and mind (psychoanalysis and yoga for me, the within and the without), and make your living space pleasant to yourself. Second, take care of the world you depend on, or there won't be any mind and body to take care of.

We live in an age of insecure and anxious attachment to both ourselves and the earth, which is reflecting back to us our own negligence as we sink into a quagmire of human suffering because of it. *As above, so below. As without, so within.*

Coming to Bali brought me full circle with nature again. As far as nature goes, it felt quite literally like coming home, albeit to a tropical version. Bali appealed to my memory of Colorado. Mount Batukaru to the north is like the San Juan Mountains near the ranch. The Ayung River below Hartland is like the Saint Charles River flowing through the canyon on Turtle Butte Ranch in Colorado. The vistas are similar—serene, gracious, composed, counterpointed with awesome storms that reveal the power of nature.

In my house, there isn't much that isn't wood and stone, not even much glass. All the water comes from natural springs. I have

A bridge connects the bedroom to the bathroom at Jambu House, Bambu Indah.

A copper-lined basket serves as a bathtub at Jambu House, Bambu Indah. Copper is renowned for its healing effects.

The bridge to the bathroom at Jambu House.

Padi House at Bambu Indah. The ample living area sits under a
ceiling of weathered old reclaimed teak.

Wastewater Gardens to filter all gray water, and a composting and seedling house. The open floor plan lets wind ventilate the house; all standing water has been eliminated for mosquito control; and the swimming pool is in an area with no trees, to absorb sunlight and warm the water. (I often hear complaints that the pools are too cold at this higher altitude.) I explored a ram pump for bringing springwater up the ridge, but it was too steep.

I would advise future architects and designers to learn as much as you can about sustainable design in school and in the field, in the context of what you want to build and where. Learn the latest technological advances, and remember that it's your job to help the client realize his own dream within his budget—not your dream. Know the difference and respect it.

I draw inspiration from nature and the best influences in my own past, from Navajo rugs to mountains. Cultivating an attitude of appreciation and respect toward the environment leads to feelings of enjoyment and an overall sense of health and well-being.

I have sought comfort and contentment in simplicity, purity, and restraint, with an awareness that impermanence presides over all things. This provides a sense of timelessness, of presence.

The design corollary is to venerate and emulate the discreet, modest, and respectful. Appreciate and be sensitive to empty space. I escape the pressures of the material world by creating lightness in my home and gardens.

Did I make any blunders? I paid a lot for a house design that I ended up not building because it was too expensive. I tried to stick everything, and everything luxurious, into it. Carrara marble from Italy, bluestone from Europe, the whole structure in buried teak—a jewel box, really. So I scrapped that design, and ended up with a modest old joglo that was redesigned by Max Jencquel; we all agreed it was better than the jewel box.

Lesson learned: Calculate your budget first? Look before you leap? Don't let Mr. Fancy Pants make the decisions? Less is more?

Also, another one—before I ever moved to Bali, shortly after I bought the property, I tore down a big, ugly concrete house that was on the land where the joglo now stands—an impulsive action, really. Not long after, I suddenly realized I had no place to live and had just torn down a house. I couldn't believe how stupid that was.

Lesson learned: Use what you have, and don't act impulsively. Whatever you do, do it gently and with love, and only after forethought.

My design signature? I'll have to think about that, but my method was to collaborate with those who made the work I love, in a context that expresses who I am.

A short time ago, we met with Richard North-Lewis, famed for his sandstone wall mural at Changi Airport in Singapore and many other carved stone interiors. He showed us his latest creation, the Koya Cabin.

After visiting Japan and a luxury mansion in West Sussex, I became inspired. I realized I had become minimalist, and what better to do during the Covid period than this project. I proceeded to go from 28 acres [11 hectares] down to 12 square meters [140 ft^2]! My concept hatched and became "gypsy caravan meets samurai warrior."

A coat from Uzbekistan displayed inside Kelapa House, Bambu Indah.

117

I built the Koya Cabin at home with my design partner, David Field. It's designed to fit into a twenty-foot container in only two pieces, and it's set on wheels of solid cast iron. You roll it out and bolt on the roof, which supports rainwater catchment and three solar panels. The cabin is graced with the best materials—it's all reclaimed teak, it's double-glazed and soundproofed, and all the doors and windows have magnetic posts. It has air conditioning and a fan, and a very slick functional kitchen, loo, basin, and shower. There's a massive amount of storage under the huge bed. The outside teak bench converts to an outdoor dining table.

The Koya Cabin, designed by Richard North Lewis and David Field: "gypsy caravan meets samurai warrior."

The Koya Cabin is designed to fit into a twenty-foot container in only two pieces.

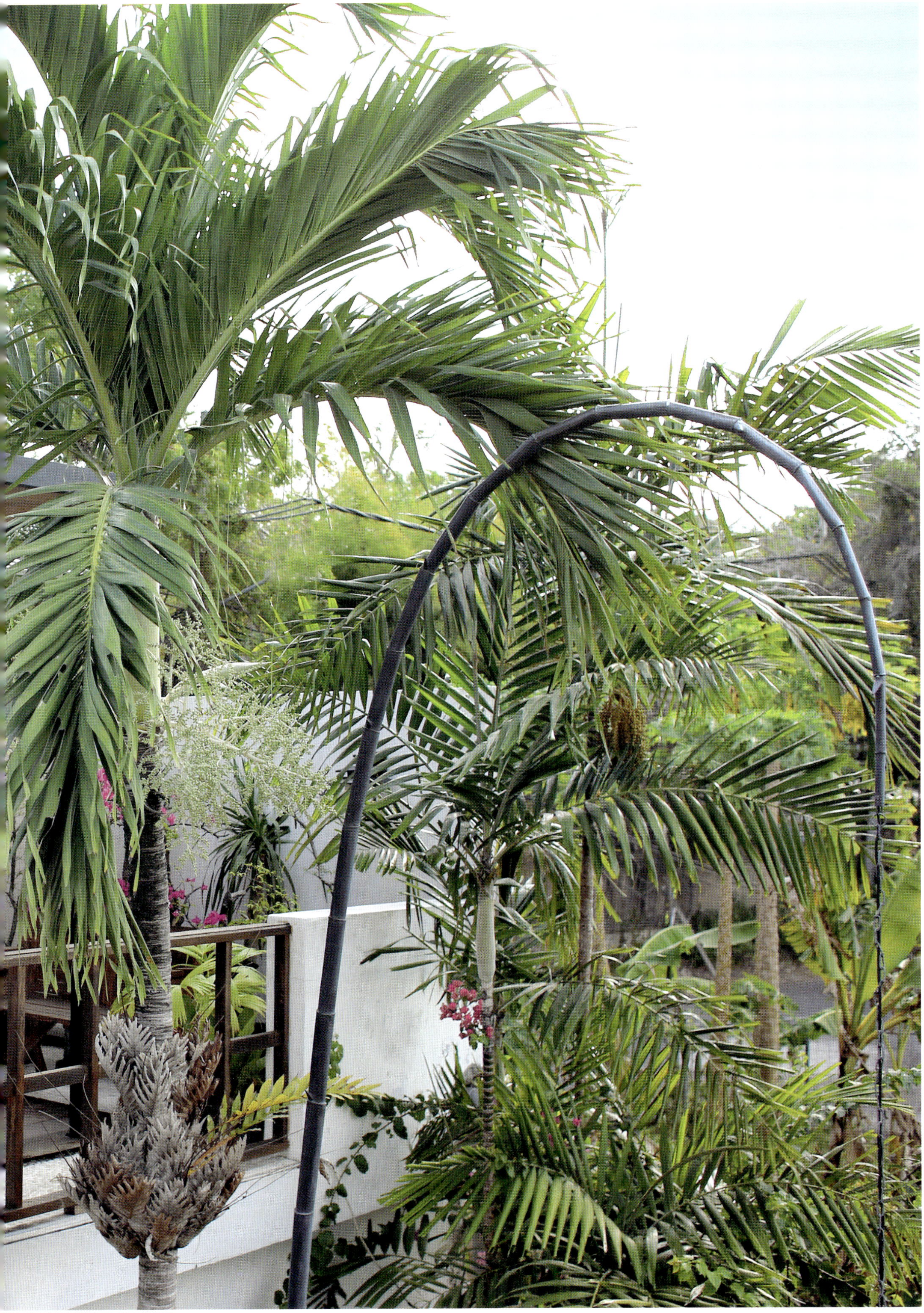

Hartland Estate, Kedewatan, Ubud, designed by Maximilian Jencquel: the open front door of the main *joglo* (knockdown wood house), with an artwork by Filippo Sciascia.

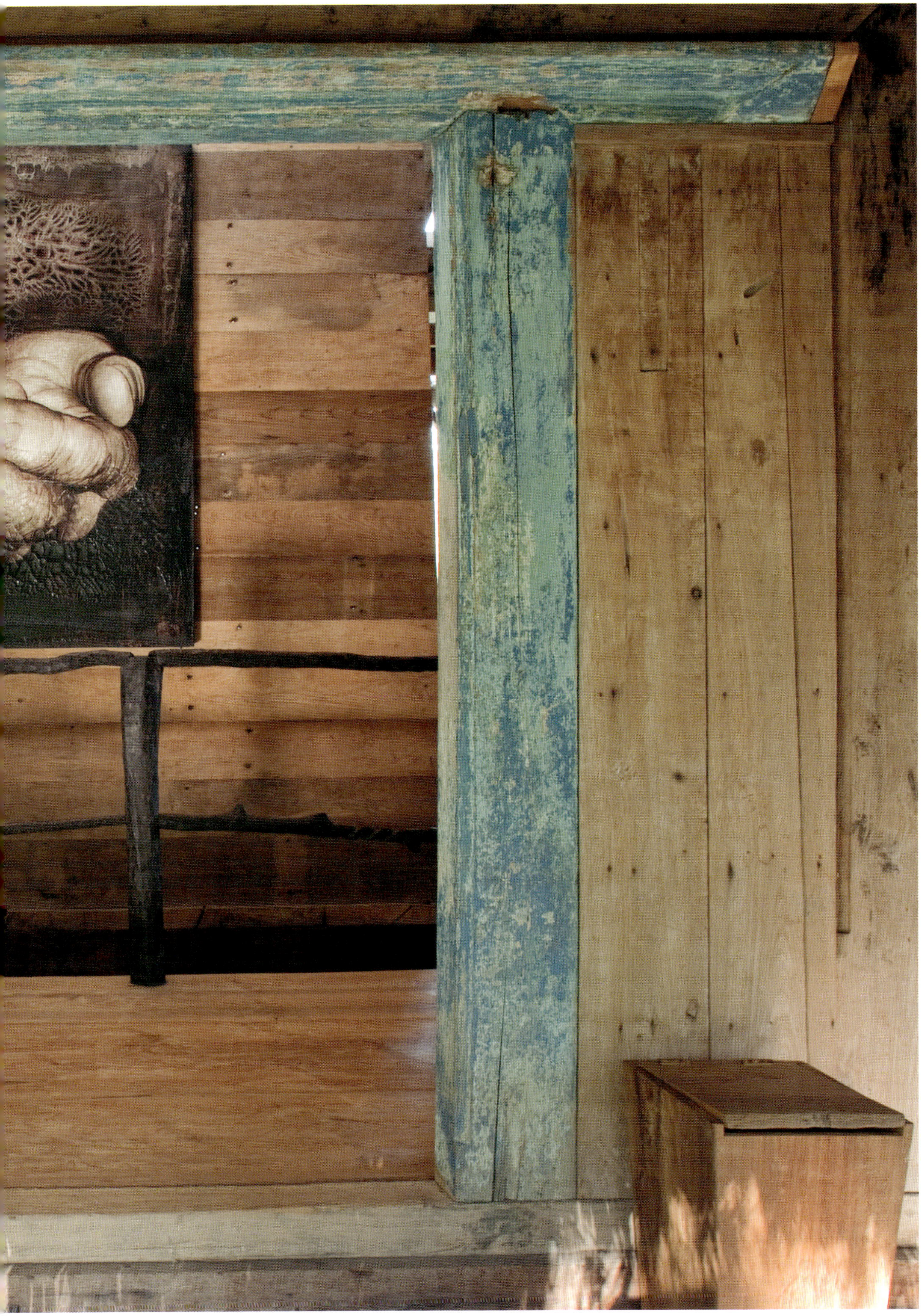

A teak *gladak* (knockdown wood house) converted to a spacious bedroom, with a bathroom and a wide veranda, at Hartland Estate.

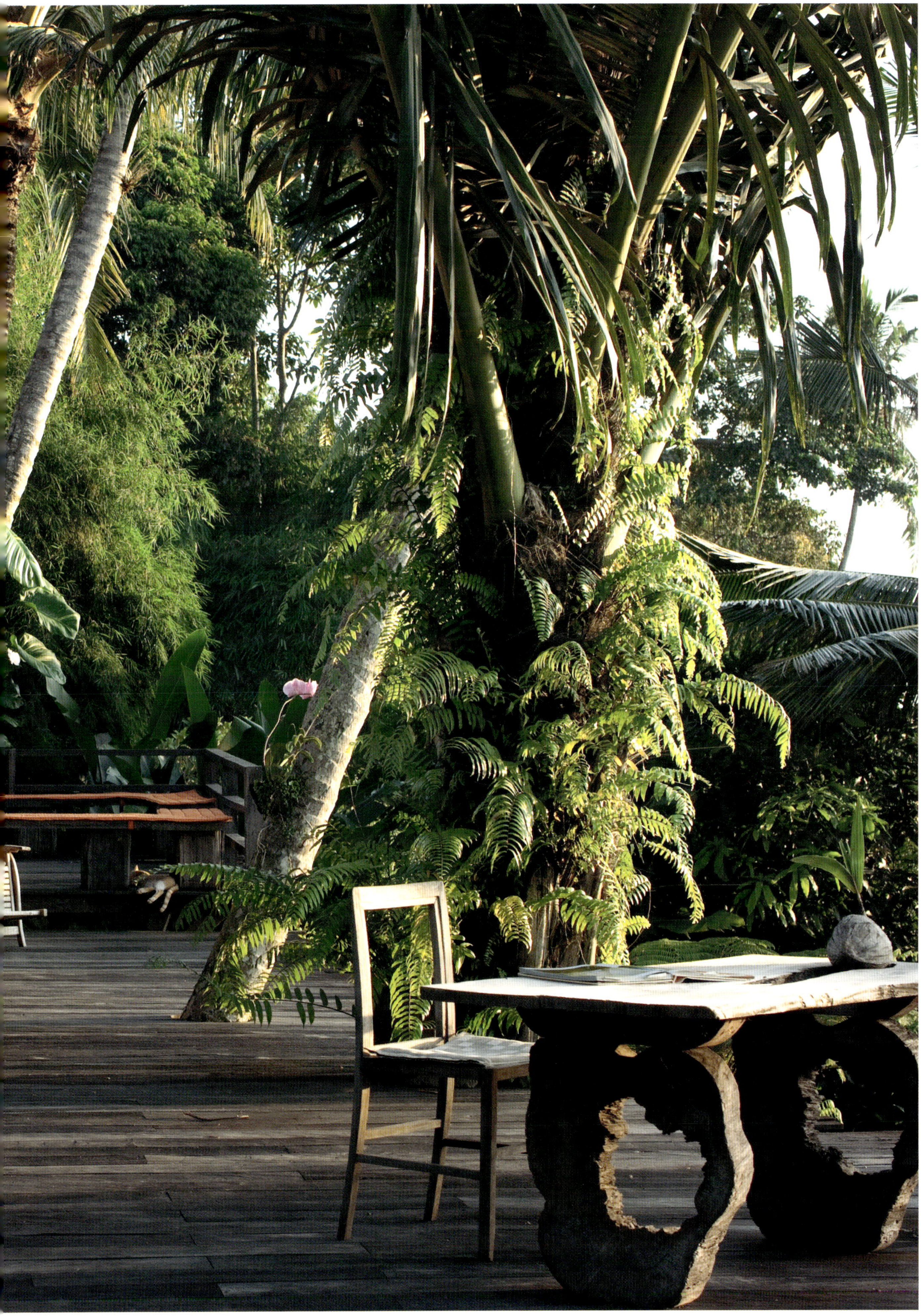

A glimpse into the living space of the main joglo house at Hartland Estate. One of the central columns is visible at left.

The central columns of the main joglo house at Hartland
Estate create a recess for the bed.

The shower in the main joglo house at Hartland Estate is set over a dark river boulder.

An exterior view of the main joglo house at Hartland Estate, revealing its characteristic roofline. The swimming pool in the foreground follows the contours of Sayan Terrace and is filled with springwater from the property.

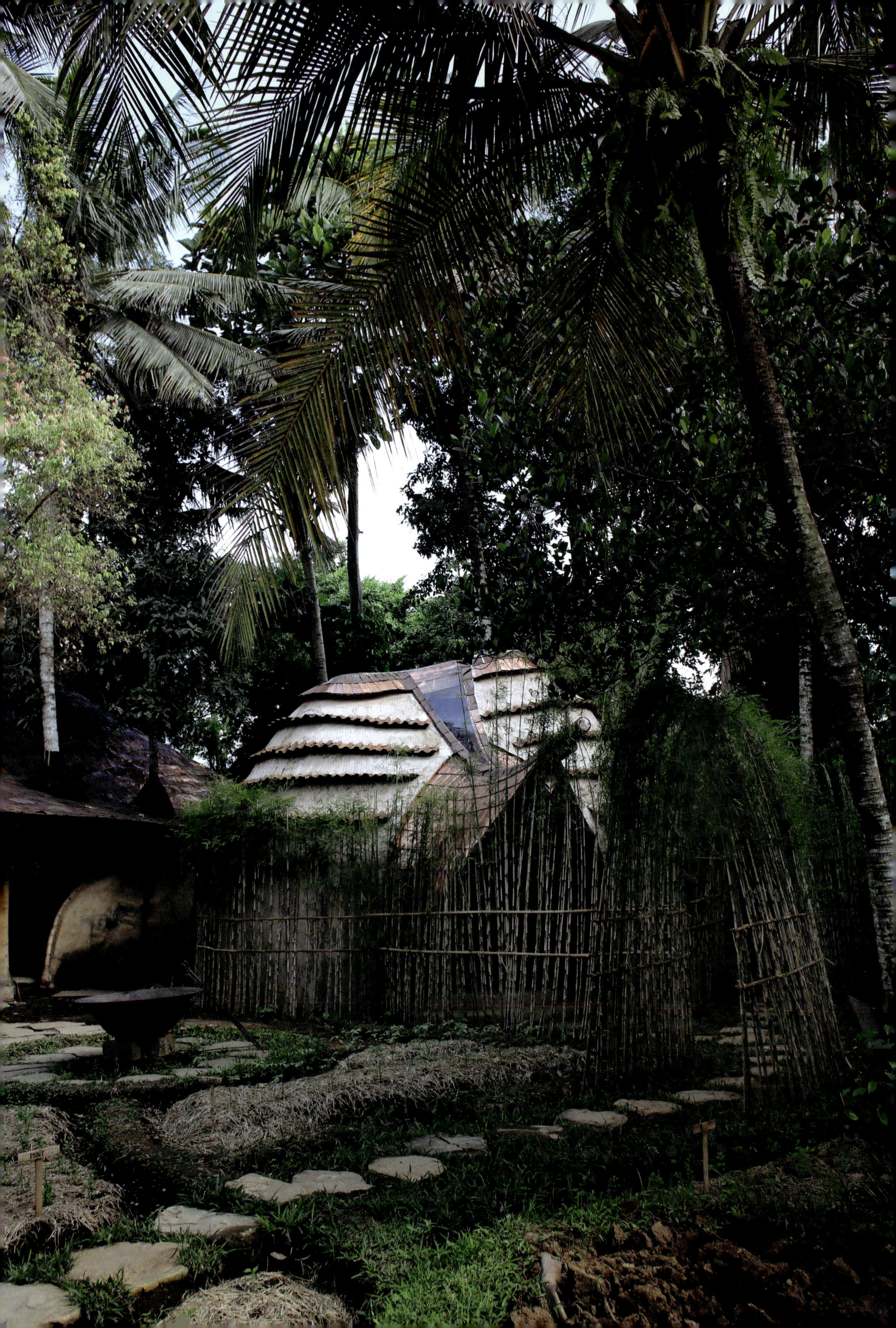

GREEN

We head off from Indobamboo, Arief Rabik's coastal factory, up the scenic volcanic slopes to meet Elora Hardy, her father John Hardy, and his wife Cynthia Hardy. The couple has also founded Bambu Indah, a resort whose guest quarters are in antique Javanese houses, and the Green School, an international primary and secondary school intended nurture curious and ecologically conscious minds. Elora has become a TED speaker and leading light in the bamboo sustainability world. She is developing a planned community of eighteen homes, the Green Village, near the Green School.

>   I first thought of eco-friendliness when I was around seven or eight. I read 50 *Simple Things Kids Can Do to Save the Earth*. It gave small tips like how to reduce the use of water in your toilet; you put a one-liter bottle of water in the cistern. I used to do things like that! It was quite clear to me in childhood that something was wrong with the environment. My parents would talk about it as part of the daily conversation, and I was worried for the future. But at the time I didn't think I had to try and create a sustainable life or anything.
>   Then, in 2002, I saw a movie called *The Next Industrial Revolution*, about the architect William McDonough and his concept of

A touch of indigo, in cloth made at TianTaru, Sebastian and Ayu
Mesdag's workshop in Puhu. Photo courtesy Zissou.

A vat of indigo dye at TianTaru.

cradle-to-cradle design, which really got to me. It wasn't about the problems but was more about design solutions. It was about super practical things and cost saving. I did manage to talk my way into an internship with McDonough one summer and sorted loads of photos out for him.

He had an architectural firm, and some of the junior architects talked me out of studying architecture, saying that it's a tough career and it'd be years before I got to make anything cool. I took their word for it.

I went to art school. I wanted a job, I wanted to be hands-on creative, but I didn't have any real goals. I met Donna Karan at the right time and got swept up into a New York fashion show and did some painting for it. I pretended I knew how to paint on fabric, and I ended up painting experimentally on super-expensive Italian silk jersey in the hallway of her offices.

Donna liked some of the work, so she put the hand-painted dresses in her runway show the next week. *Then* I had to paint exact replicas for the production run, and that led to a job doing their prints and patterns, even though there was a lot of resistance within the company.

Donna wanted a creative print designer on hand. She speaks like an artist in terms of shape, tone, texture, and mood, and I understood her. I wasn't concerned about expressing my own artistic style, and I understood what she was looking for. This lasted for five years.

Bamboo is the most sustainable of all materials, and this is what I've used in my designs for the Green Village. I wanted to use mud, but I never met the right person with all the knowledge to use it. We use some concrete for our point foundations, but not slabs. We don't use plywood, fiberglass, polystyrene, or Sheetrock. We use brass and copper and conventional plumbing and electrical wiring. I'm not an expert on sustainable materials. Right now my goal is to use this one really sustainable material, bamboo, with integrity.

The name Green Village refers specifically to the extreme sustainability of the bamboo that all the homes are built from. The other aspects are an ongoing innovation. We tried to make a bamboo-basket swimming pool, but it didn't work out.

Another innovation we came up with was to put old inner tubes between the floorboards and the bamboo to stop the squeaking. We look at problems and try to invent an unconventional way of solving them. I don't even know the conventional way, as I'm not a trained architect.

I'm not an expert on alternative energy, either, but we use natural airflow and shade to cool our houses. We don't usually use alang-alang for roofing anymore because it's not durable enough; we use bamboo shingle on a rubber liner, and sometimes aluminum.

Just picture cutting a really long bamboo pole from a ravine somewhere in Bali, then transporting it on the tiny roads, only to have to carry it to a difficult building site, in another ravine or wherever. Try turning a corner in a truck with an eighteen meter [60 ft.] pole on board. Sometimes it's hilarious and crazy. Twice in five years we've knocked shingles off a wall. We had to create a budget for the small repairs and, of course, a budget for the offerings needed for every construction and repair because that's what's expected in Bali.

My advice to student architects is to conceptualize the place while you're sitting on the land. From what I've heard, architecture students learn most of what they know sitting at a computer. Some interns are blown away that we sit in a shack on the site designing what we need and appraising the unique topography and features of the land to make it all fit together harmoniously.

My design signature? I'm not sure if it's really mine. As a team, we consider ideas together to find the best solution. A lot of it comes from what feels right. We're trying to find the curve or a shape that's right and complementary to the site.

Once we make an organically designed space, we have to furnish it. It's almost impossible to find furniture that fits harmoniously, so we design our own, mostly in bamboo. We tend to use what we're good at, which is bamboo.

My inspiration came from seeing the Green School. I was amazed at what I saw them do there: Dad; the brilliant creative director of the Green School project, Aldo Landwehr; the artisans; and the whole team. The artisans here are just brilliant; they make this all possible.

My father was in love with timber but decided to use bamboo for his showroom, at Linda Garland's urging. He and his architect, Cheong Yew Kuan, stood in a field with some petung bamboo, and they decided to make a building like the local *penjor* arches, the Kapal Bamboo, which means "bamboo boat."

The "grounding mind" that has translated John Hardy's fantasies and visions into successful businesses and organizations belongs to his wife, Cynthia.

Eco-friendliness came to me at high school in California. We had a severe water shortage in 1977, and I went around teaching children at primary schools how to reuse water. It made a big mark on me, and I've been a committed environmentalist ever since then.

When we opened the first John Hardy workshop, with eight hundred people, I commandeered most of the land and planted a garden with frangipani, cempaka, tuberoses, jasmine, and all sorts of fragrances. But we had visitors from the Northern California Permaculture Institute who said, "You guys have to plant food here." So we planted spinach, zucchini, rice, and all types of foods—we took a stand for sustainability.

John ventured into bamboo with Cheong Yew Kuan and built the Kapal Bamboo. He was a very good friend of Linda Garland and was greatly influenced and inspired by her; John is a visionary of his own sort and Linda was the bamboo visionary in Bali.

John was extremely vigilant about being "light on the land." When we built, we built off the ground and very light. In fact, Isabella may remember staying overnight on a bamboo platform thirty feet [9 m] above the ground when we were planning our first house on Sayan Terrace, in 1995. We are guests in this country, and we didn't presume to build in anything but a light, natural, and sustainable way.

We had lots of business visitors and friends arriving to Bali, so we started buying *gladaks*, the small knockdown wooden houses from Java, and put them on the land that had become available

The entrance to a tent designed by Bill Bensley at Capella Ubud, plunged into the heart of the jungle and flanked by an indoor-outdoor swimming pool.

next door. It became Bambu Indah, and it was really started as an eco-friendly, sustainable bed-and-breakfast with an edible landscape for friends. That land could be converted back into rice fields in two weeks!

I'm very sad to see how Bali is developing; I don't like condominiums and apartments. It's a shame that development has left such a heavy footprint. It's going to negatively impact tourism.

Did we make any eco-blunders? My daughters Carina and Chiara were running across a bamboo bridge we built that looked like a mini Golden Gate, and it collapsed right into the irrigation channel; we watched them fall and slide down the channel to the river. It was a small eco-blunder!

When you're a visionary, you don't have current technology at your fingertips. If you're a tech person, you have access to resources, but if your brain is thinking ahead of the technology and you're not a techie, you're really a kind of Robinson Crusoe!

My advice for anyone who builds is to listen to your land, be really sensitive to what's around, and be environmentally appropriate. Do a 360, look around, and be kind.

A little later we meet John Hardy on Sayan Terrace, overlooking Bongkasa and the Ayung River. The famous jewelry designer is dressed as usual, in a sarong and a linen shirt. We sit at a long table of solid reclaimed teak and sip from young coconuts.

I grew up in an 1890s brick house in Canada, so I never bonded with the ugly and unsustainable. I could always separate the old and real from the ugly suburban plastic in the fifties.

I didn't learn much in school. Most of the things I've learned are from people. In my buildings, I guess I've used bamboo, stone, and mud, simple things. Very simply, it's not a perfect world. If you want to use electricity, there's nothing currently eco-friendly about it. We use a lot of copper and a lot of brass for long-term things. We don't have much synergy with things like plastic; we use glass.

We started a project around seven years ago that we call the vortex; it uses a two meter [6½ ft.] drop of river water and is a promising source of energy for electricity considering the torque and speed generated. I imagine installing these in all the rivers here, because you don't have to build a dam or have any considerable heights to deal with.

We do have a beautiful solar array at the Green School, but the vortex would be the absolute solution for our energy needs. Seven years ago we dug the tunnel for the vortex, but there was local election politics involved and the guy who lost insisted that we remove one meter. It thwarted our plans. About two years later it seemed like the right time to try again. I was walking next to the river near the vortex after a big rain and the temple on the other side, built atop a huge rock in the mud, slid off and fell into the river. Of course the vortex was blamed for it! Ten thousand dollars and a year later, with a donation to seven *banjars* [villages] plus lots of ceremonies, we rebuilt the temple and started moving forward again.

The vortex still hasn't produced a single watt, but we are nearly there after seven years. The great artist Anish Kapoor, the Indian guy who made the big steel bean in Chicago, came to see the vortex and he said to me, "You can't put a generator in there, it's art!"

An eco-blunder was the first big bamboo bridge we built to cross the river to the Green School. We decided to build scaffolding under it so we could monitor the basic structure from below. While I was away a fierce raging flood came up so high that it caught on the bamboo scaffolding and dislodged the whole bridge from its footings.

My design signature is probably asymmetrical. Everything we do is flowing and curving. There's very little that's static. It's the authenticity of nature; it's comfortable and it's beautiful.

A hard modernist couch in a concrete box is for people who don't know and don't care, it's not for humans. We make a couch that you can actually fall asleep on!

Imagine if the queen planted a vegetable garden in front of Buckingham Palace and handed out eggplants: it would change the world! We need edible landscapes. The future for gardeners is to grow food instead of hiding in the bushes. Did you know that the Four Seasons has 325 acres of irrigated land in San Diego, but there's not a stick of food? It's a giant mess. What were they thinking? The drought was a real wake-up call for them. I'm starting a farm at the Green School, so we'll see how we go!

At Bambu Indah, we have a pond, a swimming pool, and edible gardens, but we don't have a water problem. The little river that cleans the pool is filtered with lava stone, and we have a hospital filter for drinking water. Electricity is a problem, but we're working on the gasification of rice husks to generate heat. At the Green School, we heat the cookstoves mainly with sawdust.

John introduces us to a young man named Matthew Bell, an industrial designer who is working on the vortex.

I grew up in an engineering environment in New Zealand, then studied industrial design. My father is a manufacturer of steel products, like LPG cylinders and water heaters, and I sort of grew up in a workshop tinkering and welding things, but I didn't study engineering. My mother was quite an activist and I remember getting dressed up as a half chicken–half frog to demonstrate against GMO in food. I was a frochicken! I grew up in an environment of questioning everything. If you have to work, it should be to address the malpractices that we see around us on a daily basis.

I got sucked into the vortex. I was with Orin, John Hardy's son, and he introduced me to his father. John asked me to make a blow-up theater for a launch of the movie *Samsara*.

We inflated the thing for the first time on the day of the screening, and it worked. It was kind of my job interview, and since then I've had continuous projects, including the vortex.

John had ordered the vortex generator, turbine, and bearing system from the Austrian inventor who designed the vortex blades. The rivers in Austria are very different from ours, and I could see that we had to make some serious modifications to address height, weight bearing, and oscillation, so we engineered a new shaft in Surabaya and it's been spinning with great stability for a few months now. We've redesigned the generator and added extra poles to generate higher outputs.

This bamboo meditation pod, designed by Matthew Bell for the Permata Ayung resort near Bongkasa, can be pulled out over the Ayung River on steel cables. Its tempered-glass floor panel offers a direct view of the water.

A dressing room with an outdoor shower in the Green Village, Abiansemal, a residential community designed by Elora Hardy and her bamboo architecture firm, Ibuku.

A mud wall overgrown with moss.

The new Moon House by the river bend at Bambu Indah, John and Cynthia Hardy's eco-luxury boutique hotel on Sayan Terrace, Ubud. This structure, with a roof of copper and brass shingles, was designed by Ibuku.

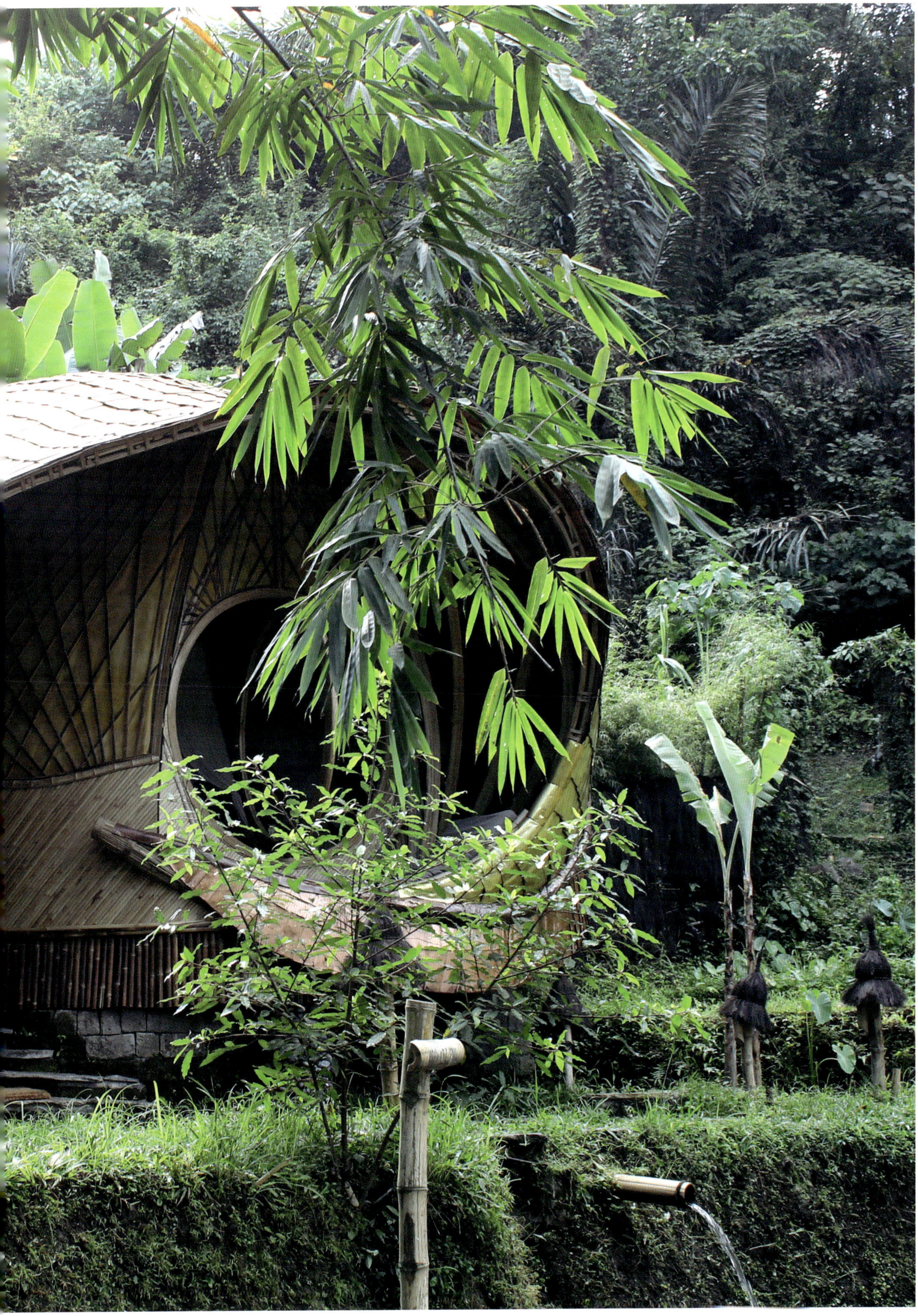

The generator was made in China, but we've customized the whole thing, and right now we're making a mounting structure from bamboo and steel. Installation isn't far away. We believe it will generate fifteen kilowatts continuously, but hopefully it will be more!

We've designed the vortex to be protected against flash flooding, wildlife, and debris, and it always allows a free flow of water to protect the ecology of the river. It will make traditional dams obsolete, because we only use a head of two meters. Hopefully before this book is published we'll have the details and proof of the outputs we're generating. It's an exciting time for me.

On July 4, 2015, just as the first edition of this book was going to press, I received an SMS from Matthew informing me that the vortex generator was finally operational with a no-load output of fifteen kilowatts, and would soon begin to supply power to the Green School.

Since the first edition of this book was published, Bambu Indah has been updated and refreshed under Cynthia Hardy's watchful eye. The *gladak* and *limasan* knockdown houses have been renovated, with some genuine comforts and luxuries, and rearranged in a "dress circle" overlooking the valley. There is now also a heavenly river playground where visitors can spend a day frolicking in the natural river pools.

We have also had the opportunity to visit another eco-conscious resort, Capella Ubud Bali, which opened in 2018. Surprisingly, this luxury tented retreat was quite busy during Covid. Its visitors from Jakarta helped greatly.

Capella Ubud is nestled between Ubud's rainforest, rice paddies, and the sacred Wos River, in an authentic Balinese artist village called Keliki. Set in lush green jungle, the resort adapts to the natural topography, respecting all trees and the surrounding ecology. Water is supplied by government lines and a deep well, but the emphasis is on conservation, with black and gray water management throughout. Supplies that are delivered to the hotel in single-use plastic packaging are transferred to reusable containers, and the plastic packaging is returned to the suppliers.

Each room has a low-impact foundation made of concrete and steel. The tents that rest atop these foundations are culturally unique, with eclectic and colorful decorations; the tent canvases were imported from France. The thrones are a humorous addition! Inspired by the early European settlers of the 1800s, designer Bill Bensley conceptualized this refined tented camp as a tribute to their spirit of adventure amidst untouched nature.

A lookout tower with a bamboo ladder and an alang-alang roof at Bambu Indah.

The Lost Lindenberg hotel in Pekutatan: a contemporary interpretation of a tree house with all the comforts at hand.

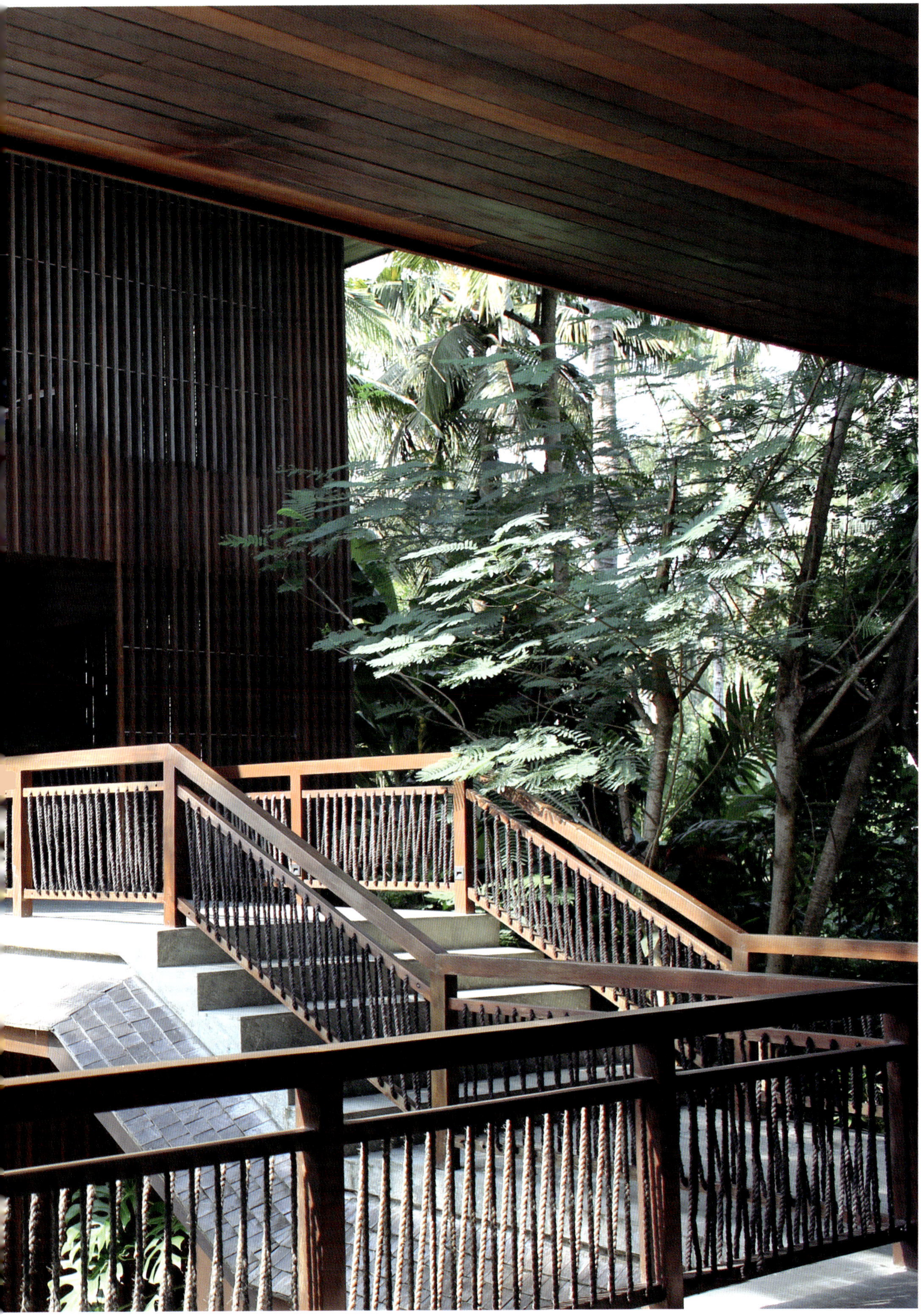

The Ibuku-designed Arc at the Green School, the international primary and secondary school in Abiansemal founded by John and Cynthia Hardy.

The dining room at the Lost Lindenberg, which serves purely plant-based vegan food. The island, in local green stone, faces a long dining table.

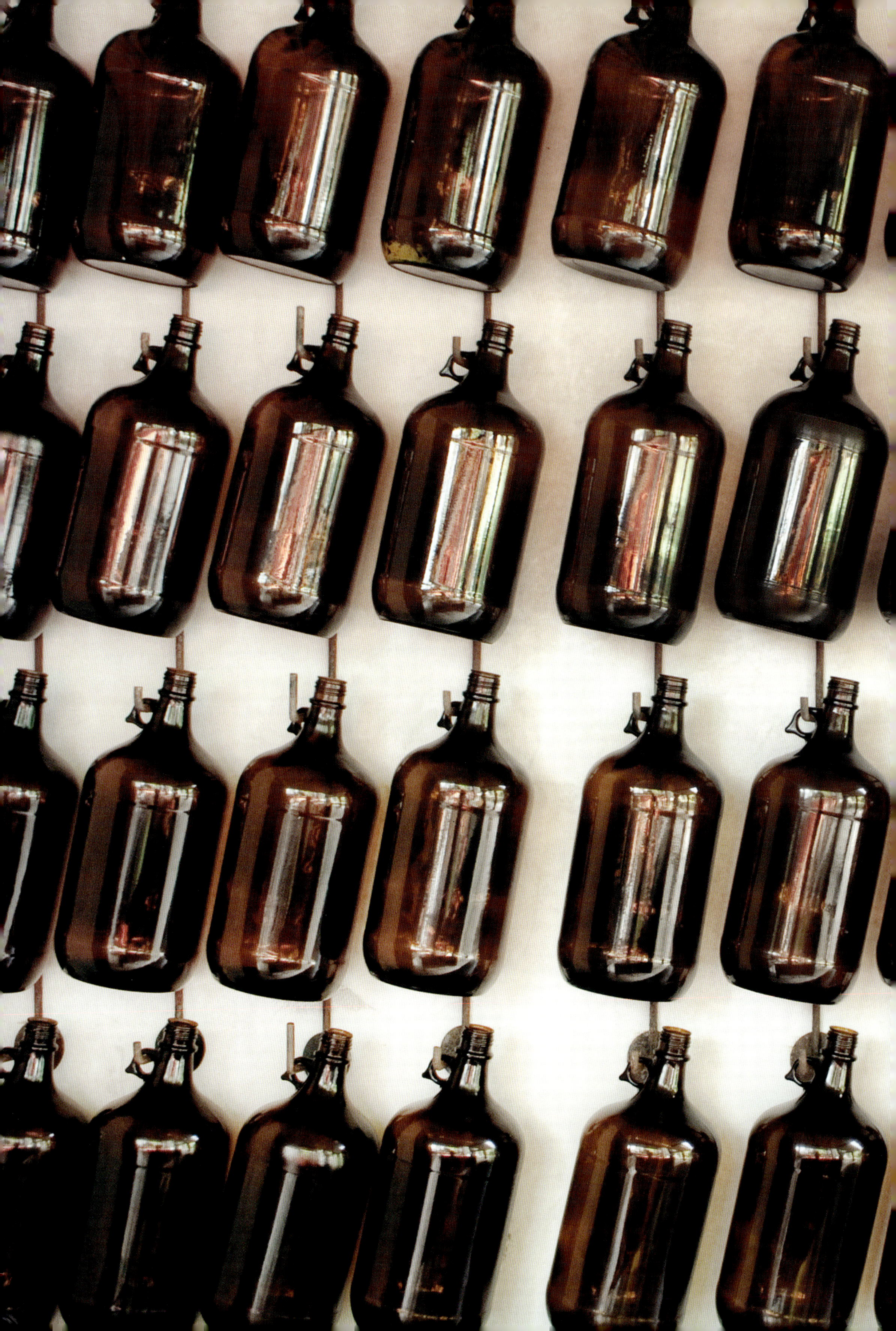

METAL AND GLASS

Glass is eco-friendly. It is easy to recycle, and there are huge deposits of silica all over the planet. The American company Corning invented Pyrex, a chemically and thermally resistant glass that represents an almost eternal material.

Metal, however, requires intensive mining operations, and vast amounts of energy are required to extract it from ore. It could be said that stainless steel is more eco-friendly than other metals, since it does not rust away. It serves its purpose without built-in obsolescence, the devilish spawn of the consumer economy.

We leave our little Bali village and motor through frenetic traffic into the heartland of Seminyak, to have light cocktails with Nicolas Robert.

Nico is a French industrial and interior designer who likes to play with light, proportion, and symmetry. He uses glass, metal, and reclaimed timbers to create houses of distinction. In the home of Damien Dernoncourt, chairman of the John Hardy jewelry company, he has achieved a contemporary Japanese feeling, using lots of glass to achieve an openness and connection to the outdoors, along with Japanese-style sliding partitions and walls.

Glass and steel structures are totally recyclable. Seventy-five percent of the building could be broken down and reassembled at a different location.

We heat the water using natural convection from the wall that gets the most sun, by channeling the hot air over water pipes at the top of the wall.

The interior gardens look Japanese and have a more mineral appearance in the red wall area, with bonsais surrounded by covered corridors to give the peaceful feeling of a convent. The exterior gardens have levels with very geometric cuts and grass slopes; a few species of bamboo have been integrated to keep the Japanese feeling, plus some bigger Indonesian tree species, trimmed to look like big bonsais. Frangipani are very Indonesian, but I felt the twisted sculptural look of the trunk matched the aesthetic, and when they flower they also remind you of cherry blossoms.

I reused as much material as possible from the original house on the land, which we demolished. Most of the concrete was used to raise the land level (to avoid flooding) or in the foundations of the new surrounding walls. All the wooden parts, like flooring, were recut and reused; the roof beams became the bridge over the pond and the six meter [20 ft.] "floating" dining table. On the wall in front of the table, I installed some wooden cones from Lombok, originally used to sift precious metals from rivers. There are also some other installations made from recycled materials, like the bottles behind the bar. The red tin boxes that make up one wall are old containers for Indonesian *krupuk* [rice crackers]. The concept for these installations comes from my love of Pop Art.

All my designs for the furniture incorporate metal and petrified wood, except for the chairs made from recycled rubber tires. Stone was sourced from Java and cut in Bali, like the balls that support the giant coffee table and the slabs for the coffee tables in front of the beige sofa. Another local material is the lava that I had gold-plated; since the client has a jewelry business, I thought it was a funny twist.

The antiques were sourced from island tribes, some from the Batak tribe, like the Singa faces, and also from the most famous tribe, the Dayaks. (Lots of men have Dayak patterns tattooed on their biceps without knowing their origins.)

We thank Nico, and he suggests that we ask Polly Purser for information about mud, as she apparently knows a women's group that specializes in mud. We text her, and she replies with an invitation to meet at her *joglo* (knockdown wood house) at midday. Polly grew up in Bali and Java and works for the John Hardy jewelry company. Her office is in the John Hardy design studio (pages 170–73), a traditional *wantilan* (pavilion) enclosed in metal and glass.

John said his company was a family practicing sustainability every day; it was about putting in a Balinese kitchen rather than a swanky German stainless steel system and planting indigenous red rice on the factory land to feed 650 employees every day and to protect the genetic inheritance of the rice. It was about both the people and the product, which has a beauty in imperfection because each item is handmade and one of a kind.

Sustainability has always been part of my world, more as it relates to community and to people as opposed to the environment. Sustainability for me was in the work I was doing in health promotion and HIV prevention, and then later in the hand-produced objects and crafts that I was making for my father's export company, Out of Asia. Sustainability was about preserving techniques and skills, and working with incredible natural materials like lontar, pandan, and water hyacinth.

When I used to eat my *bungkus* [take-out food] I would simply throw the packaging onto the ground or into the river, because it was a leaf! Now, unfortunately, plastic wrapping is prevalent, and it's not biodegradable.

The Balinese have one intention and that is balance and harmony; it is a fundamental part of who they are. They see that plastic is choking the rivers, and I have faith that they will recognize this and change their ways.

Having a child has brought a lot of home truths to me. I live close to nature. I live with the sounds and smells of pigs and chickens running wild everywhere, as I did when I was a girl. I want my child to develop this nature consciousness and to have it as I do.

The sustainability issue interests me particularly with my background in community work. Everything is interrelated, from materials to the overall health of the community. It is right for me to be living in an open house amid nature and to wash and swim in springwater, and I have a full interaction with my community. It's how I grew up and how I want to live, and I want my child to grow up the same way.

Glass may be eco-friendly, but it is not always friendly to wildlife. A great many birds die from flying into windows; I've seen literally fifty to a hundred dead birds under some glass-walled buildings in New York. Luckily, Norm vant Hoff and his son Oska, manager of Sarinbuana Eco Lodge, are in the process of creating bird-safe glass that has lines engraved within it. I had not yet seen their new product at the time the second edition of this book went to press, but I am told the second sample of the glass is being tempered. We would like to have some for our cathedral windows at home!

We are on a narrow green road cutting through Kaba Kaba on our way to Lost Lindenberg, a new boutique hotel on the southwest coast of the Island of the Gods. The coastline comes into view many times on this highway to Gilimanuk. Maximilian Jencquel collaborated with Alexis Dornier on the design of the Lost Lindenberg, and they got the volumes and scales dead right.

We have already visited some of the other beautiful architecture that Maximilian has created, such as Rumah Rubah, which has the most high-tech energy and water management of any home I've seen so far on Bali. Maximilian keeps his practice small, with the intent to grow organically. He is very selective and makes sure his clients are emotionally connected to the project:

It becomes a very personal journey. Bali has become a "brand" for modern tropical architecture, and I now get many inquiries from abroad. I invite my new clients to get involved with Eco-Mantra, as working with them is easy. They are engineers who provide eco-conscious solutions that are both sustainable and respectful.

154 METAL AND GLASS

A metal-and-glass house in Seminyak, designed by Nicolas Robert and formerly owned by Damien Dernoncourt.

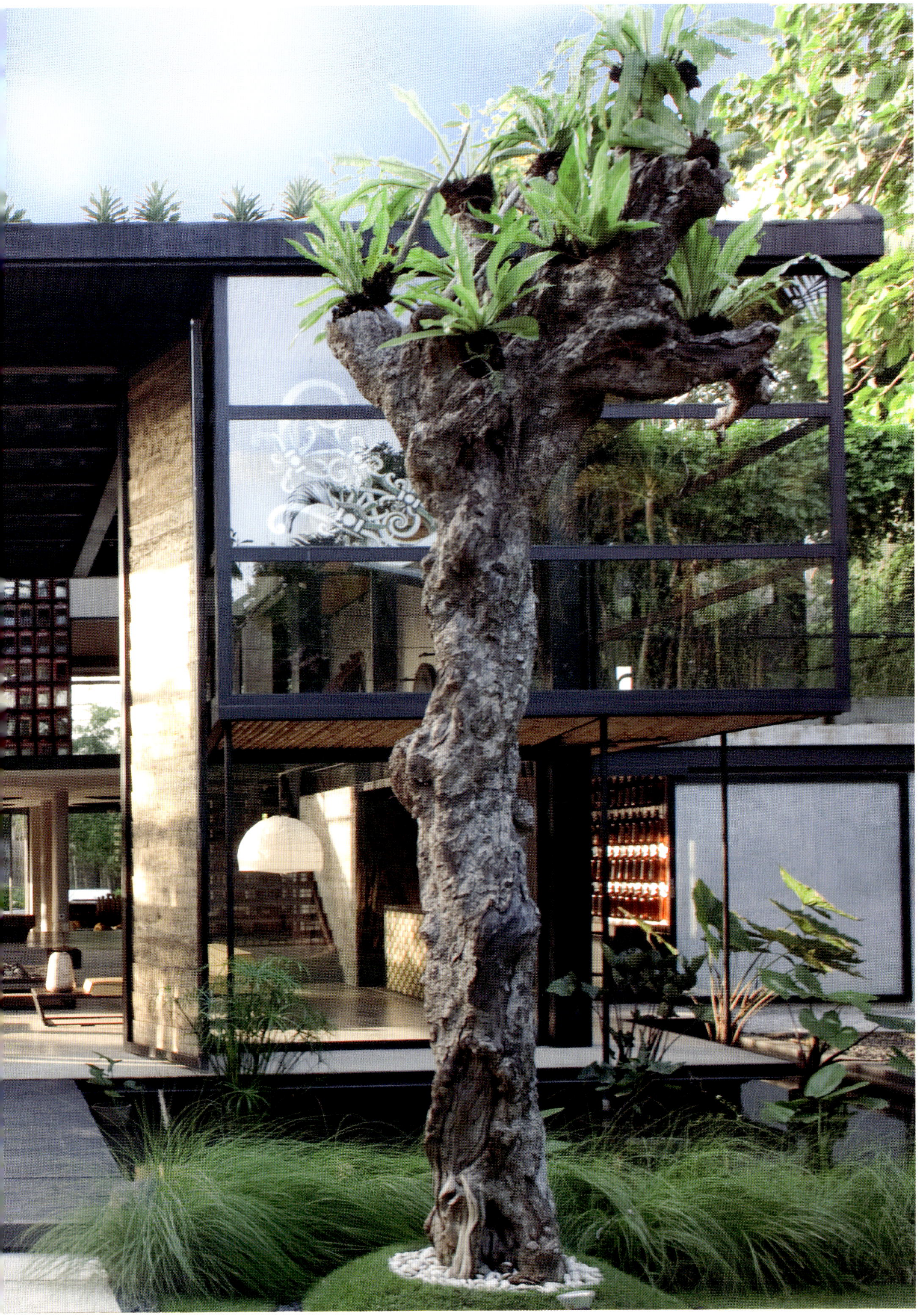

The interior of the former Dernoncourt house is designed in a Japanese-Indonesian indoor-outdoor style.

This Japanese-inspired garden in the former Dernoncourt house is surrounded by a walkway with a bamboo ceiling.

158　METAL AND GLASS

This wall of *krupuk* (rice cracker) tins partitions off the master bedroom in the former Dernoncourt house.

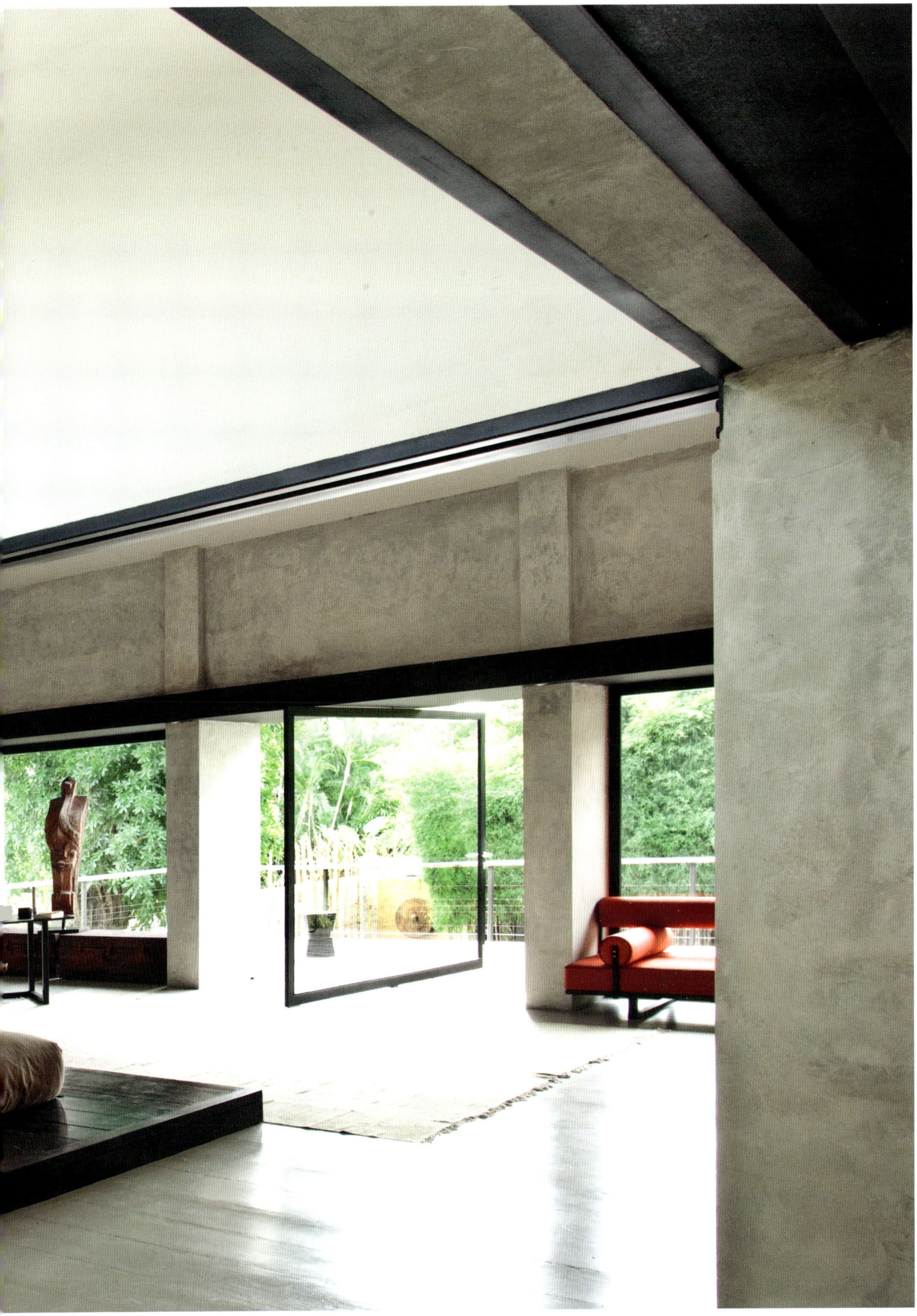

160 METAL AND GLASS

The huge gilded front doors of the former Dernoncourt house, seen from the mezzanine.

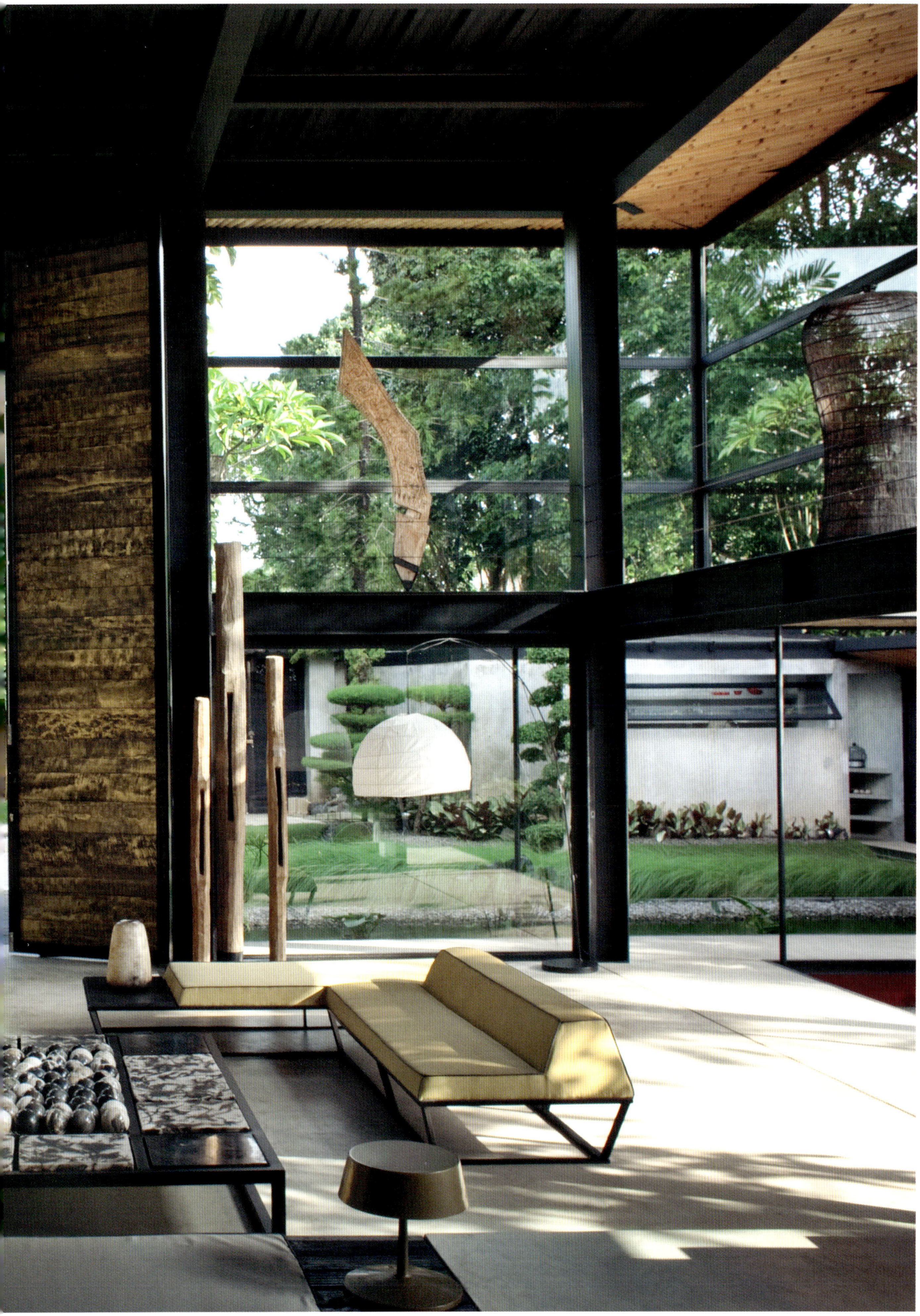

Architect Cheong Yew Kuan converted this traditional *wantilan* (pavilion) into a design studio for the John Hardy jewelry company, enclosing it with metal-and-glass walls. The building is set in the lush surroundings of the company's Abiansemal campus.

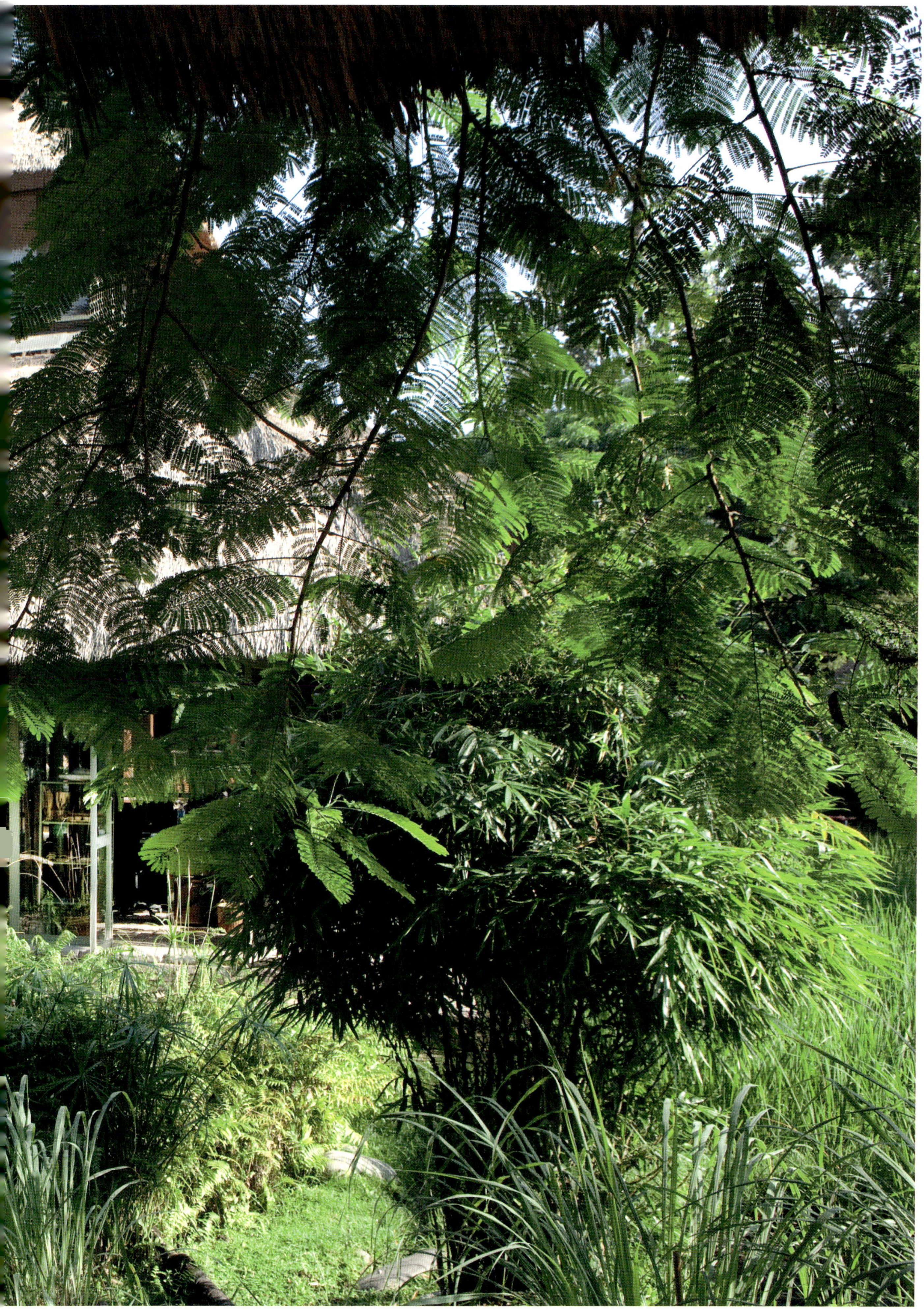

Inside the John Hardy jewelry company's wantilan design studio.

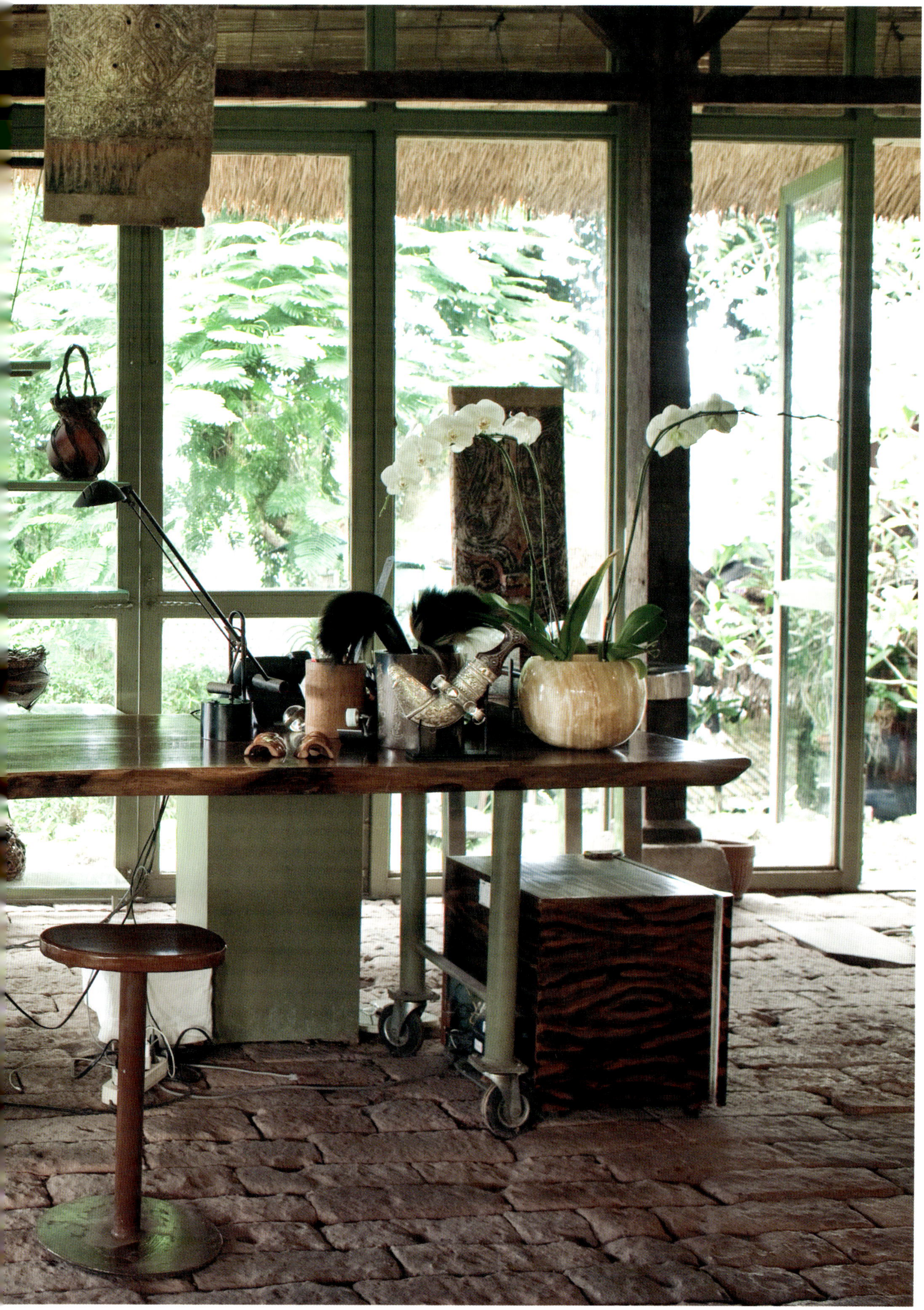

The hydroponic nursery garden at the Green School, Abiansemal, is built of bamboo and roofed with recycled windshields.

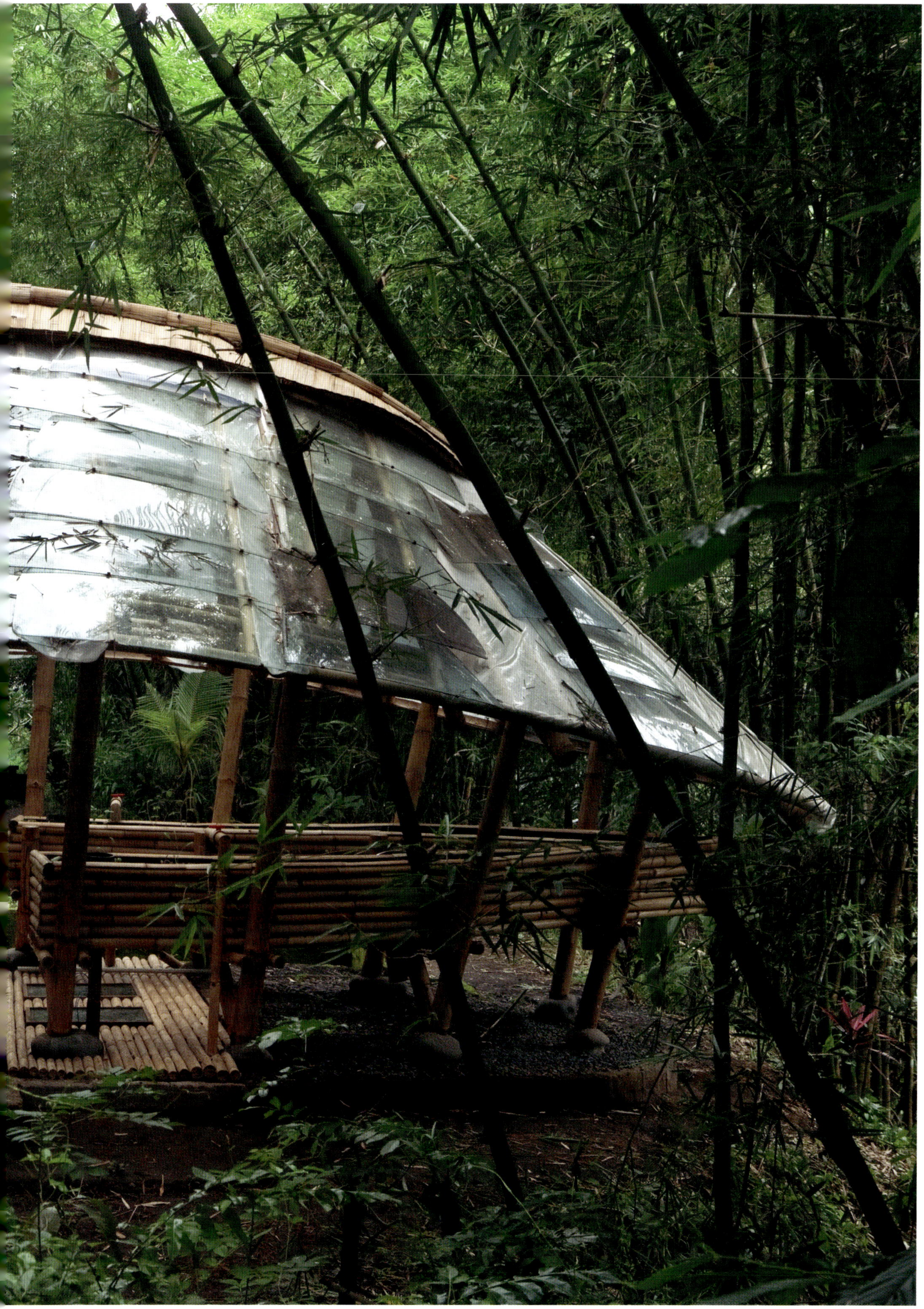

A copper bathtub and a copper wall with a pattern inspired by *bedek* (woven bamboo) at Bambu Indah, John and Cynthia Hardy's eco-luxury boutique hotel on Sayan Terrace, Ubud. Copper has healing properties.

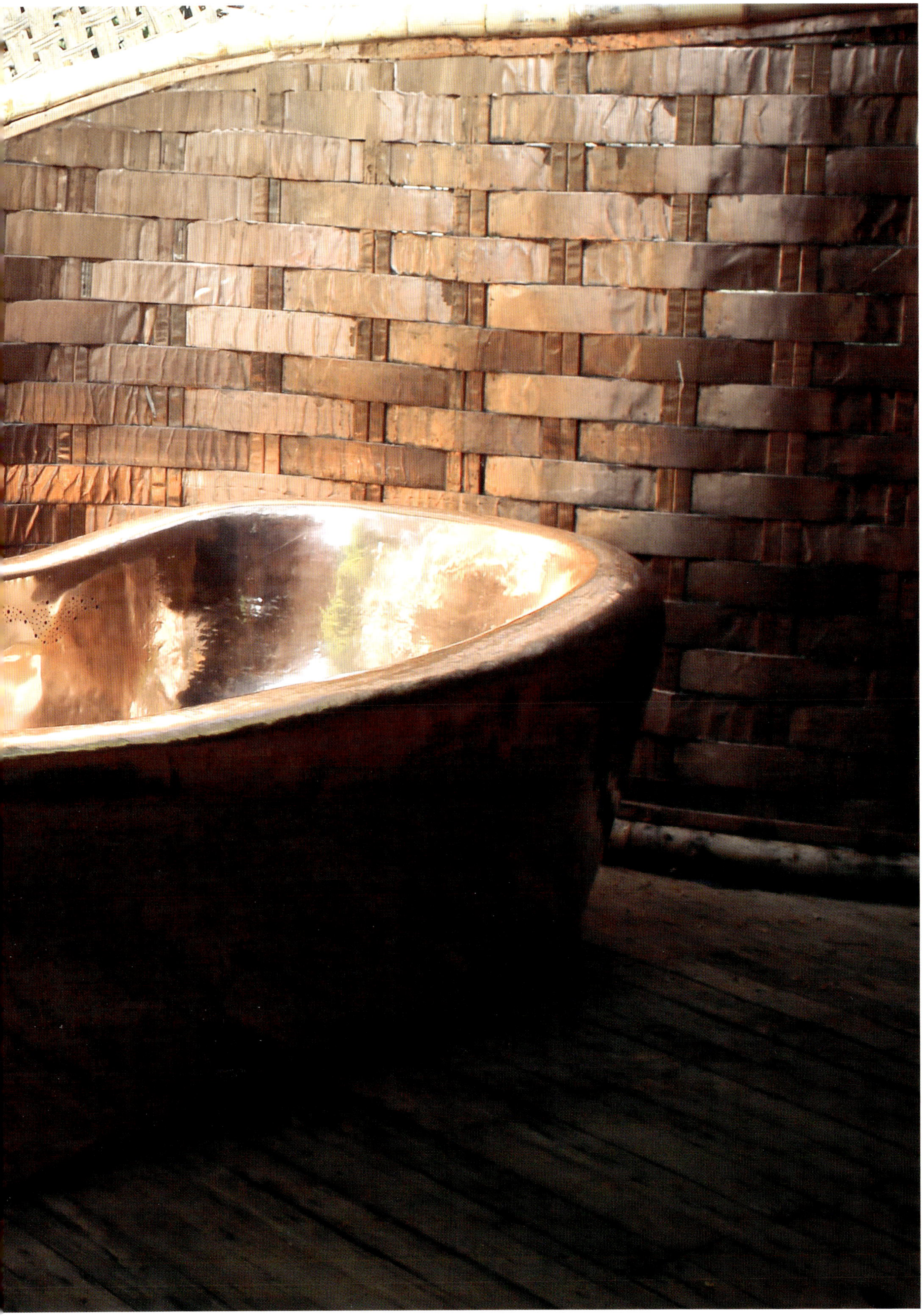

The artist and designer Jérôme Abel Seguin, known for his use of various materials recovered from the Java Sea, employed metal columns, beams, and roofing in his house at Kerobokan, in the Seminyak area.

171

172 METAL AND GLASS

The metal elements in the interior of Jérôme Abel Seguin's house create a tropical-industrial feel.

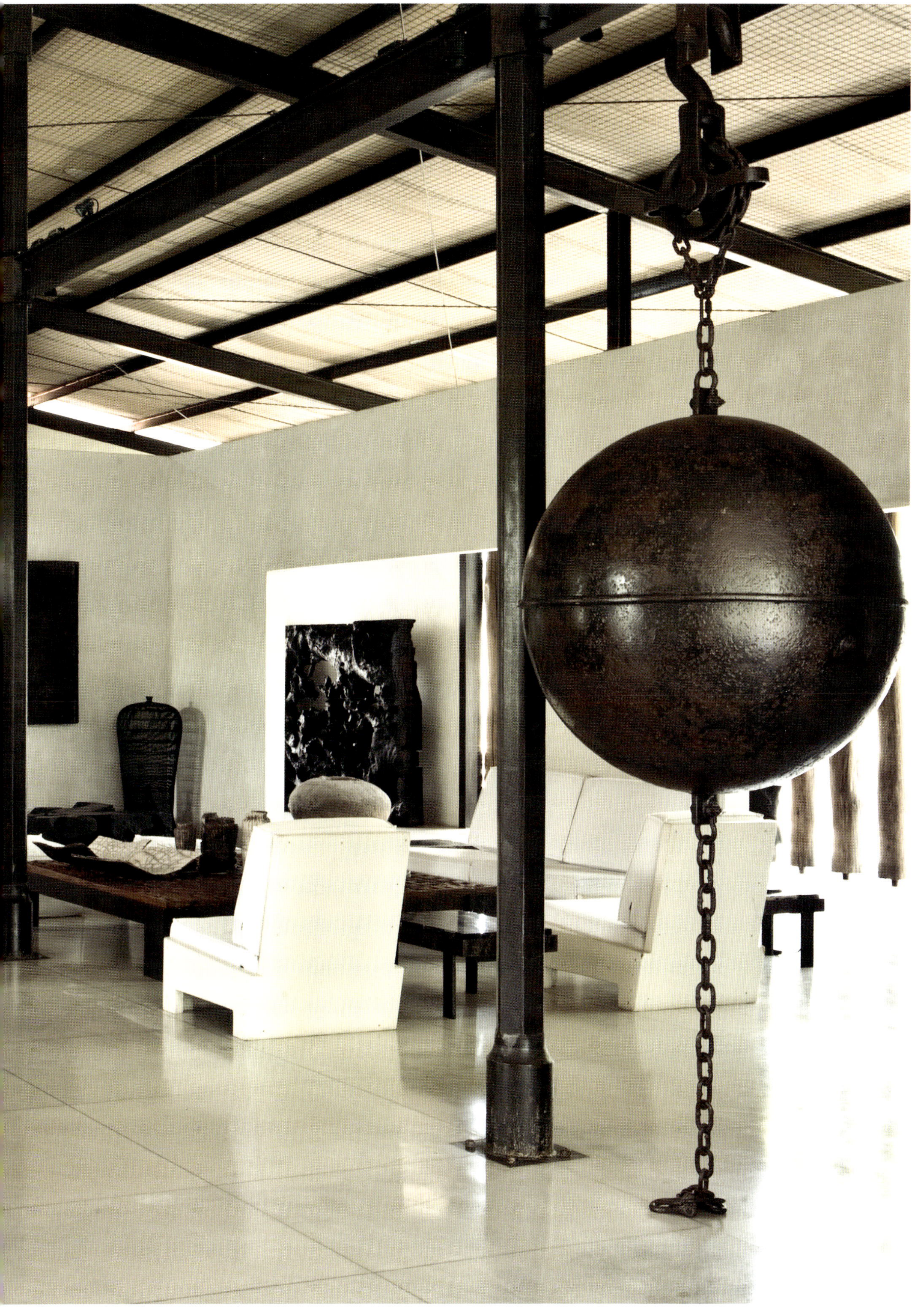

174   METAL AND GLASS

A loft space in Jérôme Abel Seguin's house, showcasing his furniture and artwork made from reclaimed roots.

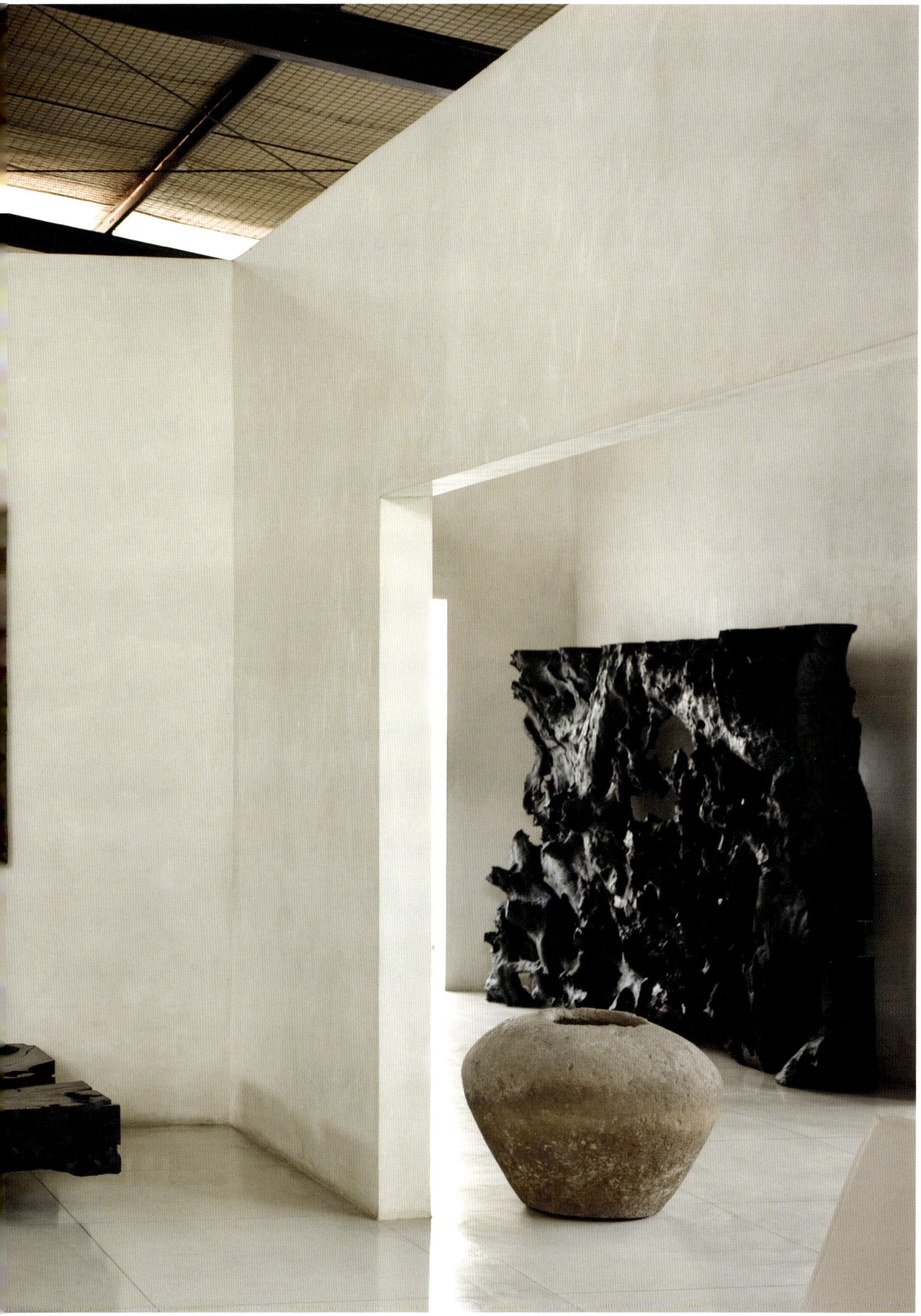

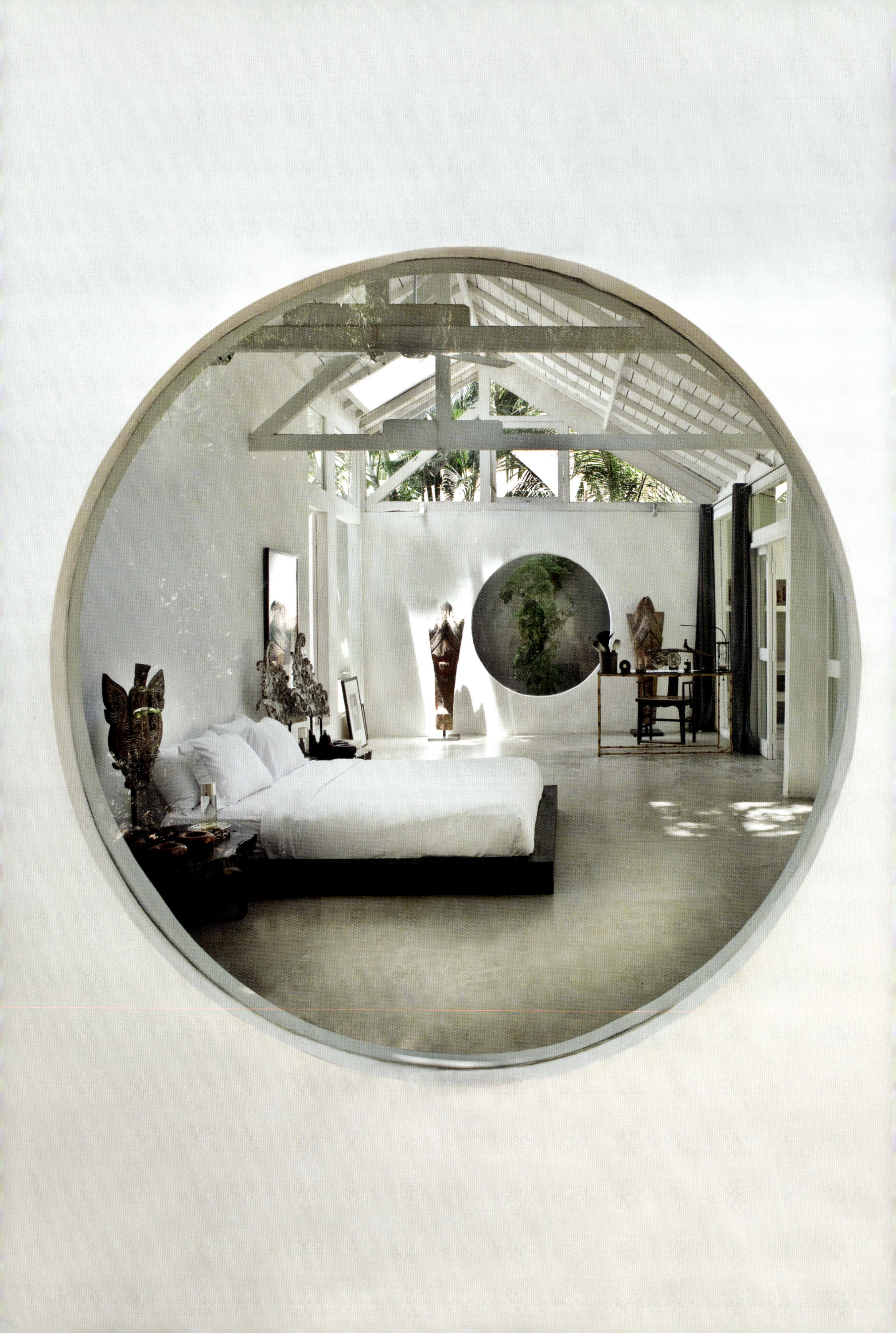

LIVING WITHOUT WALLS

The tropical climate invites living without walls. Many *bales* (pavilions) are sealed with mosquito netting that takes the place of walls, and some dwellings are constructed almost entirely with canvas. Luxury camping ("glamping") has put a new twist on the nomadic past: living in tents is now glamorous!

One pioneer is Anneke van Waesberghe, who started Escape Nomade, a company that produces high-end tent dwellings. These portable, multifunctional homes allow one to live comfortably in remote areas.

We arrive at Anneke's tented home at midday and are pleased to find how cool it is and how elegant the whole place feels. She welcomes us and serves a cool drink of lime and ginger.

> I started about thirty years ago, in 1983, with a nonprofit organization that created cross-cultural exchanges between East and West. We organized a design competition with artists, designers, and architects from both Japan and the West. From these results we analyzed the key shared influences, and they were religion and nature.
>
> The United Nations Development Programme asked me to become involved in a project to make a sort of extruded plank from jute fibers for low-cost housing. They developed a turbine that

> changed the structure of the fibers. As with a lot of projects, they
> got some initial traction but didn't really seem to catch on. Today
> I'm interested in sustainability and lifestyle—you know, how you
> can live a simple and uncluttered lifestyle. You don't really need a
> whole lot to live an elegant life.
>
> The positioning of the tents is important for cross-ventilation,
> and we fit them with fans that generate an upward draft and take
> the hot air out of the openings at the top, just like a *wantilan*
> [pavilion] roof. My designs are already sustainable and environmental, so I don't emphasize that when I'm selling my tents—
> otherwise people might think we're hippies or New Age. Instead,
> I say that my design signatures are "simplicity is the new luxury"
> and "living without walls."

We have been invited to go "glamping" at the Sandat resort, not far from Anneke's house. We head uphill into the rice fields, a few kilometers from Ubud. The final road is really a track, with the customary puddles and potholes. We are greeted by the owners, Federico Carrer and Emanuela Padoan, two gracious Italians who are living the dream. Entering the resort, we see two bamboo structures. The smaller one is used as the reception area, and the larger one is the common area for the resort, housing a restaurant with a huge teak slab table and some smaller niches, with the kitchen located out of sight behind a wall of art and framed mirrors. The bathroom has an innovative washbasin set on an antique bicycle.

The feeling at Sandat is calm and serene, and the staff are helpful and unobtrusive. Our hosts inform us that we should stay for two nights to really appreciate glamping. Tomorrow they are hosting an art opening. We concede, and have the great fortune to meet up with many friends who attend the opening.

As we sit down with Federico and Emanuela, a tropical downpour buckets onto the resort, necessitating some adjustments to our recording equipment. They answer our questions in Italian and Isabella interprets.

> It started in Italy, when we bought a corner of paradise in 2008
> near Venice. We have always loved nature and wanted to share
> this place with others who could appreciate its beauty, its sounds,
> its fragrances. From the beginning, we wanted to use tents to minimize our impact and decided to research all the possible choices.
> After installing our tents, we discovered the term *glamping* had already been coined.
>
> When we came to Bali we fell in love with the island and found
> a beautiful piece of land. We had five materials we wanted to work
> with: reclaimed wood, bamboo, cotton canvas, alang-alang, and
> stone.
>
> The canvas is from South Africa, but all the other materials
> were available locally, and we used local artisans. We didn't use an
> architect but built the whole place ourselves in one year and three
> months. We owe that to our rapport with the local community. We
> didn't make any real mistakes, and we are very lucky. We lived on
> the land in a hut for a few months first, and we didn't change the
> shape of the land at all. We wanted to use solar power, but we simply didn't have the room to install it.
>
> One thing that interests us is organic farming, and we're working with some of the farmers around us to start using organic
> techniques.
>
> One day we had a big piece of furniture delivered by a new

The decor under the gigantic bamboo roof of Uma Jiwa, a house in Ubud designed by Ibuku Studio and Earth Lines Architects.

Lines and curves stretch along the length of the bamboo ceiling, emphasizing the organic decor at Uma Jiwa.

Lamps suspended from the ceiling at Uma Jiwa.

A wide view of the dining area at Uma Jiwa.

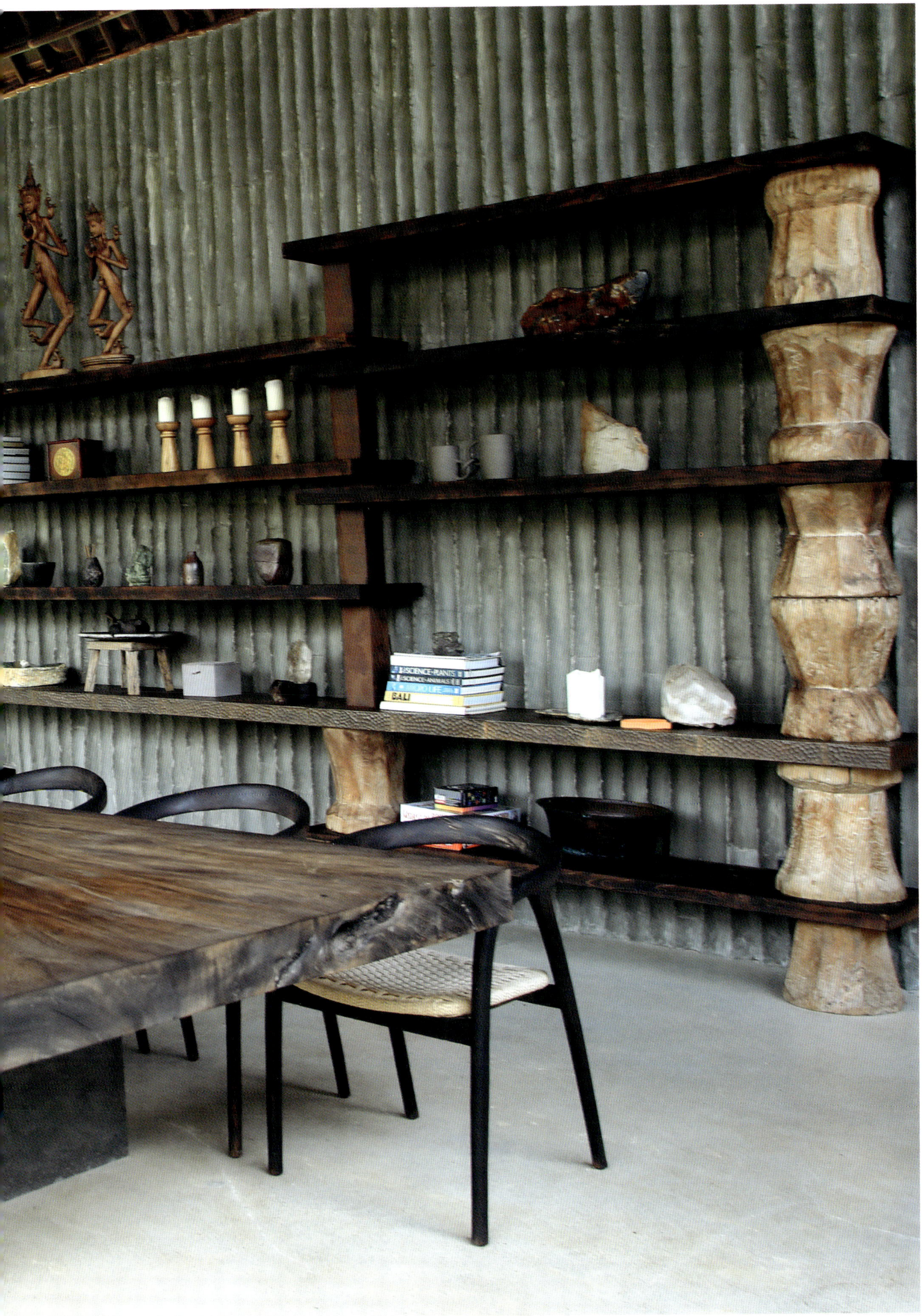
BALI

184 LIVING WITHOUT WALLS

Heaven's door: the theatrical limestone entrance to the Intaaya resort on Nusa Penida.

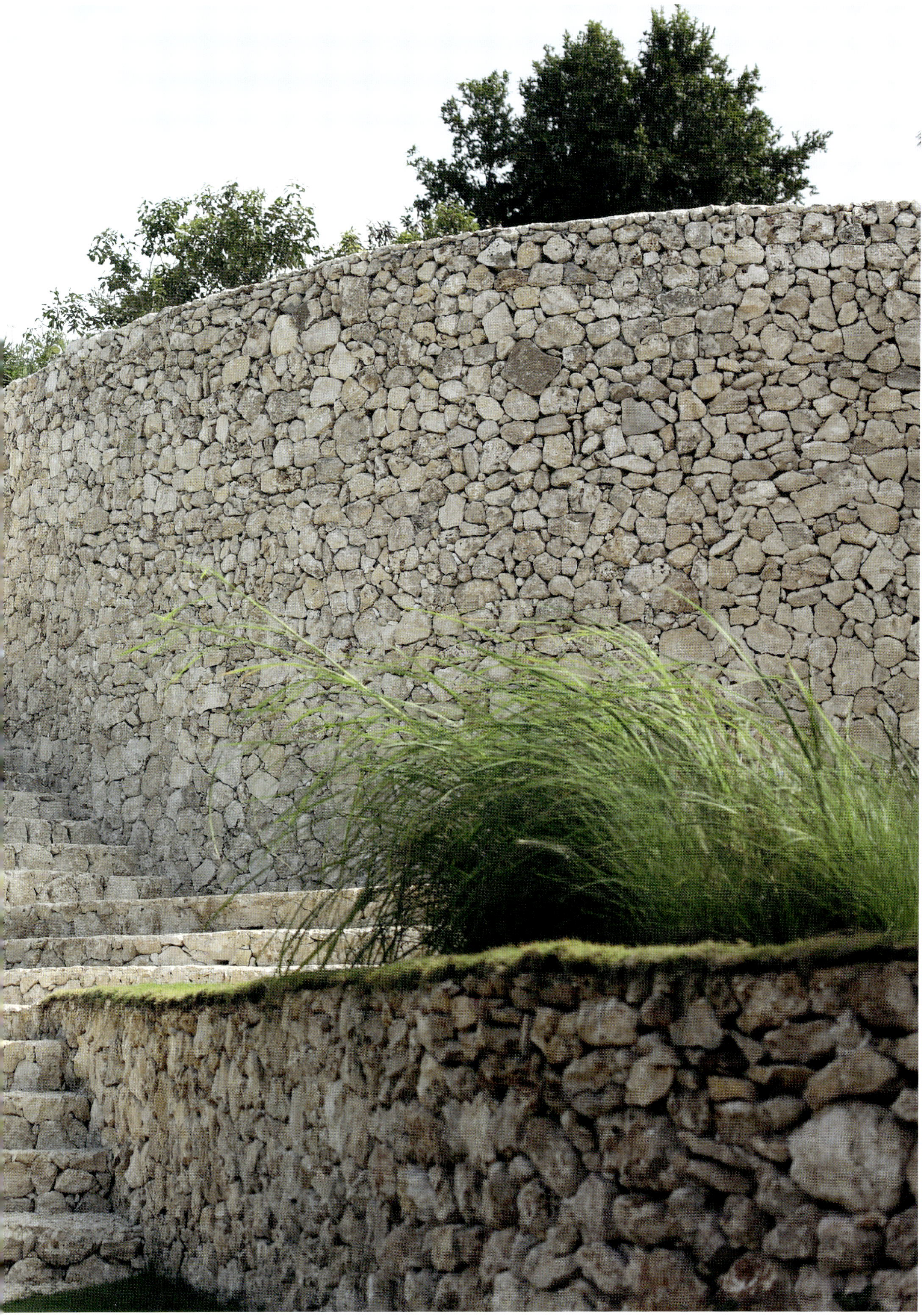

At Intaaya, precision-built glamping tents from Anneke van Waesberghe of Escape Nomade.

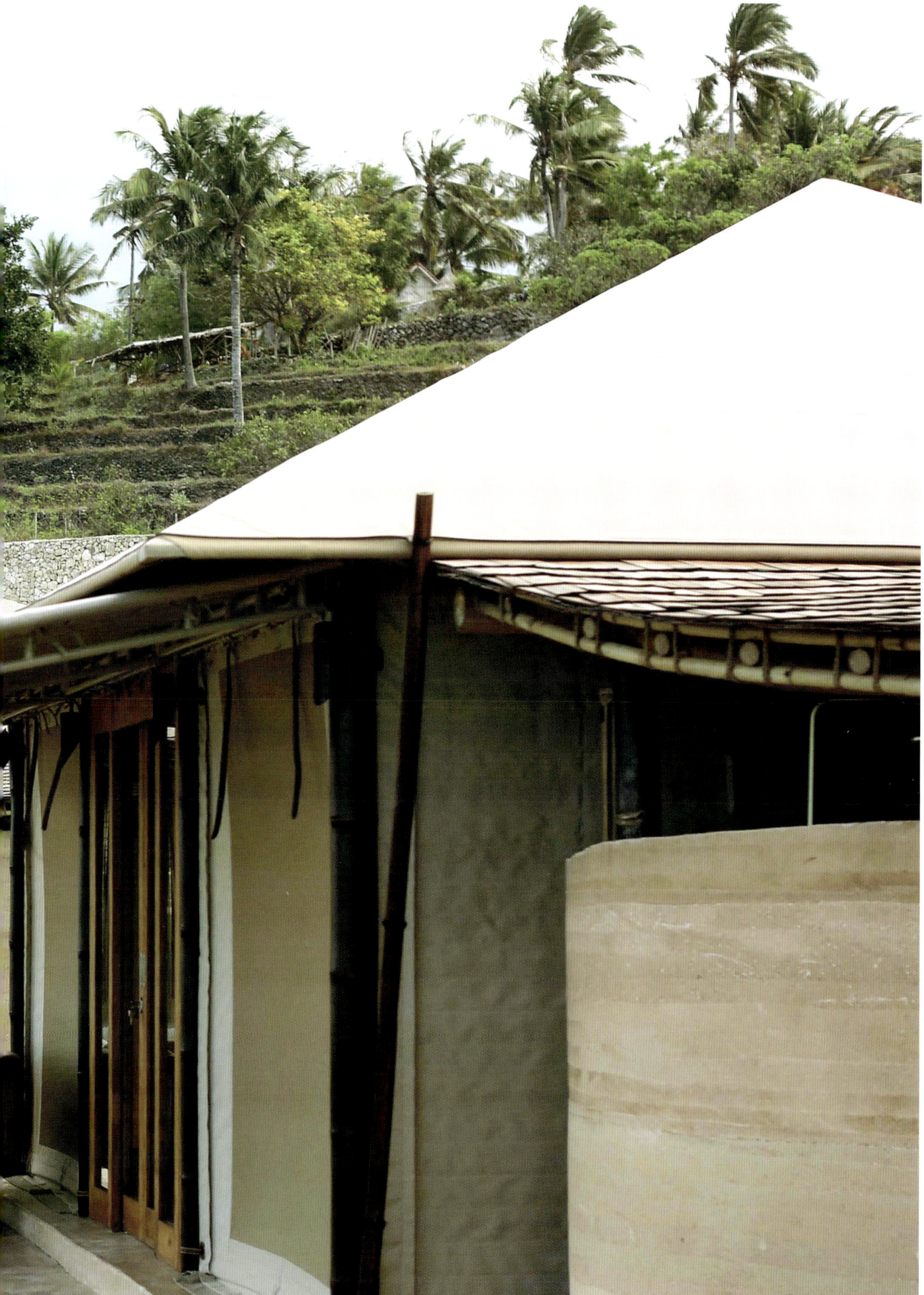

Candle-lit luxury in a glamping tent at Intaaya. The headboard is made of rammed earth.

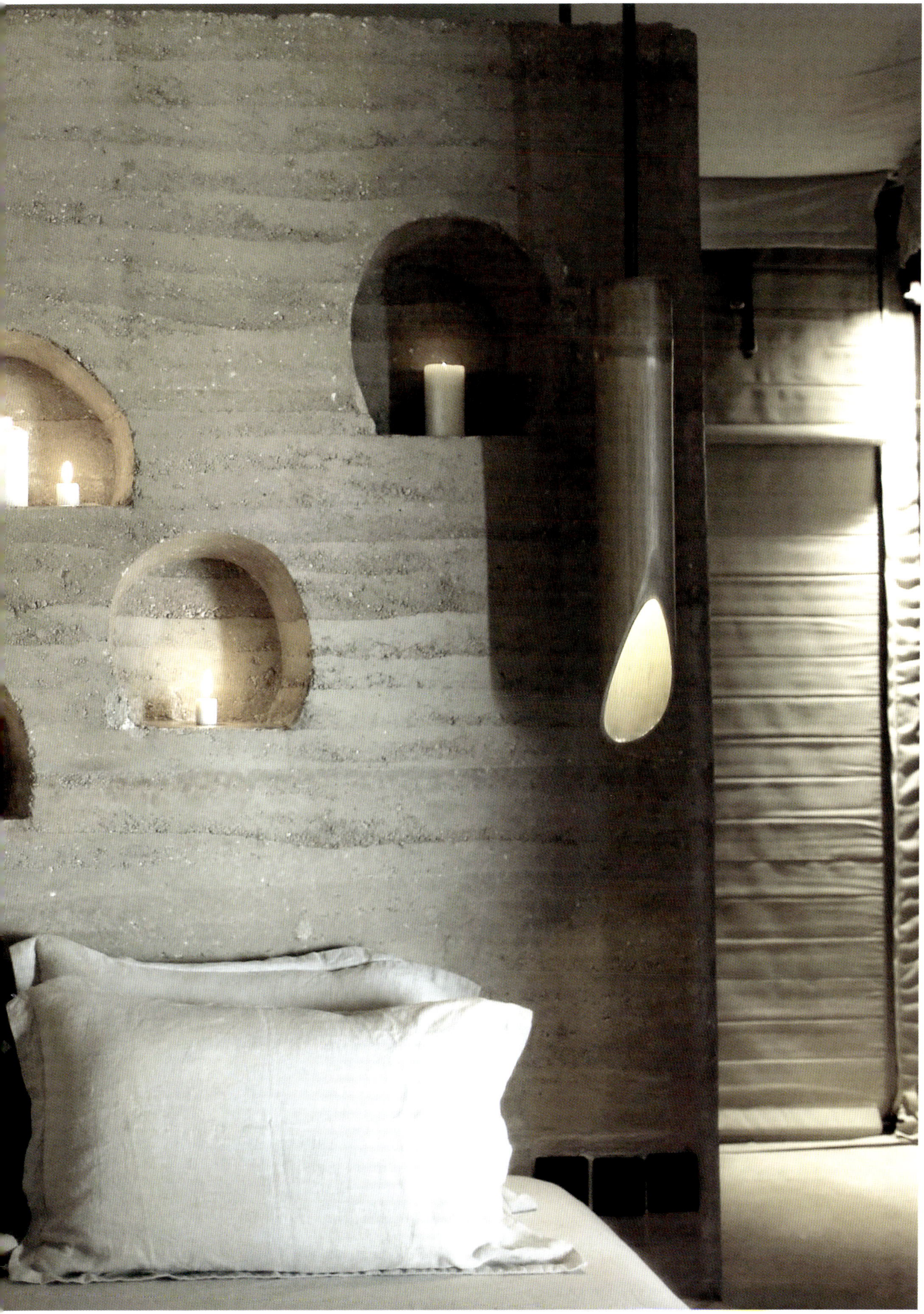

Under the awning of a glamping tent at Intaaya.

truck. When we left the resort, we found the truck stuck in the rice field gutter; it had veered and fallen off the road. We stopped and asked the two men, "Do you need help?" and they said, "No, thank you," with really big smiles on their faces. We returned six or seven hours later to find the two men still with huge smiles on their faces and still stuck. We explained that we as Westerners would be pretty angry and frustrated by now and asked why they were still smiling. They answered, "We had an accident and neither of us was killed, so we are here savoring the moment. We couldn't have done this if one of us was dead!"

In big places the guests get lost, so we believe that glamping should be small, offering real attention to the guests' personal needs.

Our design signature reflects what is in our heart.

Another proponent of living without walls is Guy Bedarida, the famed Van Cleef & Arpels and John Hardy jewelry designer. He was exposed to sustainability principles through his work with the John Hardy jewelry company and was instrumental in the creation of their factory and showroom, known for its brilliant use of bamboo and its sustainable features. Guy's Seminyak home is a beautiful series of pavilions set on lushly planted grounds.

The house is really about the environment; it's completely open, so we live with the nature. For me this is the luxury of Bali, which you don't have anywhere else in the world. Here we live outside even though we're in a completely urban environment. Plants are essential for cooling. We made sure that the existing trees and nature were completely untouched. Light is very important, too, and we have skylights in almost every room. We don't use air-conditioning, but we have fans, and most partitions are movable to maximize cross-ventilation. We will be getting a solar panel, but we've managed with a minimum of electrical usage. We have limited power waste and intend to reduce it further.

I worked for John Hardy when we built the Kapal Bamboo. It's an incredible story. We wanted a showroom that would be different, that would help elevate the jewelry and show it in the best light. We decided to build with a minimal impact, with sustainable materials, particularly bamboo and alang-alang. We agreed that wherever there was no building the land should continue to be used as it always had been.

It was very much the work of Yew Kuan, who designed the original building, but in Bali, once it goes into the hands of the artisans it transforms into something else. I was always the one who insisted that the shape and form of the land should not be changed, to the point that the rice paddy water still goes directly beneath the structure. For the floor, I suggested that we use *bedek* [woven bamboo] on top of a bamboo frame. Sure, it's not very comfortable, but it looks divine. The stories about the factory are true; we grow enough mostly organic food to feed 650 people every day from our own compound.

When I first arrived as a guest of John Hardy, he said, "Let's go for a walk." We went out into the rice fields and finally arrived at a magnificent old wantilan. I said to him that it would make a great design studio. The village was about to knock it down.

John said to me, "Okay, that's your new design studio."

A restful corner in Anneke van Waesberghe's home near Mambal, which showcases the tents produced by her company Escape Nomade.

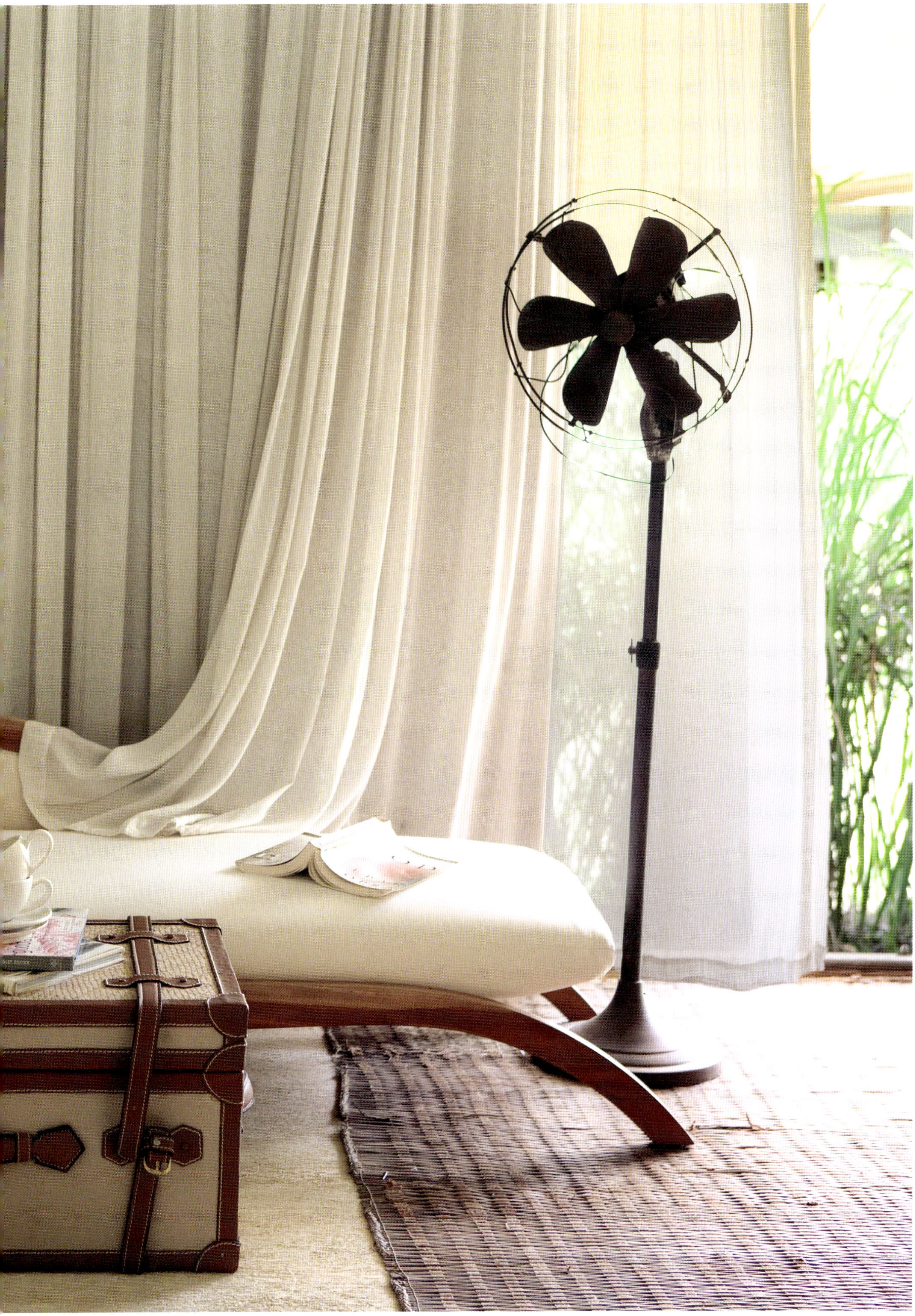

LIVING WITHOUT WALLS

The exterior of Anneke van Waesberghe's tented house.

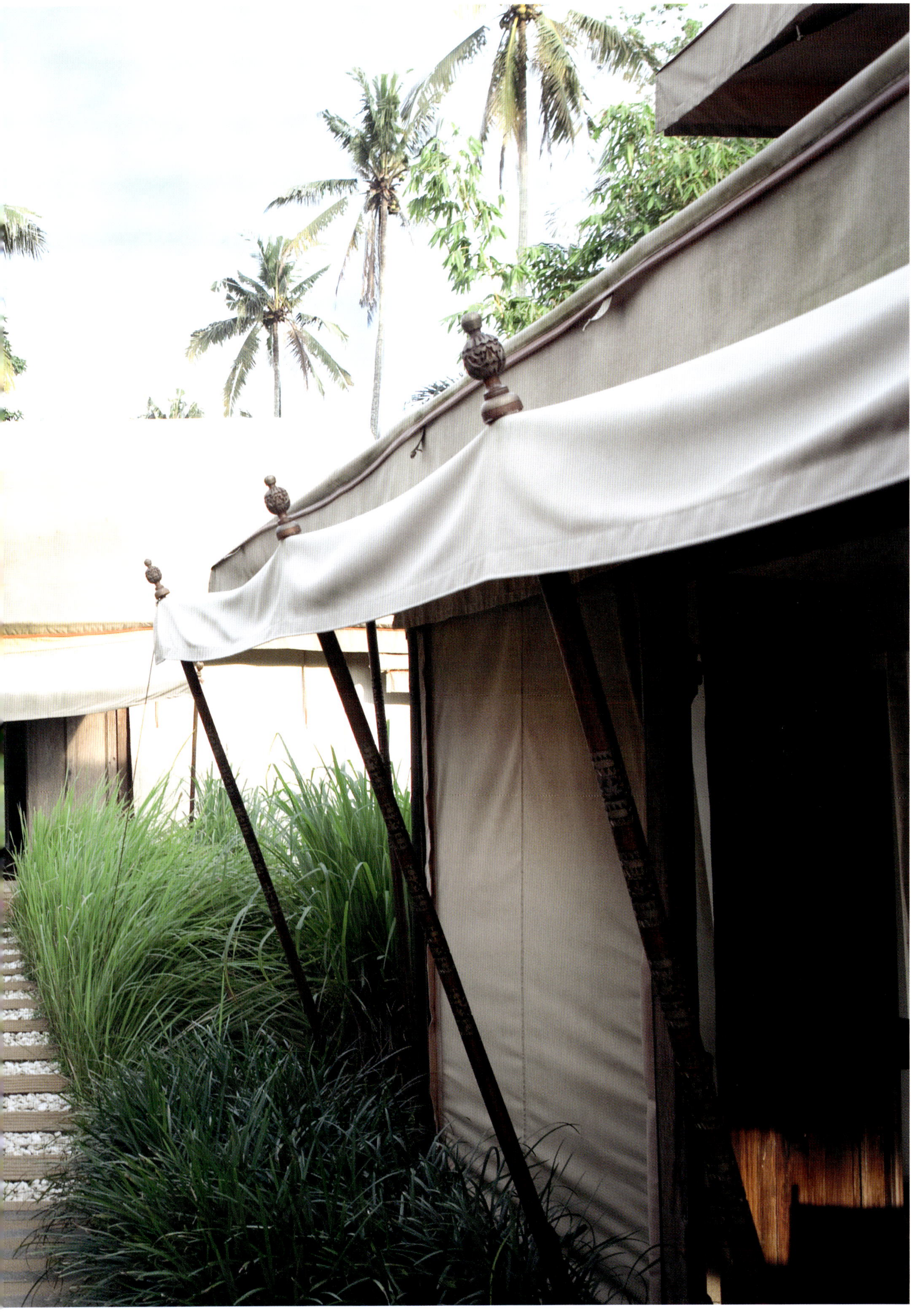

We asked Yew Kuan to redesign it with three floors, and the whole thing is closable but opens on all sides for cross-ventilation. It has no air-conditioning at all. We only put air-conditioning in the manufacturing center, as the machines generate heat and it was not pleasant for those working in there.

Wood is very interesting, especially ironwood. A hundred years ago they would cut down the tree and bury it for twenty-five or fifty years and it would harden even more; they would use it for railway sleepers and other tough jobs. This wood was just like iron and was six or seven hundred years old. The main uprights of the design-studio wantilan are all originally ironwood telegraph poles.

We used a lot of mud, and the compound walls are all in mud capped with terra-cotta tiles. Instead of adding razor or barbed wire or broken glass on top for security, we grew bougainvillea, which I can tell you not only looks lovely but has become almost totally impenetrable.

We make everything by hand. I've been using a special grass from East Bali, some black palm wood, and some bamboo in my jewelry and home creations, so we don't hurt the environment or generate any toxins we'd have to dispose of.

I was lucky enough to come from very smart parents, and when I was a kid at school in Tuscany they always taught us to not waste, not to use energy stupidly, not to use chemicals or pesticides, and to use only natural products. We used to have a compost corner, and we did things with common sense. It's more healthy to be outside. We must also make sure that we don't lose the skills and techniques of the artisans in all these varied fields.

It's 6:30 a.m., and we arrive in Ubud at first light to visit Uma Jiwa, a house introduced to us by Elora Hardy. The design of Uma Jiwa can be credited to Elora (Ibuku Studio) and Abbie Labrum (Earth Lines Architects).

We are to photograph the house first and meet the owners later. The dead-end road is so narrow that turning the car is impossible and reversing is a neck breaker. Suddenly the gate on our right opens, and we are ushered into a spacious area in front of a garage building. We park while the dogs sniff and bark at us in a friendly but skittish welcome.

The house appears to be set low compared to the horizon, and the kitchen gardens in front are green and lush with organic treats. On entering the house, we are surprised to see an exotic roof structure of intricately woven bamboo: a marvel to behold! It covers an indoor-outdoor living space bordered with a gorgeous infinity pool, all set above a magnificent gully garden view, with rice terraces layered up on the other side. A yoga shala is tucked away below the house.

This old-fashioned rattan-and-leather suitcase serves as a dresser in Anneke van Waesberghe's tented house.

This bedroom in Anneke van Waesberghe's tented house features a campaign-style desk and chair from her furniture line.

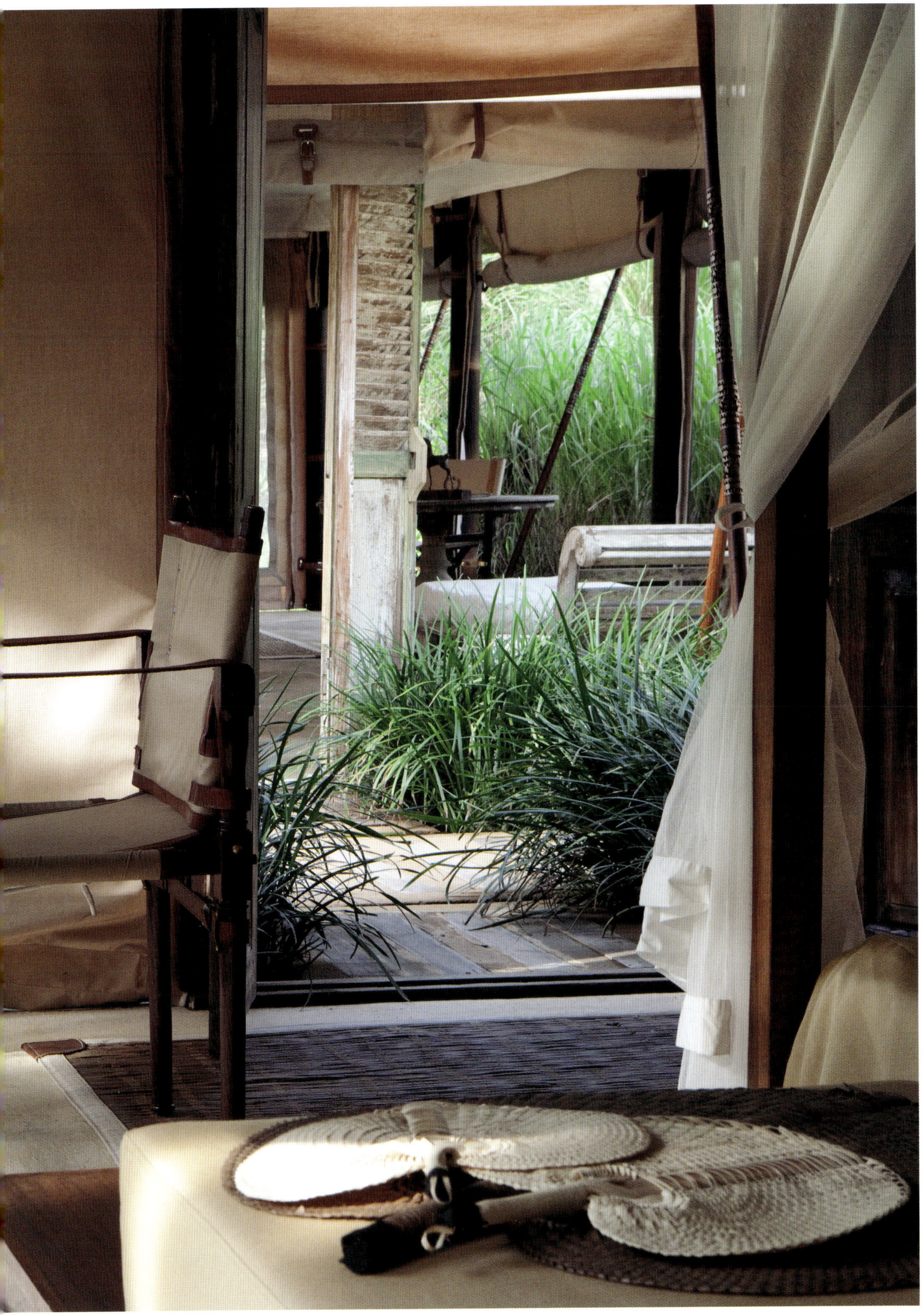

A bed with a roll-up canopy in Anneke van Waesberghe's tented house.

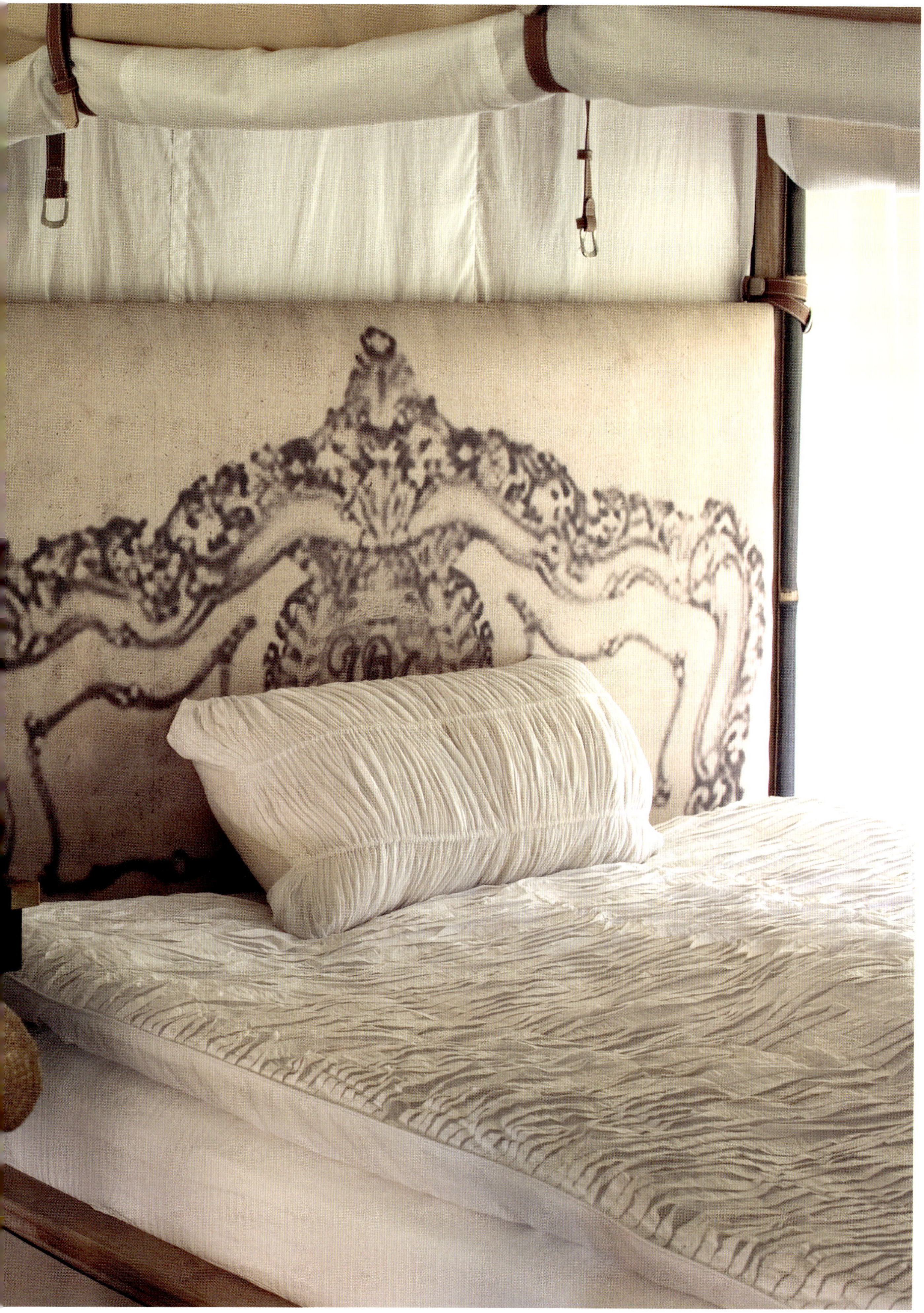

An outdoor massage tent at Anneke van Waesberghe's house.

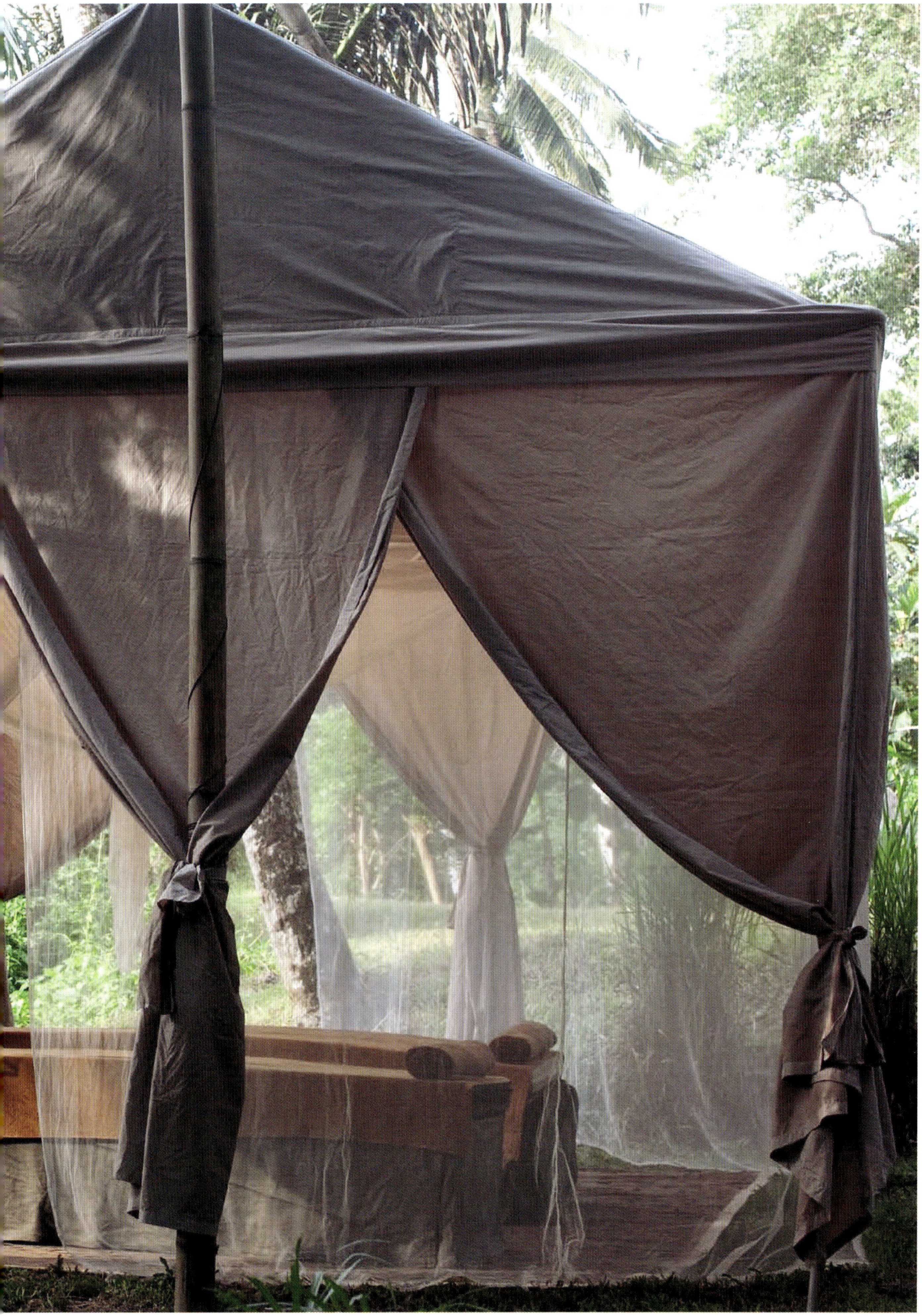

An indoor-outdoor pool at Anneke van Waesberghe's tented house.

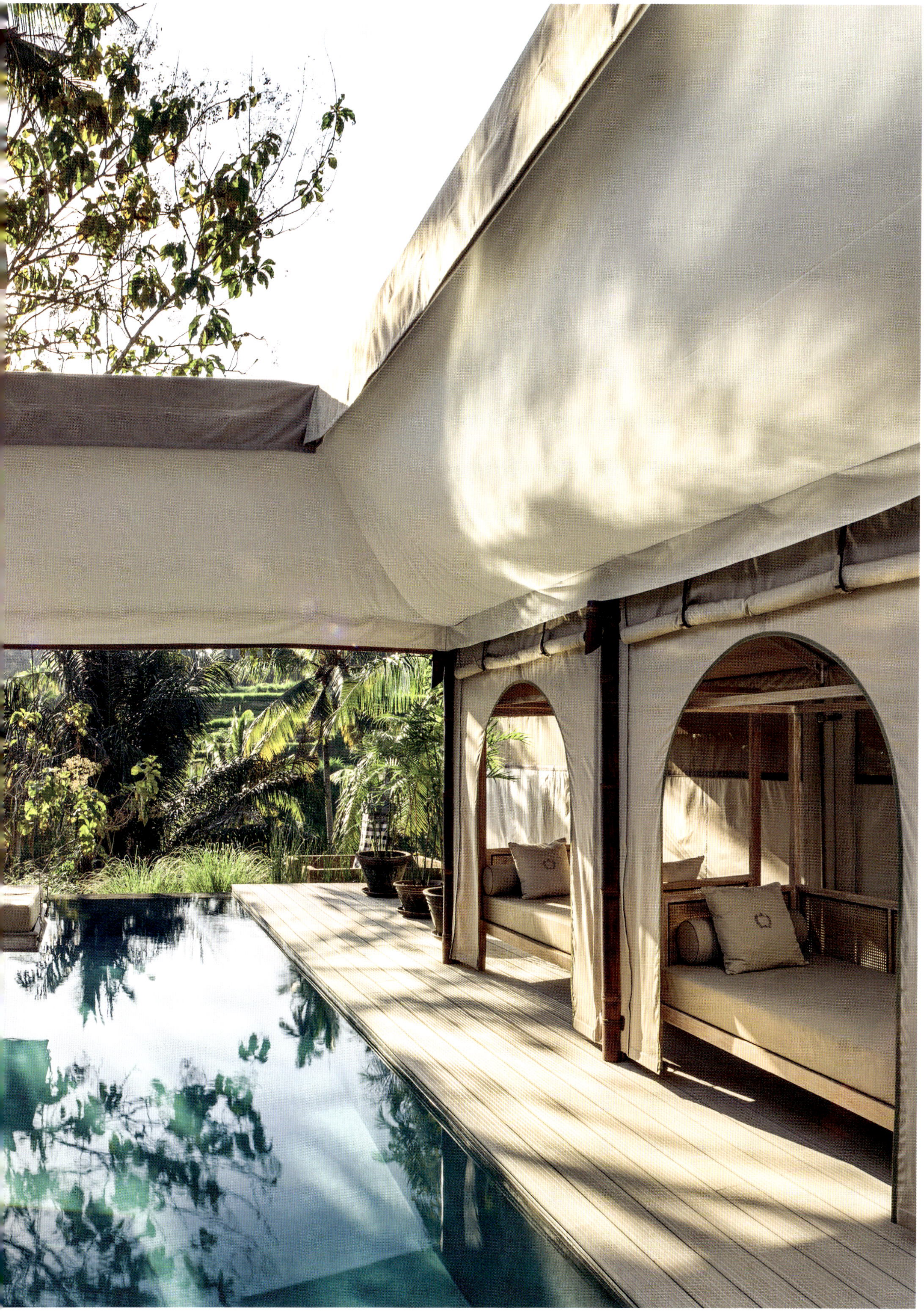

The pool and dining pavilion in Guy Bedarida and Nicolas Robert's former home in Seminyak, designed by Nicolas Robert.

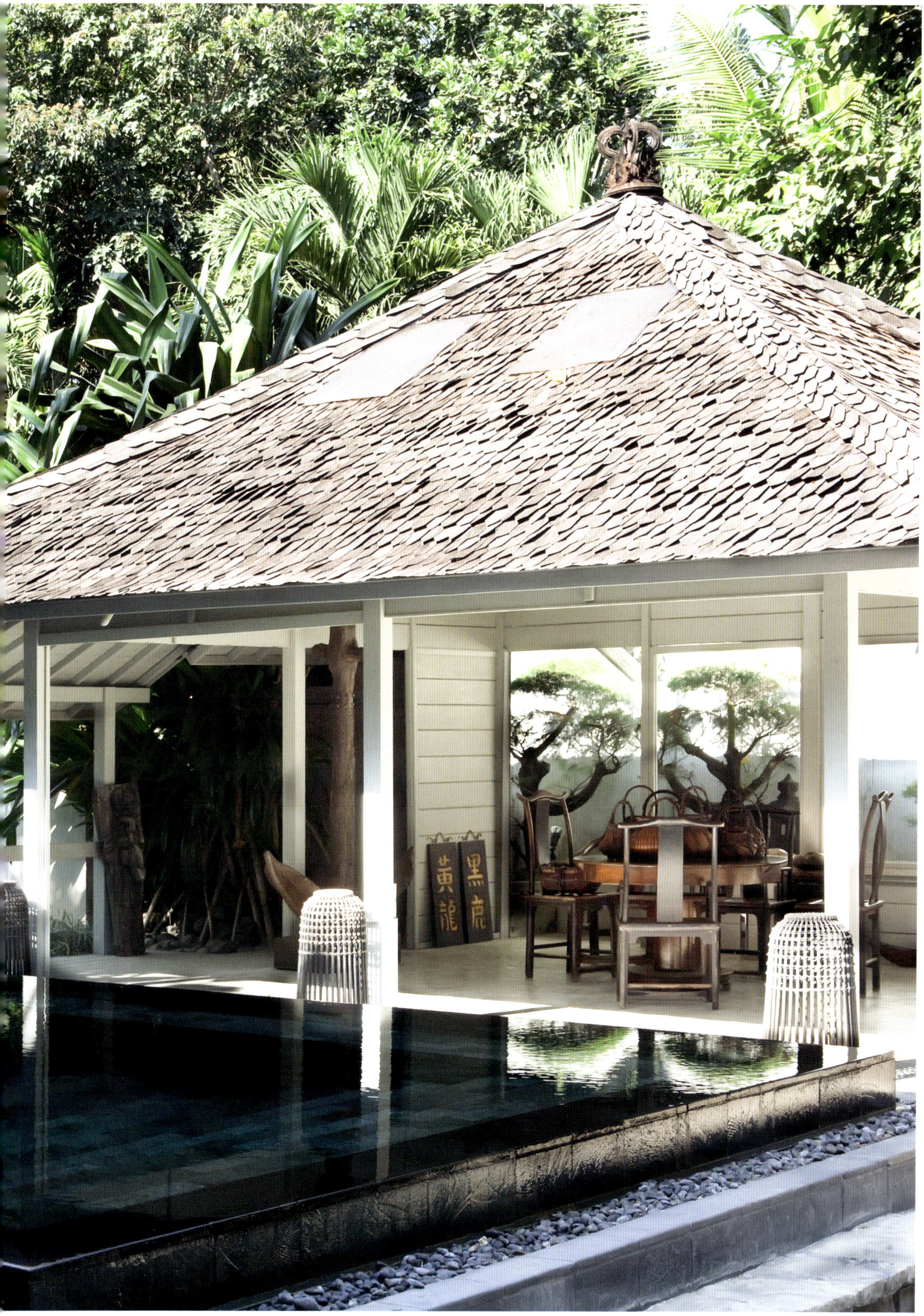
黃龍
黑虎

Chairs made from recycled car tires, designed by Nicolas Robert for the former Bedarida-Robert house.

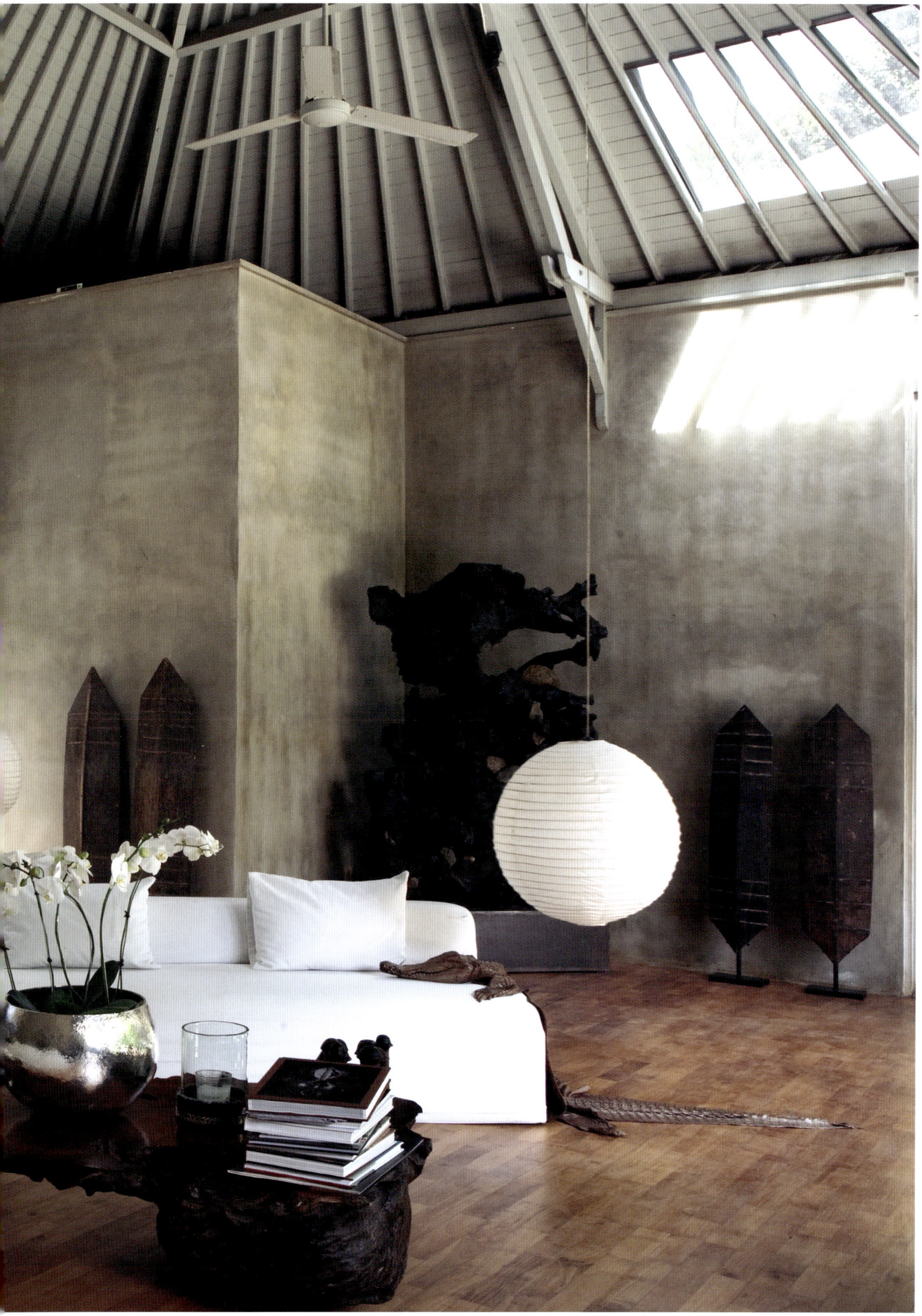

The inner side of the Lombok-style roof in a villa at Sandat Glamping Tents, modeled on a *lumbung* (rice storage hut). The chair is made from an oil drum.

In the dining pavilion at Sandat Glamping Tents, the bathroom sink is mounted on an old Javanese bicycle.

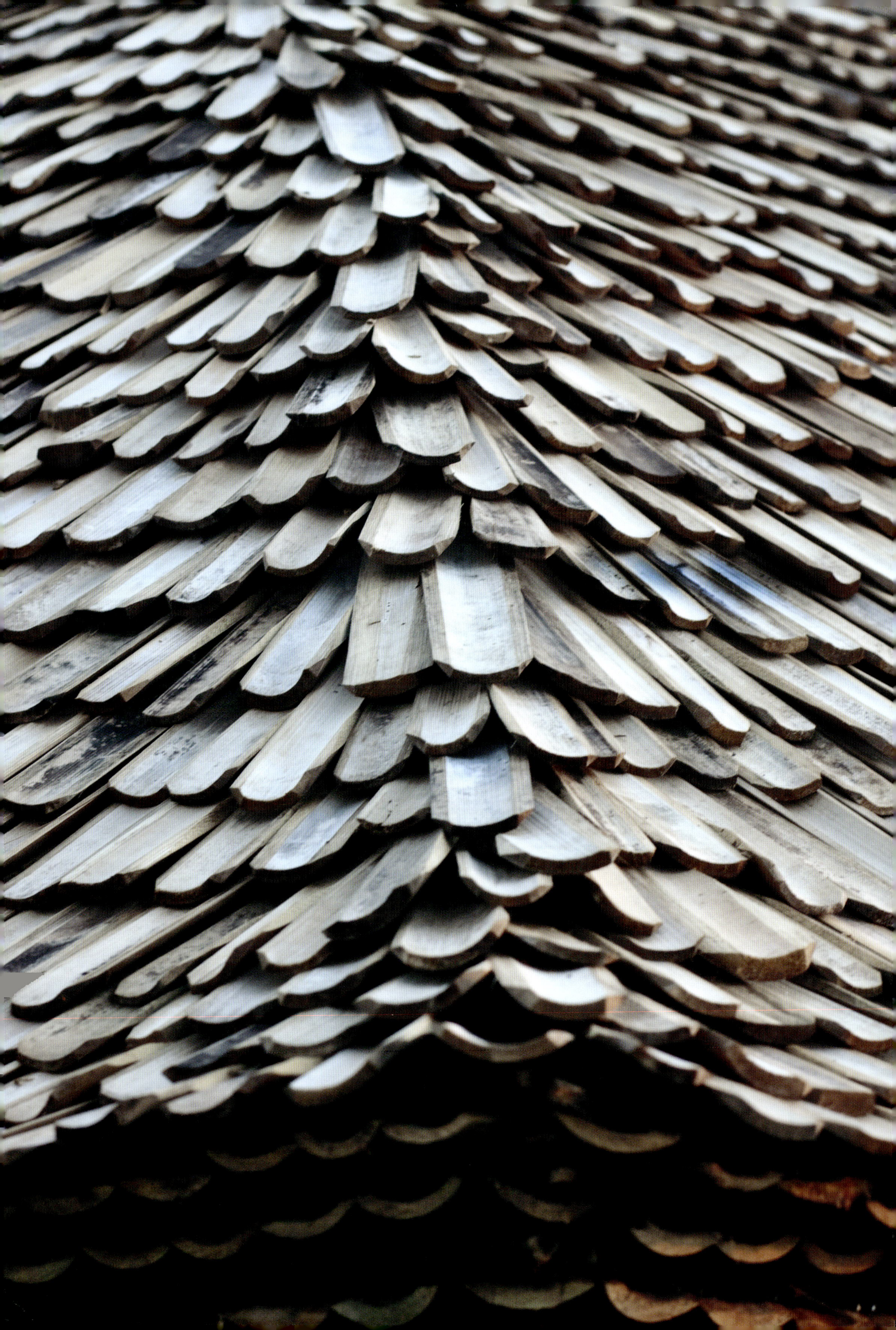

ROOFS

Since very early times, people around the world have made thatched roofs from reeds. In Indonesia and Malaysia, an indigenous species of elephant grass, alang-alang (*Imperata cylindrica*), is used for this purpose. (In Australia it is called blade grass, because of its tendency to inflict cuts.)

Alang-alang is a hardy grass that grows best in harsh conditions with poor soil. The present demand for alang-alang in Bali has led to its rapid production in fertile soils, using fertilizer for faster harvesting. The alang-alang grown this way is weaker, which shortens the life span of the roofs made with it.

Traditionally, a strong small-diameter bamboo formed the batten, or spine, of the bundles of alang-alang that are tied onto the roof, but now, due to shortages, split pieces of larger bamboo are used instead. Hence the blades of grass are wrapped around the bamboo at sharp angles rather than in smooth curves, which also shortens the life span of the thatching. The split bamboo is also prone to insect attacks, as much of its bulky cellulose is exposed.

The peak of the roof is capped with decorative terra-cotta elements. In Bali, as in Lombok and Sumbawa, the ends of the alang-alang are cut horizontally along the eaves, but in Timor, Rote, and Sumba, the grass is left uncut, drooping down like a ragged fringe.

An alang-alang roof is good insulation against heat and is attractive both

A view, through reclaimed wood columns, of Villa Lumbung, at movie director Rob Cohen's Villa Campuhan estate in Jasri, East Bali, designed by Linda Garland.

A closer view of the complex roofline of Villa Lumbung, showing also its walls of *bedek* (woven bamboo). The design of Villa Lumbung was inspired by the traditional rice storage huts of the Minangkabau people of Sumatra.

inside and out. It can last up to twenty years, although the average alang-alang roof lasts seven or eight years. The actual life span depends on many factors, such as the quality of the original material, the pitch of the roof, and whether there are overhanging trees that drop leaves onto the roof and keep it from drying off during the monsoon season.

Several other materials are used for roofing, including lontar palm and coconut palm leaves, which require different techniques in assembly and finishing. Ironwood shingles (*sirap*) originated in Kalimantan (Borneo) and were introduced all over the archipelago by the Dutch. Often found on government buildings and luxury homes, they last for at least thirty years.

Bamboo shingles have made a comeback and are now a staple of Bali's green architectural diet. Huge bamboo roofs have been built by Linda Garland, John and Cynthia Hardy, Ben Ripple and Fred Schilling at Big Tree Farms, Elora Hardy at Green Village, and Frederik Wittesaele at the Suarga resort.

Although the great majority of Indonesians now live in generic modern buildings, it used to be that each island could be identified by its distinctive roofline.

The people of Toraja align their houses, called *tongkonan*, with the Pleiades cluster in the constellation of Taurus. These dwellings stand high on wooden piles and are topped with a layered split-bamboo roof that arcs upward, pointing to the home of the mythical ancestors in the sky.

The people of Sumba build a very high, pointed roof, like a witch's hat, that serves as a symbolic link between the divine and human worlds. Sumbanese myth tells that the first ancestral house, built on the eighth heavenly sphere, was thatched with human hair gathered in headhunting raids.

In Sumatra, the *rumah gadang* is owned and occupied by the women of the family, who live there; it is passed down from mother to daughter. This type of house has a multitiered roof whose gable ends curve upward into points meant to resemble water buffalo horns. The walls are ornately carved and painted, and pierced by shuttered windows.

The roofline of a Javanese *joglo* is similar to that of a Sumbanese house, but less exaggerated. The other main types of knockdown teak house from Java, the *limasan* and the *gladak*, have gabled roof shapes.

In Bali, a *wantilan* is a wall-less rectangular public building used for community meetings or cockfights, with a double roof that provides wonderful ventilation. A *lumbung* is a rice-storage hut, usually elevated to keep the floor dry, with a tall, usually gabled roof.

The roofs of all these traditional structures are natural, sustainable, and practical for the tropical environment.

Years ago, three roofers arrived from Lombok and reroofed our whole house with alang-alang. Their cheer and athletic dexterity were stupendous and their appetite for coffee even more so, but regrettably, they did not do their work with pride and care. The new roof lasted only five years. The original Balinese work had lasted for twelve years and was much tighter, with many more tie-offs.

Traditional roofing skills are declining. And still the rain falls in sheets, the sun warps the shingles, the alang-alang slowly decomposes, and constant vigilance is required to delay the inevitable future maintenance. To have a traditional roof can sometimes seem like an exercise in frustration, but it also makes you more attuned to the patterns of nature and the life cycle of materials. It is another facet of Bali's sustainable vision.

Uma Jiwa, the sensational home that we visited in the last chapter, was built by a pair of innovators, Cezary and Kinga. When we found ourselves in the company of this visionary duo, sipping coffee in their glorious home, they told us they were developing a sustainable retreat—plus a permaculture farm to supply food—on Nusa Penida, an island about twenty miles (30 km) off the shore of Bali. Naturally our ears pricked up!

This resort, Intaaya, has now been completed, and we accept an invitation from Cezary and Kinga to take a look. We venture across from Sanur Harbor on a fast boat with miniature seats; my shoulders are the width of two seats! Long before it became a tourist attraction for its natural beauty, the Balinese believed Nusa Penida to be inhabited by dark spirits, banished to the island by the priests. It is a maze of twists and turns on very narrow and winding potholed roads, but the island has a charm all its own. It is dry, but anywhere there's water it's green!

We stand stunned on the top steps of the Intaaya arrival circle. From the top of a cliff we can see an amazing array of tasteful and intriguing visual flashes: curves, arches, open spaces, and ocean, all set with the precision and neatness of a cared-for trinket with sentimental value. "A kind of treasure!" is our first reaction. The clifftop setting allows for a dramatic ocean view; the large common buildings marry stonework and bamboo, and are accented by strategically placed precision-built tents from Anneke van Waesberghe of Escape Nomade. Our accommodations include an amazing high-tech unit that produces fresh, cold, clean water from humidity in fresh air. The rammed-earth headboard with a plethora of candles is charming. The bathroom is graced with great taste and water pressure, all surrounded by curvaceous rammed-earth walls. The air-conditioning stays off, as the cooling onshore breeze provides a welcome oxygenated boost.

Cezary and Kinga describe their vision for the resort:

> Intaaya emerged as a response to the call for a more conscious, sustainable way of living. In a world shaken by the dissonance of the Anthropocene, we strive to harmonize human existence with Earth's natural rhythms. Our structures, crafted from natural materials, are not just buildings—they are embodiments of our commitment to sustainability, designed to resonate with the energies of the land and foster a deep sense of belonging.
>
> Over the past decade in Bali, we've witnessed the exponential growth of construction projects overtaking nature. Most real estate ventures clear the land, remove vegetation, and displace wildlife. Rivers and beaches are increasingly polluted with plastic.
>
> Observing others' responses to these challenges, we were inspired by the many social businesses and individuals cleaning rivers, conserving land, and promoting conscious practices. This inspiration guided the objectives of our studio, driving us to strive for environmental harmony throughout a building's life cycle.
>
> Our aim for Intaaya is to integrate nature-inspired solutions, energy-efficient systems, and resilient structures to ensure sustainability in economic, social, environmental, and spiritual aspects. We prioritize local craftsmanship, waste reduction alternatives, renewable energy, and low-impact materials, recognizing the significant impact our design choices have on the environment.
>
> For us, sustainability is not just a moment but a way of life. As creators of this vision, we are responsible for ensuring that spaces support sustainable practices and can be maintained over time.
>
> At Intaaya, we are not just creating a retreat; we are cultivating a living sanctuary where the boundaries between nature and self dissolve. This is a place where the spirit of the land and the rhythm of the ocean guide our journey toward healing and renewal.

A play of undulating roofs and see-through structures: the reception building and Tea House at the Intaaya resort on Nusa Penida.

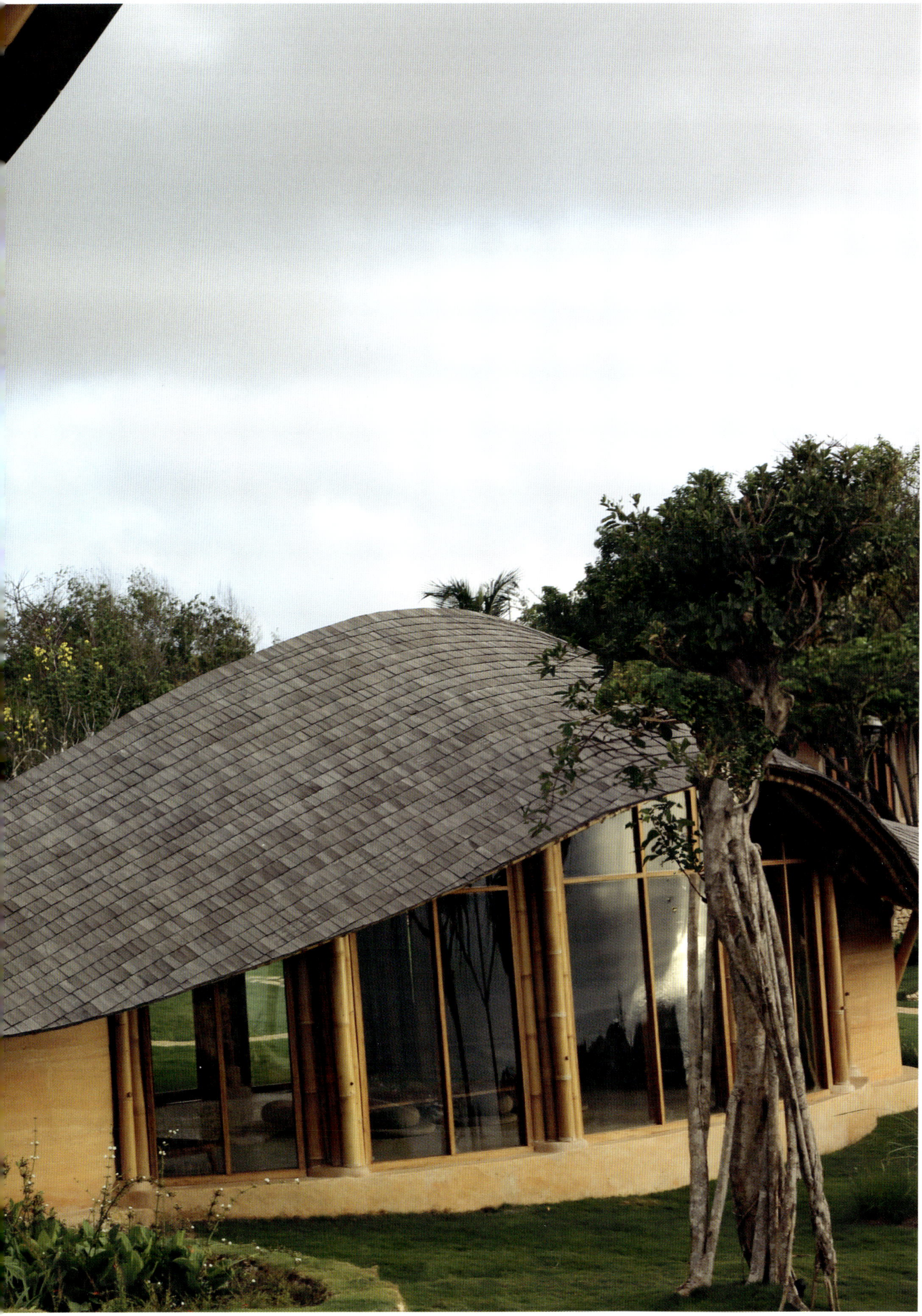

We selected bamboo as the core material for Intaaya, specifically yellow and black bamboo from Bali and other Indonesian islands. We paired this with local limestone, abundant in the area, using it for walls, retention structures, and landscaping. We also extracted lime from the stones for floors and terraces, using it as a binder instead of concrete. To seamlessly blend with the natural surroundings, we included rammed-earth walls. All our doors, windows, and furniture were crafted from locally sourced reclaimed wood. Every element, from our water systems to our solar-powered energy, reflects a harmonious balance that reverberates throughout the entire environment.

Our approach must embody tropical architecture, which offers a unique opportunity to blur the boundaries between indoor and outdoor spaces, creating environments that are in tune with natural elements. We draw inspiration from Balinese culture. We orient our buildings to harness natural light and embrace passive design elements, such as cross ventilation, to truly work with nature. Intaaya is a project fully powered by solar panels, but more importantly, we have embraced traditional practices like rammed-earth walls. These walls possess excellent thermal mass, a crucial factor for maintaining thermal stability and comfort in the spaces. Their high density slows down the passage of heat, releasing it slowly as the outside temperature decreases. Another material quality we utilized for passive energy design is the selection of light-colored floors. These surfaces have high albedo, meaning they reflect sunlight rather than absorb it, helping to maintain a stable temperature within the spaces.

We harness one of the most innovative water extraction solutions available today—the atmospheric water generator—to produce drinking water from the humidity in the air. This technology is a vital response to today's challenge of depleting freshwater resources, providing a sustainable and efficient way to ensure a reliable supply of clean drinking water. By showcasing this cutting-edge technology, we aim to encourage others to adopt sustainable water management practices in their own lives, fostering a deeper connection to and respect for our planet's precious resources.

We collaborated with Abigail Alling and Mark Van Thillo, scientists from the Biosphere Foundation. With their expertise, we built innovative wastewater gardens for the project.

One of the most memorable moments during our construction days in Bali was the blessing ceremony of the land. The entire construction team gathered to perform the Ngeruak ceremony, seeking permission from the spirits of the land for our project. Standing there with our team, surrounded by the lush greenery and the serene sounds of nature, we felt a deep sense of connection and respect for the land we were about to transform. It was a humbling experience, reminding us of the importance of honoring the local culture and traditions.

Witnessing the project come to life, especially the yoga shala built in just two months, was incredibly fulfilling. The precision and craftsmanship of our team were awe-inspiring, reinforcing our belief in the power of collaboration and respect for traditional methods. These experiences have not only enriched our work but also inspired new projects for our architects, Pablo Luna

The restaurant at Intaaya seen from the reception area.

An intricate web of bamboo in the yoga shala at Intaaya.

Studio. We are excited about the future and the possibilities that lie ahead.

Our greatest eco-blunder was believing we could achieve perfect results when working with natural materials. We learned that natural materials need space to breathe, resulting in more organic shapes and unexpected lines on the floor. The end result made us appreciate the imperfections of these materials, and we realized that they speak for themselves. This understanding has become a signature of what we aim to achieve—a blend of nature, beauty, and wabi-sabi.

We believe that a deep study of the land is essential to understanding the various kingdoms and ecosystems at play. We aim to raise awareness that any land in Bali is a little piece of heaven, and this means striving to conserve it as much as possible. At the same time, we recognize that sustainability does not end when construction is complete; rather, it marks the beginning of the most important stage—education. This includes sharing knowledge about permaculture gardens and how bamboo, wood, or any raw material can endure through time if designed and treated properly.

Listen to the land and its surroundings. The architecture of Intaaya is both innovative and environmentally conscious, using natural materials and sustainable practices to create a space that is not only beautiful but also in complete harmony with its environment.

Construction waste management played a crucial role. We made sure that no garbage, debris, or materials were neglected or fell over the cliff and that they were disposed of in a responsible, eco-friendly way.

At Intaaya, the involvement of the local community is central to our mission. Our commitment extends beyond construction; we actively support local communities by sourcing materials locally and fostering long-term employment opportunities. By prioritizing local talent and resources, we aim to create a project that not only honors the land but also uplifts and empowers the community that calls it home.

The Intaaya permaculture farm cultivates a diverse range of local plants, honoring the sustainable permaculture principles that guide our approach to farming. The food grown on our farm is served in our restaurant, creating a direct link between the land and the table and ensuring fresh, organic produce for our guests. It also supports the local farmers who are integral to this process. Working together creates a harmonious cycle that nourishes our bodies, our community, and the environment. Personal growth is not an abstract concept; it is a lived experience, supported by the Earth's wisdom and the collective energy of our community.

The yoga shala at Intaaya.

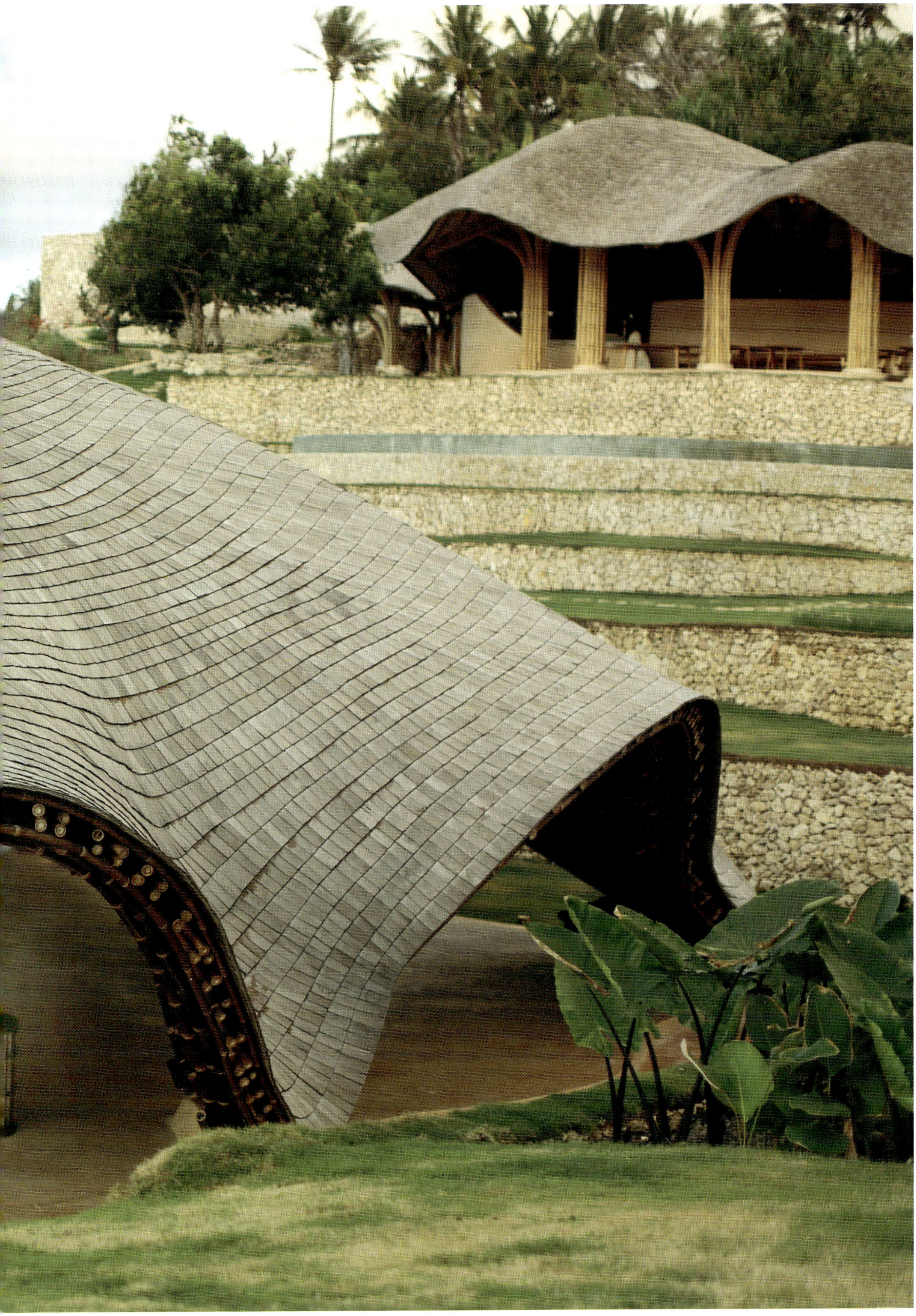

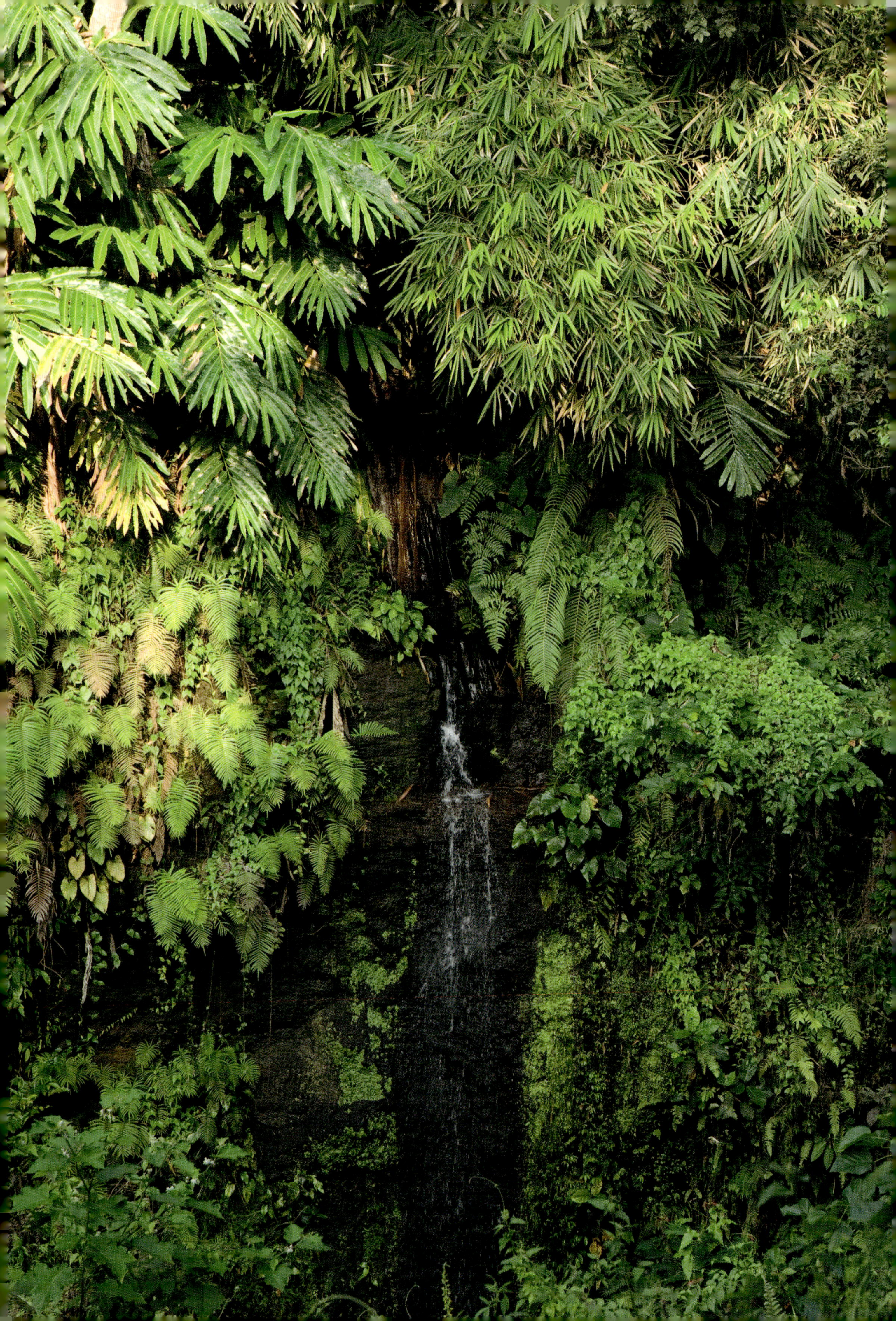

ACKNOWLEDGMENTS

To you, the visionary pioneers and eco-thinkers who by your environmental endeavors have made the second edition of this book not only possible but remarkable, our personal thanks and deep gratitude for your involvement.

Guy Bedarida
Matthew Bell
Federico Carrer and Emanuela Padoan
Cezary
Dorina
David Field
Maitri Fischer
Maria Garcia del Cerro
Linda Garland
Claude Graves
Cynthia Hardy
Elora Hardy
John Hardy
Bud Hart
Devina Hindom
Mario and Cristiana Ilotte
Maximilian Jencquel
Kinga
Abbie Labrum
Gildas Loaec
Sean Nino Lotze
Puddy Martin
Sebastian Mesdag
Richard North-Lewis
Steve Palmer
Polly Purser
Arief Rabik
Tommaso Riva
Nicolas Robert
Emerald Starr
Tomek
Norm and Oska vant Hoff
Anneke van Waesberghe
Frederik Wittesaele
Zissou

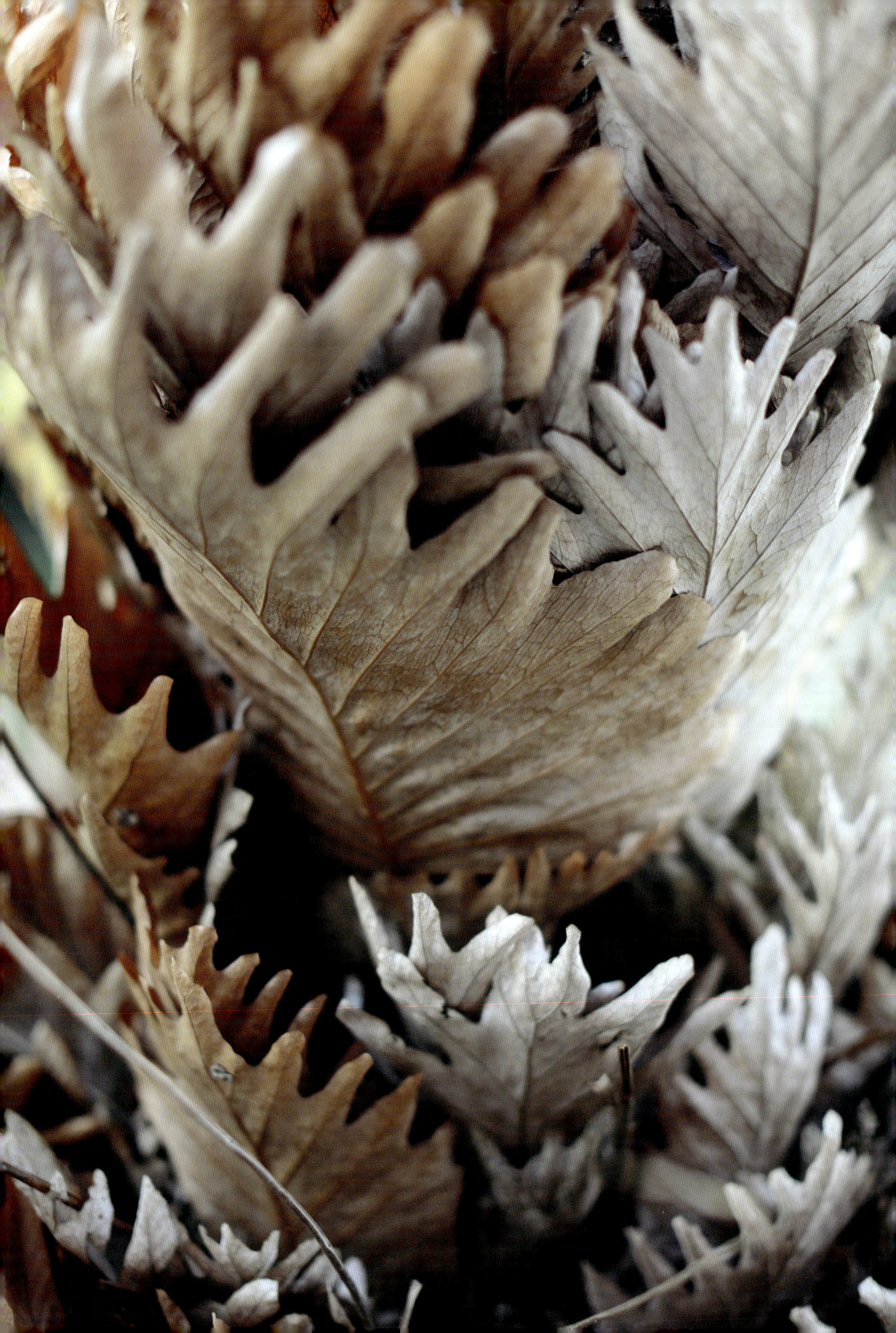

FEATURED PLACES

Bambu Indah
eco-luxury
boutique hotel,
Sayan Terrace,
Ubud
bambuindah.com

12

27

33

34–35

36

78

79

85

78

108–9

111

112

113

114

116–17

130

142–43

145

168–69

230 FEATURED PLACES

Former Guy Bedarida and Nicolas Robert residence, Seminyak

176

206–7

208–9

Capella Ubud
capellahotels.com/en/capella-ubud

136

Former Damien Dernoncourt residence, Seminyak

150

154–55

156

157

158–59

160–61

Green School, Abiansemal
greenschool.org

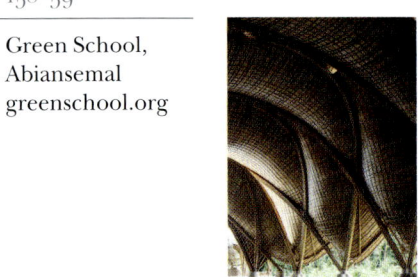

Green Village, Abiansemal
greenvillagebali.com

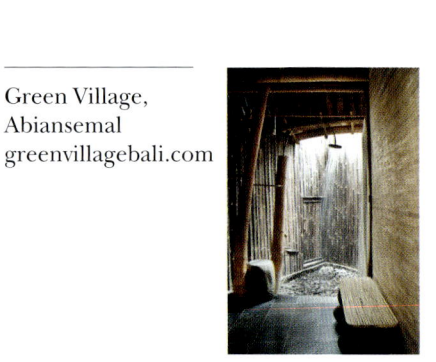

148

166–67

140

John Hardy Ubud Workshop and Showroom
johnhardy.com

162–63

164–65

231

Hartland Estate,
Kedewatan, Ubud
hartlandestate.com

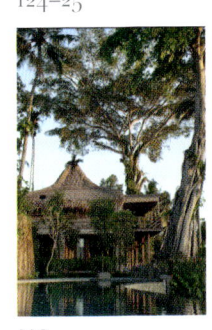

122–23

124–25

126

127

128

129

Intaaya resort,
Nusa Penida
intaaya.com

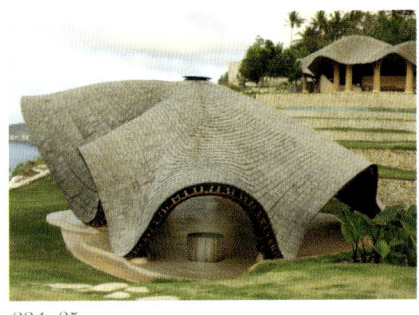

14–15

38

39

41

52

54

63

66

184–85

186–87

188–89

190

218–19

221

222

224–25

232 FEATURED PLACES

back cover

Kebek Puhu Village

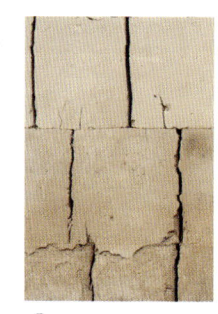

28

30–31

Koya Cabin

119

120–21

Lost Lindenberg hotel, Pekutatan thelindenberg.com/en/hotels/lost/

146–47

Lumi Shala, Alchemy Yoga Center, Ubud alchemyyogacenter.com

149

2

Panchoran Retreat, Nyuh Kuning, Ubud

22–23

64–65

Permata Ayung resort, Abiansemal permataayung.com

68–69

226

139

233

Potato Head
Beach Club,
Petitenget,
Seminyak
seminyak.
potatohead.co

11  51  80  82  84

87

Therese Poulsen
residence, Nyuh
Kuning, Ubud

72  73  74–75

Rumah Rubah,
Tumbak Bayuh
rumahrubah.com

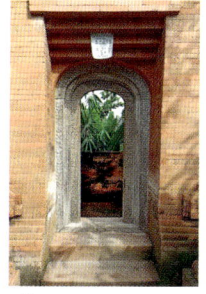

48   50  88–89  90

91  93   94  95  96  98

99

234 FEATURED PLACES

Sandat Glamping
Tents, Ubud
glampingsandat.com

210
211 

Jérôme Abel
Seguin residence,
Kerobokan

170–71
172–73 

Suarga Sustainable
Boutique Resort,
Padang Padang,
Uluwatu
suargapadangpadang.com

174–75
100–101
212 

Temple Lodge,
Bingin
thetemplelodge.com

44–45
46 
47 

TianTaru, Kebek
Puhu Village
tiantaru.com

6
132 
133 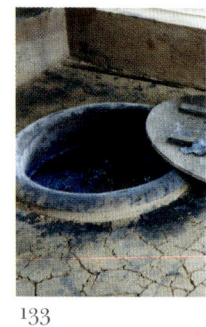 

Uma Jiwa, Ubud

front cover
26 
179 
180 
181

235

182–83

Anneke van
Waesberghe
residence, Mambal

192–93

194–95

197

198–99

200–201

202–3

204–5

Villa Campuhan
estate, Jasri
villacampuhanbali.
com

18–19

102

104–5

214

215

INDEX

Numbers in **bold** refer to interviews.
Numbers in *italics* refer to photographs.

Abiansemal. *See* Green School; Green Village; John Hardy Ubud Workshop and Showroom; Permata Ayung resort; van Weisberghe, Anneke, residence of
Agung, Mount, 13, 16, *102*. *See also* Villa Agung
AIDS crisis, 110
air-conditioning, 21, 191, 196, 217
alang-alang, 67, 178, 191; natural history of, 213; properties of, 67, 134, 213, 216
alang-alang roofs, 16, 40, *44–45*, 55, *79*, 86, *145*, 213, 216
Alling, Abigail, 220
angklung, 53
Anthropocene, 217
architecture, traditional Balinese, 13, 16, 32, 103
artificial intelligence (AI), 77
Australia, 213
Austria, 138
Aveda, 60
Ayu River gorge, *108–9*
Ayung River, 110, 137, *139*

Bahamas, 56
bale banjar, 32
bales, 8, 177
bamboo, 53, 55–57, 60–62, 67, 70, 76–77, 81, 97, 196, 223; architecture, 8, *11*, 16, 24–25, 32, *42–43*, 53, 55, 61–62, *63*, *66*, 67, *72–75*, *78–79*, *140*, *157*, *166–67*, 178, *179–81*, 191, 196, 213, 216–17, 220, *222*; as a building material, 8, 17, 53, 55, 57, 67, 86, 134–35, 137–38, *139*, 144, *145*, 178, 191, 217, 220; cultivation, 8, 17, 60, *64–65*, 70–71, 76–77, 81, 110, 152; furniture, *58–59*, 60, 135; lichen as an aging marker, 62; products made from, 53, 55–56, 60–61; resistance to toxicity, 57; shingles, 40, 83, 86, 92, 134, *157*, *179–81*, 196, *212*, 213, 216; strength of, 55, 57; sustainability of, 53, 56–57, 60, 134, 191, 223; and water tables, 57; woven, see *bedek*
Bamboo Village Initiative, 71
Bamboo Village Trust, 67, 71
Bambu Indah hotel (Sayan Terrace, Ubud), *12*, 27, *33–36*, *78–79*, *85*, *108–9*, *130*, 131, 135, 137–38, 144, *168–69*; Jambu House, *111–13*; Kelapa House, *116–17*; lookout tower, *145*; Moon House, *142–43*; Padi House, *114*; Pawon House, *34–35*; Sumba House, *78*, *79*
bangkirai wood, *94*
Bank Indonesia, 86
bars, 21, *150*, 152
batako bricks, 97
Batak people, *33*, 152
bathrooms, 16, 40, *68–69*, 86, *111*, *113*, *124–25*, 178, *211*, 217; bathtubs, 92, *112*, *168–69*
Batubelig Banjar, 103
Batukaru, Mount, 110
beaches, 62, 217
Bedarida, Guy, **191**, **196**
Bedarida, Guy, and Nicolas Robert, former residence of (Seminyak), *176*, 191, *206–9*
bebek (scooter), 62
bedek (woven bamboo), 16, *30–31*, *68–69*, 86, *104–5*, *168–69*, 191, 196, *215*
bedrooms, 8, *111*, *124–25*, *158–59*, *176*, *198–99*
Belgium, 57, 86
Bell, Matthew, **138**, *139*, **144**
bengkel, 67
Bensley, Bill, *136*, 144
Big Tree Farms, 216
Bingin. *See* Temple Lodge
biofuel, 21, 22–23
Biosphere Foundation, 16, 220
birds, 9–10, 37, *130*, 153
bird-safe glass, 9–10, 153
Blackwell, Chris, 55
Blue Economy, The, 60
blue-green algae, 56
Bongkasa, 137, *139*
Boom Festival, 62, 67
borax, used to treat bamboo, 57, 86, 92
Borneo, 86, 216; East Borneo, 86
bougainvillea, 196
Bovill, Joanna, 62
Bowie, David, 55
Branson, Richard, 55
bridges, 86, 97, *111*, *113*, 137–38, 152
Brown, Ben, 57, 62, 71
Buckingham Palace, 138
Bukit Peninsula, 40, 83, 92
bungkus, 153
BYO Living, *84*

California, 24, 135
Canada, 56, 137
Capella Ubud, *136*, 144
Capra, Fritjof, 60
Caribbean, 56
Carrara marble, 115
Carrer, Federico, **178**, **191**
Catholic Church, 71
Cezary and Kinga, 9, 216, **217**, **220**, **223**
Cheong Yew Kuan, 135, *162–63*, 191, 196. *See also* Green School; John Hardy Ubud Workshop and Showroom
Chicago, 138
China, 92, 144
Chopra, Deepak, 62
Climate Breakthrough Foundation, 71
climate of Bali, 8, 177
cob, 32, *36*
coconut palm roofs, 16, 216
Cohen, Barbara. *See* Villa Campuhan estate
Cohen, Rob. *See* Villa Campuhan estate
Colombia, 57
Colorado, 110
community, 13, 16–17, 20–21, 32, 37, 49, 76, 92, 153, 178, 223; planned, 131, *140*. *See also* Green Village
conservation, 56, 77, 144, 217, 223. *See also* energy conservation
cooling, natural means of, 29, 191, 217
Corning Incorporated, 151
corridors, *87*, 152
Costa Rica, 25
Covid, 115, 144

Dayak people, 152
Dernoncourt, Damien, former residence of (Seminyak), *150*, 151–52, *154–61*
design studio, *80*, *84*, 152, *162–65*, 191
dining areas, *90*, *94*, *96*, *149*, *182–83*, *206–7*, *211*
dining tables, 118, 152
doors and doorways, *48*, 67, *98–99*, 118, *126–27*, *160–61*, 220. *See also* entrances
Dornier, Alexis, 153
dressing room, *140*
driftwood, *106*. *See also* reclaimed materials
Dubai, 77

Earth Construction Bali, 38
Earth Lines Architects, 9, 26, *179*, 196, 239
East Bali, 16, *18–19*, 62, 196, *214*. *See also* Villa Campuhan estate
eco-friendliness. *See* ecology; sustainability
ecology, 16, 32, 53, 55, 60, 62, 70, 77, 81, 97, 110, 131, 135, 137, 144, 151–53, 223; ecological problems in Bali, 8–9, 16
Eco-Mantra, 9, 103, 153
Ecospecifier, 67
Ecuador, 57
Edison, Thomas Alva, 61
electrical power, 7–8, 32, 61, 92, 97, 110, 137–38, 191. *See also* solar

power; vortex generator; wind power
El Niño, 71
energy conservation, 56, 92, 97, 103, 134, 137, 196, 217, 220
entrances, 34–35, 48, 56, 72, 87, 136, 184–85. *See also* doors and doorways
Environmental Bamboo Foundation, 55, 57
Environmental Protection Agency, 7
Escape Nomade, 177, 186–87, 192–93, 217

Field, David, 118, *119–21*. *See also* Koya Cabin
50 Simple Things Kids Can Do to Save the Earth, 131
Fischer, Maitri, 9
Flanders, 83
Flores, 57, 76
forests, 17, 32, 37, 53, 56–57, 61, 67, 144; forestry, 62, 67, 70–71, 77; reforestation, 61. *See also Towards Resilient Bamboo Forestry*
Forest Stewardship Council (FSC), 86, 97
Fourth International Bamboo Congress, 60
Four Seasons, the, 138
France, 144
frangipani, 135, 152
furniture, 62, 152, 178, *198–99*; in bamboo, *58–59*, 60, 135; from reclaimed materials, 103, 110, 152, *174*, 220

Gaborit, Elie, *38*
gardens, 16, 24, 67, 92, 135, 138, *166–67*, 223; organic, 110, 196; traditional Balinese, 16. *See also* Japanese-inspired gardens; Wastewater Gardens
Garland, Linda, 16, 24, **55–57**, **60–62**, 135, 216; bamboo sofa of, *58–59*. *See also* Panchoran Retreat; Villa Campuhan estate
gasification of rice husks, 138
Germany, 67
Gilimanuk, 153
Ginanneschi, Isabella, 8, 135, *178*
Gingrich, Newt, 60
gladaks, 8, 107, *124–25*, 135, 144, 216
glamping, *178*, *186–90*, 191, *210–11*. *See also* Sandat Glamping Tents
glass, 8, 110, 137, *139*, 151–53, *154–55*, *162–63*, 196; fiberglass, 134; sustainability of, 151–53. *See also* bird-safe glass; metal-and-glass construction
Good Energies Foundation, 71
Graves, Claude, 9, **17**, **20–21**, **24–25**. *See also* Nihiwatu Resort; Haweri resort
Graves, Petra, 17, 20
Gore, Al, 17
Green School (Abiansemal), 131, 135, 137–38, 144, *166–67*; Arc, *148*
Green Village (Abiansemal), 131, 134, *140*, 216
Gresik (East Java), 86
Grigio Argento marble, *95*
guesthouses, *18–19*, *104–5*, 131

Hall, Margaret "Peggy," 56
Hardy, Carina and Chiara, 137
Hardy, Cynthia, **135**, **137**, 144
Hardy, Elora, 9, 25, **131**, **134–35**, *140*, 196, 216. *See also* Green Village
Hardy, John, 24, 57, **137–38**, 151–52, *162–63*, *164–65*, 191. *See also* John Hardy jewelry company; John Hardy Ubud Workshop and Showroom
Hardy, John and Cynthia, 9, *12*, *27*, *33*, *78*, *85*, *108–9*, 131, 135, *142–43*, *148*, *168–69*, 216. *See also* Bambu Indah hotel; Green School
Hardy, Orin, 138
Hart, Bud, **107**, **110**, **115**. *See also* Hartland Estate
Hartland Estate (Kedewatan, Ubud), 107, 110, 115, *122–29*
Haweri resort, 24
Hawken, Paul, 71, 81
Hearst, William Randolph, 17
hemp, 17, 24, 76–77
hempcrete, 24–25
Hemp for Victory, 17
Hiroshima, 57

Ibuku Studio, 9, *26*, *140*, *142*, *148*, *179*, 196, 239
IKEA Foundation, 71
Ilotte, Cristiana, 40, *44–45*, 49. *See also* Temple Lodge
Ilotte, Mario, **40**, *44–45*, **49**. *See also* Temple Lodge
Inconvenient Truth, An, 17
India, 56–57
Indian Ocean, 83
indigo, 6, 9, 32, 37, 40, *132–33*
Indobamboo, 131
Intaaya resort, *14–15*, *38–39*, *41*, *52*, *54*, *63*, *66*, *184–90*, 217, *218–19*, 220, *221–22*, 223, *224–25*
International Development Research Centre (IDRC), 56
ironwood, 86, 196; reclaimed, 83, *96*, *102*; shingles, 16, *96*, 107, 216
irrigation, 8, 37, 137–38. *See also subak*
Island of the Gods, 153
Italy, 40, 115, 178

Jakarta, 83, 86, 92, 144
Jalan Karet, 86
Jambu House. *See* Bambu Indah hotel
Japan, 61, 177; Japanese folklore, 103; Japanese-inspired architecture, 115, 151, *156*
Japanese-inspired gardens, 152, *157*
Jasri. *See* Villa Campuhan estate
Java, 8, 17, 62, 103, 107, 110, 135, 152; Central Java, 86; East Java, 86; Java Sea, 170
Jencquel, Maximilian, 9, *48*, *88–89*, **103**, 115, *122*, 153. *See also* Hartland Estate; Rumah Rubah
joglos, 8, 107, 115, *122–23*, *126–29*, 152, 216
John Hardy jewelry company, 151, *162–65*, 191, 196
John Hardy Ubud Workshop and Showroom, 135, *162–65*, 191, 196
Jokowi (Joko Widodo), 60
jute, 177

Kaba Kaba, 153
Kalimantan (Borneo), 56, 216
Kapal Bamboo, 135, 191
Kapoor, Anish, 137–38
Karan, Donna, 134
Kebek Puhu Village, *6*, *28*, *30–31*, *32*, *132*
Kelapa House. *See* Bambu Indah hotel
Keliki village, 144
Kenya, 17
kitchens, 21, 32, *42–43*, 92, *95*, 118, 152, 178, 196
Klungkung, 62
knockdown houses, 8–9, 107, 110, 115, 118, *119–29*, 135, 144, 152, 216. *See also gladaks*; *joglos*; *limasans*
Koya Cabin, 115, 118, *119–21*
kris, 78
krupuk, 152, *158–59*
Kuta, 17, 62
Kyoto, 61

Labrum, Abbie, 9, 196
Lam, Wayan, 9
Lamb, Max, 103
land ownership, Balinese conceptions of, 8
Landwehr, Aldo, 135
Laudato si' (*Praise Be to You*), 70–71
lava, 103, 138, 152
Legian, 17
limasans, 8, 40, 107, 216
limestone, *41*, 97, *184–85*, 220
lingam, 40
Little Tree Bali, 97
living areas, *94*, *114*, *122*, 196
Loaëc, Gildas, 103
Lombok, 9, 152, *210*, *213*, 216
lontar palm roofs, 16, 216
lookout tower, *145*
Lost Lindenberg hotel (Pekutatan), *146–47*, *149*, 153
Lotze, Sean Nino, 9
lumbungs, 8, *210*, 216

Madura, 92
Mahakam River, 86
Maison Kisuné, 103
Malaysia, 213
Mambal, *192–93*. *See also* van Waesberghe, Anneke, residence of
mangroves, 17
massage tent. *See* tents
Masulin, Lim, *84*
Matin, Andra, *80*
McClure, F. A., 57
McDonough, William, 131, 134
Mentawai, 33
meru, 67
Mesdag, Ayu, *6*, 9, *132*
Mesdag, River, 32
Mesdag, Sebastian, *6*, 9, *25*, **32**, **37**, **40**, *132*
metal, 151, *170–73*. *See also* metal-and-glass construction
metal-and-glass construction, 151, *154–55*, *162–63*
Minangkabau people, 215
Mitchell, Joni, 9
Moon House. *See* Bambu Indah hotel
mud as a building material, 8, *12*, 16–17, *28*, *29*, *30–31*, 32, *33–36*, 40, *42–47*, 55, 110, 134, 137, *141*, 152, 196; advantages, 29; history, 29

NASA, 61
Nashville, 17
natural convection, 152
Natural History Museum (London), 56
nature-based solution (NBS), 70
Nelson, Mark, 16
New York City, 49, 110, 134, 153
New Zealand, 138
Next Industrial Revolution, The, 131
Ngeruak ceremony, 220
Nihiwatu Resort (Sumba), 9, 17, 20, 21
Northern California Permaculture Institute, 135
North-Lewis, Richard, **115**, **118**, *119–21*. *See also* Koya Cabin
Nusa Penida, 9, *14–15*, *38*, *54*, *184–85*, 217, *218–19*. *See also* Intaaya resort
Nyuh Kuning, Ubud. *See also* Panchoran Retreat; Poulsen, Therese, residence of

Oak Foundation, 71
Office for Metropolitan Architecture (OMA), *80*
offices, 134, 152. *See also* design studio
organic farming, 20, 178, 223. *See also* gardens, organic
organic food, 40, 191, 196, 223
Out of Asia, 153

Pablo Luna Studio, *54*, 220, 223
Packard Foundation, 71
Padang Padang, *100–101*, *212*. *See also* Suarga Sustainable Boutique Resort
Padang Padang Cove, 97

Padi House. *See* Bambu Indah hotel
Padoan, Emanuela, **178**, **191**
Palmer, Stephen, 97
palm oil trees, 22–23; palm oil, 81
Panama, 25
Panchoran Retreat (Nyuh Kuning, Ubud), 22–23, 55, 57, 68–69, 226; bamboo plantation, 64–65
Panyaden School (Chiang Mai), 86
Paris Agreement, 70
Pauli, Gunter, 60
pavilions, 8, 16, 67, 68–69, 86, 152, 162–63, 177–78, 191, 206–7, 211. *See also* bales; wantilans
Pekutatan. *See* Lost Lindenberg hotel
Perini, Susanna, 67
permaculture, 16, 217, 223. *See also* Northern California Permaculture Institute
Permata Ayung resort, 139
Philippines, the, 25
plastics, 24, 70, 76
poleng, 55
pool houses, 44–45
pools, 16, 21, 40, 44–45, 93–94, 110, 115, 129, 134, 138, 196, 206; indoor-outdoor, 136, 204–5; natural, 22–23, 27, 85, 108–9, 144
Pop art, 150, 152
Pope Francis, 70
Portugal, 62
Potato Head Beach Club, 9, 11, 51, 80, 82, 84, 87, 103
Potato Head Design Studio, 80, 84
Potato Head Studios, 103
Poulsen, Therese, residence of (Nyuh Kuning, Ubud), 67
Puhu. *See* Kebek Puhu Village
Purser, Polly, **152–53**
Pyrex, 151

Quad-block construction, 67, 73–74

Rabik, Arief, 9, 57, **62**, **67**, **70–71**, 72, **76–77**, **81**, 131
Rabik, Karim, 62
Rabik, Pak Amir, 62
rammed earth, 32, 38–39, 41, 188–89, 217, 220
reclaimed materials, 8, 40, 104, 178, 214; bicycle, 211; bottles, 84, 103, 150, 152; car tires, 152, 208; concrete, 152; driftwood, 40; ironwood, 83, 86, 96, 102, 196; Javanese sliding doors, 67; from Java Sea, 170; mud, 8, 40; oil drum, 210; roots, 174–75; rubber pipes, 92; stone, 8, 40, 83, 88–89, 178; teak, 40, 46, 83, 86, 97, 114, 118, 137; timber, 55, 151; window shutters, 82, 87, 103; windshields, 166–67

religion, Balinese, 13, 16
responsible development, 17, 20–21, 25
rice fields, 8, 16, 37, 55, 137, 144, 178, 191
rice husks. *See* cob; gasification of rice husks
Ripple, Ben, 216
Robert, Nicolas, 150, 151, **152**, 176, 206–8. *See also* Bedarida, Guy, and Nicolas Robert, former residence of; Dernoncourt, Damien, former residence of
Röckstrom, Johan, 71
Ropp, Paul, 67
Rote, 9, 49, 77, 213
rumah gadang, 216
Rumah Rubah, 48, 50, 88–91, 93–96, 98–99, 103, 153
Rüsters (Ubud restaurant), 25

Sacred Mountain Sanctuary, 16
Saint Charles River (Colorado), 110
Samarinda, 86
Samsara, 138
Sandat Glamping Tents, 178, 210–11
San Diego, 138
San Juan Mountains (Colorado), 110
Sanur Harbor, 217
Sarinbuana Eco Lodge, 153
sawdust, as fuel, 138
Sayan Terrace. *See* Bambu Indah hotel; Hartland Estate
Schilling, Fred, 216
Sciascia, Filippo, 126–27
sculpture, Balinese, 16, 55
Seguin, Jérôme Abel, 170–75
Seminyak, 151. *See also* Bedarida, Guy, and Nicolas Robert, residence of; Dernoncourt, Damien, former residence of; Potato Head Beach Club
sewage treatment, 92
showers, 38, 92, 118, 128; outdoor, 140
Singa faces, 152
Singapore, 56; Changi Airport, 115
skylights, 191
Smithsonian Institution, 61
solar power, 8, 21, 24, 92, 97, 118, 137, 178, 191, 220
South Africa, 40, 178
spa. *See* Intaaya resort
Starr, Emerald, **16–17**, 18–19
stone carving, 16, 115
Stonehenge, 40
Suarga Sustainable Boutique Resort (Padang Padang), 83, 86, 92, 97, 100–101, 212, 216
subak, 8
Sumatra, 33, 55, 62, 215, 216; Sumatran carpenters, 18–19. *See also* Batak people; Minangkabau people

Sumba, 9, 17, 20–21, 24, 92, 97, 213, 216. *See also* Nihiwatu Resort
Sumba Foundation, 17, 20–21
Sumba House. *See* Bambu Indah hotel
Sumbanese roofs, 216
Sumba stone, 83, 92, 107
Sumbawa, 213
Surabaya, 86, 138
sustainability, 7–10, 16–17, 21, 25, 56, 62, 70–71, 92, 97, 103–110, 131, 134–35, 178, 237–38; definitions of, 7, 9, 32, 92, 152–53, 217, 223
sustainable architecture, 7–9, 25, 216. *See also* Bambu Indah hotel; Intaaya resort; Rumah Rubah; John Hardy Ubud Workshop and Showroom; Suarga Sustainable Boutique Resort
Sustainable Development Goals (United Nations list), 70
Sustain a Clump, 62
Switzerland, 20

Tahiti, 49
Tao of Physics, The, 60
Tapscott, Don, 67
teak, as building material, 16, 86, 91, 95, 99, 103, 107, 110, 115, 124–25, 216; furniture, 104–5, 178; reclaimed, 40, 46, 83, 86, 97, 114, 118, 137
TED conferences, 131
tekor, 13
Temple Lodge (Bingin), 40, 44–47, 49
temples, 13, 16, 37, 42–43, 55, 137. *See also* Temple Lodge
tents, 136, 144, 177–78, 186–90, 192–95, 197–205, 210–11, 217; massage tent, 202–3
Thailand, 25, 86
thatched roofs, 16, 213, 216. *See also* alang-alang roofs; coconut palm roofs; lontar palm roofs
TianTaru workshop, 6, 132–33
Tibetan pagoda, 62
Tika, the, 80
tiles, 47, 55, 107, 196
Timor, 213
Tirta Gangga Water Palace, 16–17. *See also* Wastewater Gardens
Toogood, Faye, 103
Toraja, 216
tourism, 8, 21, 24, 55, 137, 217
Towards Resilient Bamboo Forestry, 57, 60, 62, 71
Tumbak Bayuh, 48, 50, Turtle Butte Ranch (Colorado), 110
Tuscany, 196

Ubud, 9, 25, 32. *See also* Bambu Indah hotel; Capella Ubud; Hartland Estate; Panchoran Retreat; Poulsen, Therese, residence of; Sandat Glamping Tents; Uma Jiwa

Uluwatu, 100–101; Uluwatu surf break, 40
Uma Jiwa, 9, 26, 179–83, 196, 216
United Nations Development Programme, 177–78
USAID Environmental Services Program, 62
U.S. Department of Agriculture, 57
Uzbekistan, 116–17

Van Cleef & Arpels, 191
Van Thillo, Mark, 220
vant Hoff, Norm, 9–10, 153
vant Hoff, Oska, 153
van Waesberghe, Anneke, **177–78**, 186–87, 217; residence of (Mambal, Abiansemal), 192–95, 197–205. *See also* Escape Nomade
Vélez, Simón, 57
Venice, 178
verandas, 32, 104–5, 124–25
Verschelden, Karolien D. A., 83
Villa Campuhan estate (Jasri, East Bali), 16, 18–19, 104–5; Villa Agung, 102; Villa Lumbung, 214–15. *See also* Wastewater Gardens
villages, traditional, 8, 16, 20, 29, 32, 37, 55, 77, 81, 137, 191
vortex generator, 24, 137–38, 144

Wabi-sabi aesthetic, 93, 223
Waldorf School, 40
wantilans, 8, 67, 68–69, 72, 90, 98, 152, 162–65, 178, 191, 196, 216
waste management, 56, 71, 191, 196, 217, 223; zero waste, 103
Wastewater Gardens, 16–17, 18–19, 26, 92, 104–5, 110, 115, 220
water catchment, 8, 57, 97, 110, 118, 217, 220
water conservation, 21, 24, 57, 92, 97, 103, 131, 135, 153, 220
West Sussex, 115
wetlands, constructed, 16–17, 92. *See also* Wastewater Gardens
Whole Earth Catalog, 97
Wikinomics, 67
Williams, Anthony D., 67
windows, 37, 46–47, 62, 97, 118, 153, 176, 216, 220
wind power, 8, 21, 24, 92; windmill, 110
Wittesaele, Frederik E. A., 83
wood carving, 16, 48, 107
Wos River, 144

Yoga shala, 196, 220, 222, 224–25

Zero waste. *See* waste management
Zissou, 132

Front cover: Indoor-outdoor living under a supersize bamboo roof that, with imagination, recalls the shape of a *gelungan*, the ritual headdress worn by Balinese and Javanese women on important occasions. Uma Jiwa, a house in Ubud designed by Ibuku Studio and Earth Lines Architects.

Back cover: A play of veiled curves with a clifftop view of the sea at Intaaya, a resort on Nusa Penida designed by Pablo Luna Studio. Fishing nets animate the lines of the bamboo structure.

Page 2: Lumi Shala, Alchemy Yoga Center, Ubud. Designed by Ibuku Studio. Photo courtesy Tommaso Riva.

Page 4: Leaves and a palm front impressed in the surface of a path, revealing nature's silhouettes and providing traction underfoot.

Page 6: A touch of indigo. Making indigo cloth at TianTaru, Sebastian and Ayu Mesdag's workshop in Puhu. Photo courtesy Zissou.

Page 12: A passage through a hollow mud circle at Bambu Indah, John and Cynthia Hardy's eco-luxury boutique hotel on Sayan Terrace, Ubud.

Page 28: Detail of a mud-brick wall in Kebek Puhu Village, near Payangan, north of Ubud.

Page 52: A dance of arches and columns created by the harmonious juxtaposition of "see-through" buildings at Intaaya.

Page 82: The facade of the world-famous Potato Head Beach Club in Seminyak is made from 6,600 antique shutters sourced from all around Java.

Page 106: Shades of driftwood.

Page 130: An aviary for the many species of birds to be found at Bambu Indah.

Page 150: Nicolas Robert's Pop art–inspired installation of bottles behind the bar at Damien Dernoncourt's former house in Seminyak.

Page 176: A circular window looking into the bedroom of the former home of Guy Bedarida and Nicolas Robert in Seminyak, designed by Nicolas Robert.

Page 212: Inside-out bamboo shingles on the roof of the Suarga resort in Padang Padang.

Page 226: A cascading natural spring at Panchoran, designer Linda Garland's former estate in Nyuh Kuning, Ubud.

Page 228: A curious plant embracing the trunk of a palm.

Isabella Ginanneschi is a photographer based in Bali. She began her career in Milan as an art director collaborating on special projects with Condé Nast and numerous fashion labels, including Diesel. Later, in New York, she worked with luxury brands such as Barneys, John Hardy, Cole Haan, and Hunter. Her experience working on high-profile campaigns with the most illustrious fashion photographers led her to explore further creative assignments with her camera in hand. Since then, she has worked with *Elle Decoration*, *Marie Claire Maison*, the *Robb Report*, and *Architectural Digest*, among others. Now, as an "artographer," Ginanneschi has drawn on her fascination for creating images and her experience to develop a body of work that reveals unexpected harmonies by connecting different objects from different places, ultimately eliciting dreamlike emotions that urge the viewer to reconnect with nature. Her selected work can be viewed at the Ralph Pucci, Staley Wise, and Robin Rice galleries in New York.

Duncan Murray Kirk was educated in England and worked for CBS Records and Canon in Australia. He first visited Bali in 1980, and the island became a catalyst for his creative endeavors. His company Zenergy produced eco-friendly accessories for fashion labels such as Monsoon, Jigsaw, Portmans, and Esprit, and he developed Meshglass, a new type of stained-glass decor surfacing that combines traditional Balinese craftsmanship with digital design. His intent is to reconcile the natural and scientific worlds; his passion is aroused by sustainable design, integrity, tolerance, and kindness. Kirk has witnessed Bali's changes over forty years, and using this knowledge he has written not only the present book but also *In the Spirit of Bali* (Assouline) and several works of fiction: the Rollo Trilogy and *The Wetiko Killers*.

See the preceding page for captions to the jacket images and chapter openers.

A note about the materials used in this book
The paper, manufactured by the Oji Zunma company, is FSC (Forest Stewardship Council) certified.
The binding boards are made of 100% recycled materials.

Editor: David Fabricant
Production editors: Greg Villepique and Austin Allen
Designer: Misha Beletsky
Production manager: Louise Kurtz

Photographs copyright © 2015, 2025 Isabella Ginanneschi. Text copyright © 2015, 2025 Duncan Murray Kirk. Compilation, including selection, order, and placement of text and images, copyright © 2015, 2025 Abbeville Press. All rights reserved under international copyright conventions. No part of this book may be reproduced or utilized in any form or by any means, electronic or mechanical, including photocopying, recording, or by any information retrieval system, without permission in writing from the publisher. Inquiries should be addressed to Abbeville Press, 655 Third Avenue, New York, NY 10017. Printed in China.

Second edition
10 9 8 7 6 5 4 3 2 1

ISBN 978-0-7892-1503-1

A previous edition of this book was cataloged as follows:
Library of Congress Cataloging-in-Publication Data
Ginanneschi, Isabella.
  Bali : sustainable visions / photography by Isabella Ginanneschi ; text by Duncan Murray Kirk.
    pages cm
  Includes index.
  Summary: "A visual survey of environmentally sustainable architecture and interiors on Bali and other islands of the Indonesian archipelago. Photographs of homes, resorts, and other spaces, as well as interviews with the architects, designers, and entrepreneurs who created them"—Provided by publisher.
  1. Sustainable architecture—Indonesia—Bali (Province) I. Kirk, Duncan Murray. II. Title.
  NA2542.36.G56 2015
  720'.470959862–dc23
                    2015023230

For bulk and premium sales and for text adoption procedures, write to Customer Service Manager, Abbeville Press, 655 Third Avenue, Suite 2520, New York, NY 10017, or call 1-800-ARTBOOK.

Visit Abbeville Press online at www.abbeville.com.